YOU CAN'T TAKE MY SON

JOSEPH TRIOLO

outskirts
press

Introduction

TODAY WAS THE second happiest day of my life. It was a beautiful day in Charleston. The sky was bright blue. The scent of spring was in the air. It was a day, that only a short time ago, I never dreamed possible. It was my day, our day- a day that belonged to us. Parents sat in folding chairs, lined up in military fashion, eagerly awaiting the procession about to enter the grounds of the Cistern. As the music began, the dignitaries and the scholars entered to the cadence of the symbolic graduation song. Suddenly, two huge doors opened from the administration building. A sea of students began to slowly emerge onto the commencement stage. I observed the proud faces of the parents, friends, and relatives as they intently searched for some familiar characteristic that would enable them to recognize their son or daughter.

Looking for my son, I soon became aware of his presence. It wasn't difficult for me to locate him. I recognized his smile and deep-set dimples because I knew him when he was unable to smile. I recognized his wavy brown hair, long curled eyelashes, and full eyebrows because I knew him when he had no hair, eyelashes, or eyebrows. I recognized his steady gait because I knew him when he was unable to take a single step, when he had to be carried in my arms. I also recognized his strong healthy frame, because I knew him when he was frail, sickly, and fighting death at every turn. I listened to the scholars and college officials as they spoke of life in general; each remarking in their own particular style how lucky the students were as they embarked on life's journey. I smiled thinking that many of them are, for the first time, about to venture into this vast world. Sitting there, I could not help feeling that at sometime during each of their lives, the mettle of every graduate would be tested. At that time I hoped that they would be able to rise to the challenge, to stare the demon in the face, and to slay it at its door. There was one young man on that stage who would have no trouble fighting demons for he had already fought one. There was one young man on that stage whose courage and desire to live was already tested. Yes, on that stage stood my son, who at the tender age of thirteen taught his father what it was to be a man. When others would have quit, he did not. When most people would have thrown in the towel because every fiber in their body told them not to go on, he continued. When morphine offered little comfort, he trudged forward. Even when surrounded by the cries of children who would never see another birthday, he persevered. Today, there was a valedictorian on that stage but not the one all would applaud for academic excellence. No, that was a valedictorian of other sorts. The one I am referring to is a young man named Joe who had the courage to fight cancer and to win.

This is his story and mine. It is the story of a father raising three children as a single parent. After having read it you may ask yourself, given the opportunity, would I have made the same choices? Only you will know the answer to that question. I did not write this story so people would forget it. I wrote it for the wonderful parents that I met along the way- the ones who will never know life as it could have been, but only as it was. I also wrote it for all the single parents who have been, and will continue to be, faced with the tiresome never-ending job of parenting. Perhaps they can derive some solace knowing that someone previously traveled down the same road. I hope that they will learn from my accomplishments as well as from my failures.

Today, God opened the doors of heaven to share with me the joys of his creation. Yes, this was the second happiest day of my life. The first is in the book. You will know it when you find it.

Chapter 1

THROUGHOUT TIME MOTHERHOOD has always been considered an entity comparable only to God and nature in reverence. Children are tied to their mothers at birth through her umbilical cord sharing life's precious blood, air, and nourishment. Regardless of what fathers may think, mothers have been the force, the omnipotent power, the center of the household from which everything has evolved. Mothers raise children. They guide them, love them, and comfort them in their times of need. Humanity recognizes this fact.

Today, however, we are faced with a new worrisome question. Are women following in the footsteps of men? Are they too leaving the household? With this event seemingly becoming more common, there is only one certainty, children are the ones who lose. Shouldn't it matter if children are raised by an aunt, friend, or some distant relative? Shouldn't it matter if they lie crying in their beds at night waiting for a parent who is no longer there to give them one last kiss before they go to sleep? And, shouldn't it matter if no one is there to give them a nourishing meal, to comfort them when they are sick, to see them in a school play, or help them with their homework?

In our society, the word love defines the word parent and the word parent defines the word love. They are synonymous. A father, or mother, should never leave their children. A parent should be the one that exemplifies all that is good in life. Children need their parents to play a game of catch or to see them all dressed up for their senior prom. When a father leaves the household, the children must learn to fend for themselves. It rocks them to their very core. The probability exists that if he should return, the father child relationship will remain poor. One day the child may elect to abandon the father and also have a difficult time committing to others. However, the catastrophic consequences felt by children when abandoned by a mother is immeasurable. All the negative effects of a mother leaving her children are not presently known. It is a relatively new issue. When comparing the present to the past, is it easier today for parents to leave their children? In today's culture, it appears there are very little consequences, if any at all. Family, friends, and acquaintances will still associate with a parent who has walked out on their children.

Children will try to forgive and understand their parent's selfish act. They may even blame themselves for the parent leaving, when the parent should be the one shunned by all for this ungodly deed. Consequences are a necessary part of life.

I cannot begin to express the emotions that I experienced when first confronted with the reality of my divorce, especially because it was not my choice. I never understood why our marriage ended. Perhaps, like others from our generation, we married too young or I just assumed that we would always be there for each other. The hardest realization I had to make was that the person I loved most stopped loving me a long time ago and I was the only one unaware of it. To be honest, I felt an emotional withdrawal on my wife's part but nothing to indicate the magnitude of what was about to transpire in my life.

Going on with my life was not the problem, making it through the day was. I knew that I had to survive the moment hoping to see tomorrow, until one day, with any luck, my tomorrow's would all become yesterdays taking with them my pain and despair.

I recall leaning over the kitchen counter saying, "I can't do this. It's too much for one person." I had no idea where to begin. What about the cooking, cleaning, ironing, and everything else? My God, I can't do any of that. I remember the anxiety, fears and solitude. Most of all I remember the loneliness. I thought I would never feel more helpless than I did at that moment. I was wrong. Life would become much harder. I knew that, with me, the children had a chance. Without me, they would never make it in this world. It would be all over for them before they had the opportunity to begin. It was now entirely my responsibility to provide for their simplest needs.

At the time of my divorce, my oldest daughter Claudine was

sixteen-years-old. My middle daughter Tammy, fourteen and Joseph, the youngest, was ten. Claudine was in France for the summer studying with an exchange group. My wife said that she wanted to be on her own and waited for Claudine's departure before breaking the news to us. With her mind made up, she moved quickly without regard for her family. Suddenly before me was a different person. What was taking place reminded me of an old movie. My wife closed her eyes, fell to sleep, and while she was sleeping a pod resembling her was left in her place. Nothing about her was the same. It appeared as though a spell was cast over her. I eventually discovered she was involved with someone else, a family friend. All that seemed to matter to her was her new love and her own wellbeing. Overnight she abandoned her family and marriage; leaving with someone that she had only known two months. It happened that quickly. Regardless of how hard I tried to uncover the cause of her unhappiness her answer was always the same, "I don't want to talk about it." It was my job to explain to the children what was taking place but how could I explain something I did not fully understand myself? All I could say was, "Mom is unhappy and wants to start a new life. She is trying to find herself."

The everyday painful emotional aspect of a pending divorce was beyond expression. Here was a person that I had known since she was fourteen years old. We were children who grew up together. We were supposed to grow old together, and along the way share in the joys and hardships of raising our children. Didn't we promise to love each other for all time, for better and for worse? Wasn't that the deal? Now my wife, and the mother of our children, wanted out of the deal. There would be no one to climb into my outstretched arms tonight, no one to share my inner most thoughts. The dreams of tomorrow no longer existed. They all disappeared in twenty-four hours. I stood there wondering how could I take care of my children when I was incapable of taking care of myself? All that was left was an emptiness, a hole that seemed to have no bottom. The pain was so great that I thought I would never be able to climb out of the abyss I was in. At night I watched my ten-year-old son run to his bedroom window to see if the headlights of a passing car was bringing his mommy back home. It broke my heart to see his disappointment as each car drove by without stopping. No matter how shattered our present condition, I knew that I would have to be able to think clearly or we would not be able to go on as a family. But how could I accomplish that when every membrane of my body was filled with my own impassive agony?

Chapter 2

IT WAS DINNERTIME and the children were seated at the table. I was standing near the stove when I noticed them staring at me. They didn't have to say a word. The expressions on their faces said it all. They were hungry and I knew it. Finally, one of them mustered up enough nerve to ask, "What's for dinner, Dad?" I didn't answer.

After a few seconds, I turned to them asking, "Is it really necessary for you to eat?" With a quizzical look on their faces I continued, "Look at all the children starving all over the world. Look at how thin they are. I mean, don't you kids want that look? Just think, no cholesterol problems, triglycerides at an all time low. Joey, no hidden dimples because of excessive fat."

One of them interrupted, "Next thing, Dad, you will be telling us is that it's good to have flies all over your face."

"Come on, Dad, what's for dinner?" they barked. "How about soup?"

"In July! Dad, it's ninety-seven degrees outside."

"I know, but soup is always a good choice. Haven't you ever seen that television commercial where they say, 'Soup is good all year round?' That's the trouble with you kids, you don't watch enough television."

I proceeded to heat up some soup. They ate it, as did I. I knew I had a problem of monumental proportions on my hand. I hadn't the first idea of what cooking entailed. Until now my main purpose around the kitchen was chewing and swallowing. When I was a boy my mother would call me into the kitchen to taste the spaghetti to determine if it was cooked, and on many occasions I failed the taste testing spaghetti test. Now, I was quite aware that something had to be done and soon. The children went from a mother who had a master's degree in culinary arts to me. Talk about a step down, this was more like an elevator crash. We could, I thought, continue to eat out every night at various fast food restaurants. So what if it reduced our life span by about fifty years. Did these kids expect to live forever? After a few seconds I eliminated that alternative.

Gathering my thoughts I picked up the phone, called my friend's wife, and explained my problem to her. Her immediate reaction was to laugh. I was really delighted that everyone was enjoying my predicament. However, she also knew that I would have to resolve this matter for the health and welfare of the children. Her advice was to start on tomorrow's dinner tonight. She went on to explain that I didn't have to cook it today but that I should at least plan the gourmet event. I listened as she instructed me on the preparation of tomorrow's dinner. After hanging up the phone, I ventured over to the local supermarket and purchased an oven stuffer roaster. I selected one with that little gizmo that pops up when it's cooked, a can of corn, and some carrots. Okay, now bring on tomorrow and those kids who foolishly believe they need food to survive, I thought.

The next evening I washed the chicken and sprinkled it with some salt and pepper. I could not tell if the salt was coming out of the shaker so I gave it a double whammy just to make sure. I sprinkled a little garlic powder on the bird to remind him that we were of Italian origin. Placing the chicken in a pan I added a few dabs of butter, heated the oven to 350 degrees, and stuffed the stuffer in the oven. Next, I peeled and sliced the carrots placing them in a pot on the stove burner. The can of corn was emptied into another pot and placed on a burner next to the carrots. The first lesson I learned was that no matter how long you leave a pot on the rear burner, the food will never heat up if you turned the front burner on by mistake.

After waiting for what I thought was a long enough time, I removed the chicken from the oven. Surveying the situation I came to the conclusion that it was taking the chicken too long to cook. Looking at my prospective meal I realized that the popper wasn't popping. Just what I needed, I thought, a chicken with a defective popper. I dislodged the popper to examine it. After inspecting it I concluded, who really needs this thing anyway. After all what did people do before this innovation came along? I threw the popper in the garbage believing that neither I, nor the chicken, would miss it, and he certainly wasn't registering any complaints. My first chicken dinner turned out to be a pleasant surprise.

That night I went to bed determined to get a handle on this cooking thing. After much contemplation I deduced, if you can read, you can cook. Pursuing this line of thinking I decided to look for recipes that appeared relatively simple to concoct. Any recipes containing garlic, salt, pepper, onions, and butter would make the list. Those that required a dab of this or that, referring to unknown ingredients, would be quickly eliminated. They would be placed on my later list. I slept better that night knowing that I had a plan.

The next day, with my mind preoccupied with thoughts of cooking, I walked over to the kitchen table to reach for a chair and discovered that there wasn't a chair to be found. Tammy stared at me with an astonished look on her face.

"Dad, I don't know how to tell you this but Mom came by while you were out and took the kitchen chairs."

"Took the chairs? And what in the world does she expect us to sit on?" Tammy shrugged her shoulders. She appeared to be as dismayed over the dilemma as I was.

The following night I returned home to find most of the pots, pans, and dishes gone. Gazing about, I observed that the walls had a different look. Many of them were bare. Several of the pictures and paintings that covered the walls were no longer there.

"Dad, can't you stop her?" Tammy asked. I didn't respond. I was too shocked at what was occurring to say anything.

The very next evening I was walking into the dining area of the kitchen when I hit my head on the overhead light fixture. This had never happened before and the reason was rather simple. There was formerly a kitchen table there to prevent me from hitting my head. I noticed Tammy walking through the kitchen.

"The kitchen table too?"

Without missing a step she nodded yes as she continued on her way. Well, at least this resolved the problem of not having any chairs to sit on during dinner, I thought. The house looked extremely messy so I asked Tammy to give it a quick vacuum before going out for a bite to eat.

"I can't."

"Not the Kirby?" "Yes, the Kirby."

I was floored by what was taking place (I had witnessed riots where looters had taken less).

"What kind of person would take another person's Kirby?" I yelled.

This was the straw that broke the camel's back. I didn't mind the chairs, table, pots, pans dishes, new car, and pictures, but the Kirby? How could we live without the Kirby

"Dad," Tammy replied, "I think this is what's taking place. She wants to turn the house that she is now living in into what our house is, and by taking everything out of our house and bringing it into that house, that house is becoming our house."

Pausing for a second, I said, "Tammy, you lost me in the first house. I think that I understand what you are trying to say, and if what you are saying is correct, then in about another week we should all move into that house. As a matter of fact, I'm so confused, I'm not certain I'm not in that house right now."

"Dad, "I think you got it." "Oh, I got it all right."

Joey looked up at me with a questionable look on his face, "Dad, is she going to take my bed too?"

"Joey," almost laughing, I replied, "Don't worry. I believe your bed and baseball cards are safe." If she really wanted to take something, why doesn't she take the stove? I thought. At least that would give me a reason not to cook. "Look, tomorrow I'll talk to her. This has to end." I knew that she was entitled to half our belongings but not like this.

At first I thought of changing the locks on the doors. After contemplating this alternative I realized that it would not bode well with the children. She could easily manipulate this action into an act of aggression on my part that would most likely accentuate the problem. The children might also view it as my preventing their mother from visiting. Despite her present conduct, this was still mommy and I knew how much they loved her. I had to tread lightly. It would be wiser for me to remain in the role of victim for the time being. However, I would speak to her concerning the disappearing house. The last thing I wanted was to come home one night, walk into the house, look up, and see the Big Dipper shinning brightly overhead.

During the course of the week, I approached her and asked that she not remove any more items because it was upsetting the children having to eat dinner on the floor.

"It's just not conducive to good digestion," I said.

With all the vehemence and hatred a person could render she said, "You have even turned my children against me." One and one no longer added up to two. I was now dealing with an alien. Her next move was to try to access the children's college savings.

"I need the money to start my life over again," she said.

"Well, you aren't going to get it. We saved that money for their education and that's what it is going to be used for."

Let them go to a two year college," she snapped.·

At that point, I knew all was lost. There was no hope for us as a family. I would now be forced to protect the children and myself from their mother. I found this concept terrifying. I was certain that I would now have to be the one to raise the children. I came to the hard realization that their mother, now a stranger, would not be able to place them first in her life. At the very least they would be third in her lineup. I made up my mind to fight as hard as necessary to keep my children. Not that I wanted to deprive her of them, or them of her, but it was becoming apparent that I loved our children more than she did. I knew in my heart that because I loved them I could do whatever was required of me to raise them. Plus, I was now the only game in town.

It was time to initiate a full-fledged attack on the cooking situation. The piranhas were hungry and I had to make some progress.

At first, each part of a meal was ready at different times. Sometimes we ate carrots, followed by roast beef, followed by a whole bowl of mashed potatoes. The next time I prepared the same meal it might be served completely in reverse. It certainly made for variety. I never believed that I would be able to serve all the courses simultaneously. I soon learned to remove the batteries from the smoke alarm before cooking commenced. If, by some chance, I neglected to complete this task I would find myself in the hall foyer, magazine in hand, swinging wildly trying to disperse the heavy smoke that I always managed to generate.

One day I was thumbing through the school adult education pamphlet when I observed a listing for a gourmet cooking class scheduled for Tuesday evenings at the local high school. I glanced at the ad then walked away. A little while later I returned, picked up the course description, and read it. Thinking, why not? I wrote out a check and mailed my fee along with the registration form. Two weeks later my day of destiny arrived. I was walking through the corridors of the high school looking for the home economics classroom. After finding the room, one observation became immediately apparent. I was the only man in the class. As I entered the room all heads turned in synchronized unison. I felt very strange. I now had two choices. I could either ask, in a deep baritone voice, for the location of the automobile repair shop, or I could say hello and put on an apron. I chose the latter. I was bent on learning how to cook and what better place to start than a gourmet cooking class. My children were going to eat meals just as they had before their mother left or I was going to burn down the house trying. One thing was for certain: I was going to try.

The instructor broke us into two groups of three. We were all handed a recipe. The idea was for all groups to prepare a specific dish. At the conclusion of the allotted preparation time, each dish formed part of an entire dinner.

One of the women asked me to retrieve an egg from the refrigerator. After taking the egg out, I placed it on the counter top. As I walked away I heard a splat. My egg rolled off the counter onto the floor. I felt somewhat embarrassed as all cooking teams stopped to stare at this pitiful specimen wearing pants. I meekly apologized and cleaned up my mess. With a reddish face I opened the door and removed another egg. Only this time I was smarter, or so I thought. I placed the egg farther back on the counter thinking that surely now it was safe to walk away. As I was approaching my group I noticed a white object starting to move in the distance, and it was picking up speed at an incredible rate. I dashed to cut it off at the lip of the counter while saying, "Look at this egg go." This had to be the egg from hell. Stretching my hand out to arms length, I could feel the egg kiss my fingertips before meeting the same fate that his relative had encountered only a few minutes before. If my first accident caused everyone to stare this one almost caused them to stop breathing. Each woman looked at me as though I was an escapee from a mental institution. Finally one lady broke the silence by saying, "Why don't you place your egg in a bowl?" How simple a solution for such a complex problem, I thought. With tips such as these how could I go wrong? This was certainly worth the fee, if not for any other purpose then to learn the secret of the rolling egg trick. I returned home that night and told the kids about my experience in gourmet cooking 101. They laughed, and so did I.

The next day while Tammy and Joey were attending school I decided that it might be the perfect time to test a few of my new recipes. To my surprise it didn't go badly. Of course I had to constantly run from the stove to the counter to triple check each ingredient. After a few cuts and burns to my extremities I was on my way. Now all I needed was a potential victim to taste my gourmet delight. I made up my mind that the first one home from school would be it. That seemed only fair. I heard the front door open. It was Joey. Poor kid, I thought.

"Joseph, little buddy," I called, (as he foolishly entered the room). "Sit down, I want you to try tasting this new recipe. I think that you are going to be pleasantly surprised."

He looked at me for a moment as though to exclaim, "not me!"

"Come on, Joey, try it. We can always have your stomach pumped later on." He shook his head no. It was now time to resort to plan B. I would bribe him. Bribing always worked with children.

"If you try it I will take you to Friendly's after dinner." I watched as he carefully placed some food in his mouth. Then came the swallow. Okay, I nervously asked, "How was it?" "Not bad."

"Alright! I'm on my way!" I shouted.

For the next few weeks I attended every cooking class. Within a short time I became friendly with everyone in the class. They all greeted me warmly. Sometimes I would join them in enjoying our nightly preparations and at other times I would bring home the night's meal for the children to taste. Soon, I was moving about the kitchen like Mario Batali. There wasn't anything I couldn't prepare from stuffed Cornish hens to eggplant Parmesan. I learned how to bake pies, cakes, and even came up with a few recipes of my own. The children would make a suggestion as to what they would like for dinner and I would prepare it. Knowing that, at times, I might not be home to cook a nightly meal I would prepare a few meals in advance for them to eat.

We could have lived on fast food but that is not what I wanted for my children. When their mother lived at home, she prepared dinner every night. We sat at the kitchen table as a family conversing about the events of the day. That wasn't going to change.

Chapter 3

GROWING UP IN an Italian family in Brooklyn, it was not uncommon for children to be raised by their grandmother. Yes, the little old lady who always dressed in black, wearing her gray hair in a bun, and mourning someone who died twenty years ago. In reality no one knew whom she was mourning. That little tidbit of information was lost somewhere with the passing of time. It was enough to know that there was always someone to mourn.

Italian funerals managed to bring out all the emotions family and friends could deliver. They were a sight to behold. The crying never ceased. If in the rare event there was a momentary pause in the emotional display, you could be certain that the next person approaching the casket would bring on another howling rendition surpassing the first. The crying would start all over again with "too soon," and "why?" No matter how old the deceased, it was always too soon. I wondered what was too soon about dying at ninety-three years of age?

Everyone offered condolences and kind words of solace guaranteeing the poor deceased was with God. No matter how decadent people knew this individual to be, today, he was with God.

I was dumfounded. Was there no accounting for taste? If this miserable specimen of a human being made it to heaven and is now residing with God then who is keeping the devil company? God keeps some pretty awful company, I thought. At any rate, all the carrying on was a ruse because on the way home you would hear how awful this individual really was and how the world was now a better place without him. Although this opinion could quickly be altered if one discovered that they had been named in his will.

Back then there was a need for an Italian grandmother. Both mothers and fathers found it necessary to work, not for the benefit of luxury items, it simply took two paychecks to make ends meet. Most men frowned on the fact that wives had to work. At least they expounded this opinion in public. However, they always welcomed that second check rarely allowing their spouses to keep any of it for her personal needs.

My grandmother raised my two brothers and myself. We loved her dearly. After all she was the one we hid behind when my mother chased us with the wooden spoon. You see the main purpose of the wooden spoon was not to stir the sauce. Oh no, that's what everyone thought it was used for. It was really a weapon used by my mother to inflict pain upon us anywhere she could connect. (I always believed that the armed forces should not be issued rifles but instead be issued wooden spoons.) These spoons broke easily upon contact so a loving mother would always keep a spare on hand. Our job, as children, was to seek out and destroy this Italian vehicle of torture before ending up on the receiving end of its wrath. When no one was home I would break any and all wooden spoons I was able to locate, on the open window sill, they were then flung into the back yard to take up residence with the tomatoes and the fig tree. With any accuracy one might be able to hit the pail resting on the fig tree's shoulders.

My grandmother arrived here from a small town in Sicily. She married young, giving birth to seven children, four boys and three girls. Owning and operating a vegetable store, in Brooklyn, she toiled side by side with her husband. In addition to endless hours of work, she cooked, cleaned house, and lived the life of a diligent housewife. She taught her children to be respectful to others and loving towards one another.

The family was the focal point of her existence. Within the family all problems could be solved. Being part of an Italian family was extremely comforting. Her family, as with most families of her generation, was ruled by the husband. It was he who made all the important decisions. His word was conclusive on all issues. His decisions were never to be questioned or bartered. His mandates never violated. He was as close a thing to God that ever came down the pike. Did his children violate his rules? Certainly, kids are kids. However, the price one paid if caught was extremely severe.

My grandfather, in his later years, abandoned his wife and children. He met another woman, moved out of the house, and set up residence with the new apple of his eye. Yes, even back then men had indiscreet affairs. What they did not do was desert the family. This was unheard of in an Italian family. This incomprehensible act was a violation of God and man's law. The price he paid for committing such an abhorrent deed, for violating the dignity of the family, was death. Not in the customary way that we know death, but a sentence by all family members to a life of nonexistence. His name would never be spoken again by any member of the family. It was as though he never left a shoe print on the face of the earth. The boys now ran the household with the oldest son assuming the duties and responsibilities of the father.

Years later I heard that my grandfather showed up on my grandmother's doorstep asking for forgiveness. I believe that she would have taken him back, but her sons closed the door in his face and that was the last time she, or any of her children, ever saw or heard from him. Through the rumor mill they discovered that he had passed away. I remember asking my mother where her father was buried. She didn't know, nor did anyone else in the family. In all the years that my grandmother lived with us I never heard her mention my grandfather's name. You would never know that she was once married.

I will always remember my grandmother in this light. At eighty years of age she became stricken with cancer. One afternoon I was walking her to the doctor's office when she tripped and fell crossing the street. As I reached down to grab her arm she pushed my hand aside. Reaching for one last moment of dignity she picked herself up, pointed her nose towards the sky, and proudly continued on her way. Three weeks later she passed away. In her heart, and in her life, her children always came first. Reflecting, I wish that I could have given her one more hug.

Unlike the past, as parents today abandon their children in search of their own happiness we realize there are very few consequences for their acts. People do not seem to understand that there should be a price to pay for disparaging behavior. You cannot leave your family today without tomorrow being different. The mores of true love, faithfulness and honesty should be what guides every member within a family. Violate these values and face the known consequences. Tomorrow's consequences has to be the price for today's mistakes. As strange as it may seem, it was easier for me to understand the old ways.

Chapter 4

LIFE WAS BECOMING more difficult. The children missed their mother. We all did.

Tammy was the closest of the children to her. On her fourteenth birthday her mother had left her with relatives in upstate New York while disappearing to be with her new love.

A beautiful blond with sky blue eyes that expressed the German half of her heritage, Tammy's nature was that of a loving caring child. She only saw the goodness in the world and all that was in it. She was not in any way mean spirited but kind and gentle. I was worried about her and what she was feeling; frightened that she might be internalizing her thoughts and emotions. One day attempting to pick up her spirits, I turned to her and said, "Why don't you go upstairs and start packing your bags."

"Why?"

"We are going to Europe." "To Europe?"

"I thought I had already said that, Tammy," I joked.

I knew the one person who might be able to cheer her up was her older sister and the only way for that to happen was if I made it happen. They were sisters and friends. The two of them would be more comfort to each other than I could ever be.

"Can I go too?" Joey asked.

"I wouldn't think of leaving you behind." "Dad, can I bring a friend?" Tammy inquired.

"Why not? If that's what you would like then bring a friend."

At this stage, I wasn't about to turn down her request. Nothing so trivial mattered. With my life turned upside down, my heart torn from my body, and my thoughts scattered, adrift somewhere in the ionosphere, why should any request upset me? The more, the merrier.

A few days later we boarded a charter plane for Paris. I had a feeling that my finances would soon be heading for an all time low so why not enjoy what might be one last vacation with the children. I wondered if the airlines offered a dysfunctional family fare?

After retiring from the New York City Police Department, I became a limited partner in a private security company. My partners, realizing my family situation, knew that I would not be able to partake in the everyday running of the business. Fortunately, the combination of my pension and business investment allowed me to make ends meet.

We drove into Manhattan to update our passports. Thirteen hours later I pulled into our driveway. During the course of the day, my car was towed to the west side pound for parking in a restricted area. The cost: fifty dollars for the ticket; one hundred and fifty dollars for the pound fee; ten dollars for the cab ride to the pound, and ten dollars for the tunnel toll. Numb from the day's occurrences, I couldn't help thinking that this was not a very good sign of future events. There was still one major hurdle that I would have to circumvent before we departed for France. I had always been terribly afraid to fly.

Passing the pilot as we boarded the 747 charter I said, "Don't forget the flaps." He looked at me with a strange expression on his face. My comment made perfect sense to me. Almost every airline crash that I had read about was caused by pilot error. The number one reason for this, in my mind, was someone forgot to either raise or lower the flaps. I didn't want to tell him what to do with the flaps because I wasn't sure if he should lower or raise them upon take off. Suppose I gave the pilot the wrong information and he listened to me, I could be signing my own death warrant, I thought. Yes, I was coming to the realization that I would have to stay on my toes during this entire trip.

As we searched about the plane for our seats, I told the children that I would have to sit by a window. "Don't worry I won't be disturbing you by getting up to use the bathroom because I won't be moving out of this seat for the entire flight."

"Dad, you won't be moving out of your seat for the entire flight?" Tammy asked. "Of course not, I have to watch the engine that's why I need a window seat." "Watch the engine? Watch it for what?" Tammy laughed.

"Yes, watch the engine, and the wing too, for sparks, loose bolts and wing fatigue. If I see anything like that starting to occur I'm out of here. Tammy, why are you having a hard time understanding all of this? To me it makes perfect sense."

Joey was deriving some sick pleasure observing my rather pale complexion getting whiter by the second. He loved to fly. The more turbulence, the more he liked it. Oh, just great, I thought, I'm on my way to Europe with two teenage girls, to meet another teenage girl, with a son who's highlight of the trip is going to be watching his father receive a shot of epinephrine in order to restart his heart.

Our first stop was Gander, New Foundland for refueling. As we approached the runway, I was amazed at the vast emptiness below, causing me to wonder why anyone would want to live in the middle of the North Atlantic? The more I looked, the more beautiful the great expanse became. Perhaps I should move here? What modern day problems could these simple people be faced with? I thought.

Tammy and her friend asked if they could spend a few moments browsing about the airport stores while the plane took on fuel. I thought for a second and said, "Sure." Joey elected to stay with me. It wasn't long before the other passengers started to reboard the plane. I tried my best to stall the flight attendant hoping that the two girls would show. I was starting to become concerned that the plane would take off without us. "Dad, do you want me to find them?" Joey asked.

"Okay, but make it quick." It wasn't long before the girls came walking down the boarding ramp.

"Thank God," I said. I was about to lecture them when I noticed that Joey wasn't with them.

"Tammy, where is your brother?" "What brother?"

"You know, the same brother that you always had. Tammy didn't you see him? He went looking for you."

The flight attendant looked at me as though to say, "Have you ever thought of taking this show on the road?"

"Hey, look, I'm new at this," I said. "So, I misplaced a child, big deal."

A few minutes later with my bevy conveyed together we re-boarded the plane. I reminded the flight attendant about the flaps and we took off on the final leg of our trip to Paris. Sitting in my seat I asked myself, "Why am I doing this?" Once again I fixed my eyes on the huge engines hoping that the deicer worked better than the one in my refrigerator did at home. Tammy looked at me with my nose stuck to the Plexiglas window and asked, "Still not going to relax Dad?"

"No, not until I'm on the ground where I belong."

As the plane took off, I closed my eyes and squeezed the arm rest and repeated, "Why am I doing this?" A single father surrounded by children in a strange country. What could I have possibly been thinking at the time I made this suggestion?

It was wonderful to see Claudine again. She was enjoying her summer residing with a french family in the Britannia region of France. I was quite impressed with the fluency of her French. She had made great strides in such a short period of time. Then again, she always had a knack for foreign languages. She seemed to speak every language but mine.

Prior to arriving in France, I decided to give the children a lot more freedom then was my custom. I wanted them to have fun, to enjoy themselves. I knew that in a short time they would be drawn back into the conflict of a pending divorce. I came to the conclusion that they needed a little room. If I pulled back too hard on the reins, they would rear up. If I held the reins too loosely, they would run wildly out of control. At this stage, they needed a little slack on the reins. I fell in love with Paris and yet something was missing. I wanted to be able to share it with the one special person that was no longer in my life. No, this trip wasn't for me. It wasn't my moment. I was here to nurture and bring a smile to what was now the most precious thing in my life, my children.

With Claudine serving as our guide, we remained in Paris for a few days taking in the sights. I enjoyed art and wanted to visit the Louvre. I convinced Joey to join me because I promised him that I would treat him to a bumper car ride we had noticed within close proximity of the museum.

It was July with the temperature soaring outside. The temperature inside the Louve was the even more stifling. Joey immediately wanted out.

"Okay, Joey, I promise if you will be a little patient in a few minutes we will be on our way."

I no sooner finished my statement when I noticed an unusually large crowd standing in front of one particular painting. All heads were tilted back as they appeared to marvel with adoration at the sight before them. I knew why they were staring. Only one painting could create this type of fuss and enthusiasm. I turned to Joey asking, "Do you want to see the Mona Lisa?" "What's that?"

"Well, it's probably the most famous painting in the world. A man named Leonardo De Vinci painted it a long time ago. It portrays a lady with a mystic, captivating smile. Men have written songs about her and have been intrigued by her magnetism and beauty. Let's take a look."

Fighting the crowd we positioned ourselves in front of the Mona Lisa. Joey's face said it all. He flinched as he looked up at the painting. His face looked as though he had just swallowed a sour ball. I knew the meaning behind his expression.

"Dad, she is ugly!"

I looked at him, then at Mona, after a few seconds, I said, "Joey, you're right she really is pretty homely." To Joey, Mona was like caviar, if it's so good why do we have to work so hard at persuading people to try it? Never argue with the honesty of a child, I concluded. "Joey, come on buddy, let's go on the bumper cars." A smile came across his face that said, "finally." A little boy was made happy in Paris with a simple gesture of love.

After spending a few days in Paris, I rented a car that comfortably held four. Somehow I managed to wedge five people into it, along with enough luggage to fill the first floor of Bloomingdale's, and headed south towards Nice. The children loved the warm air, balmy breezes, and relaxed demeanor of the French Riviera. Once again I allowed them a little more flexibility than usual. A few days later we departed the French Riviera with all its beauty.

Our next stop was London. Joey started to run a fever. Not knowing the cause of his temperature I called for the hotel doctor to examine him; he rendered a quick diagnosis of pneumonia. With Joey's temperature nearing a 104, I made a decision to cancel the trip two days short of our intended stay. The last thing I wanted was one of the children hospitalized several thousand miles from home.

Arriving at the airport I was told the airlines overbooked our flight. They asked that I find a hotel to remain in until the next day when there might be some passenger availability. I looked at Joey sitting in the lounge area of the terminal and knew that I couldn't allow him to remain here in his condition for another day. The airlines might not have known it, but we were getting on that flight. I would, if necessary, create a scene that would be remembered by all who witnessed it for years to come, but first I would ask nicely. To my surprise, they understood my situation and somehow found four available seats. Sometime later we arrived unscathed at Kennedy International Airport. Joey didn't register a complaint during the entire trip home. It was obvious that he was longing for the tranquility of his bed. Finally arriving home I made him comfortable. I then asked Tammy to keep an eye on him while I ran to the local supermarket to pick up a few staples.

Chapter 5

FOOD SHOPPING HAD never been one of my favorite pastimes. Within the walls of the supermarket, I was out of my element. This was a bastion for women as they made their daily haj to purchase groceries. Here, I was outnumbered ten-fold. After doing the family grocery shopping for the last few weeks, I was amazed at how women moved about the store. They appeared to move in slow motion, picking up, touching, and squeezing anything that allowed itself to be picked up, touched, and squeezed. I was afraid to stand still for fear of being picked up and squeezed. Whether they wished to purchase it or not didn't matter. They squeezed it anyway.

Another observation I made was that women abandoned their shopping carts in the middle of an aisle disappearing in search of a specific item. The manner in which they shopped was similar in many ways to the way they operated a motor vehicle. It was very clear that no rules of the road existed here. Some pushed their carts on the right side while others used the European approach by hugging the left, and a few came right down the middle. The one thing they appeared to have in common was that they were totally oblivious to anyone around them, especially me.

When searching for a grocery item, I could position my cart right behind theirs. If I didn't pretend to clear my throat they would never know that I existed. It was as though I was invisible. In order to pass I would meekly say, "Excuse me," which always managed to meet with a bewildered look on their faces. Kind of like, "Oh, where did you come from?" Of course they would let me pass, but I was fascinated at how I would wind up behind the same woman in another aisle. With all their squeezing and touching, how did they manage to get ahead of me again? Once again the whole scenario had to be repeated. A few women in the same aisle could cause a backup worse than rush hour on the Long Island Expressway and yet it never seemed to disturb them. Somehow, this was part of the program.

The coupon scene at the register was another fiasco. From somewhere deep within their pocketbooks, these women kept a smaller pocketbook. After ten minutes of searching, they succeeded in pulling out a pile of coupons that were held together by the world's oldest rubber bands. Next, they browsed through them in search of each coupon that matched the item they were purchasing. Many of the coupons were expired, but had not been discarded because they kept trying to pass them off on different cashiers.

This particular day, I knew I was in trouble when the lady in front of me pulled out a coupon that read ten cents off a tube of Ipana toothpaste. She also tried to receive twenty five cents off a roll of paper towels. The clerk informed her that the coupon had expired causing her to ask to see the manager. The manager confirmed that a discount could not be given. Her reply, "In that case, I don't want to purchase it." Now, a credit had to be deducted from her bill. With this completed, the last event took place. It was time for her to pay. Once again she opened her pocketbook. Inside the smaller pocketbook was a purse containing her cash. I laughed thinking, what a way to go through life.

After what felt like a lifetime, the expedition was completed. Of course payment had to be made to the exact penny. I wanted to scream, "Why didn't you have your money out and ready ten minutes ago? Did you think that all this food was for free?" Instead, I elected to remain silent. The final insult occurred as she started to walk away from the register. "I'm not coming back here again they take much too long," she said.

I knew that shopping would never be a pleasurable task, but a necessary one nonetheless. Yes, I could do this with time to spare but it would be wiser for me to food shop at two o'clock in the morning. In a few days, Joey was feeling better. Seeing any of my children sick always upset me, but in the past there was a partner, a wife, a mother who made life so much easier. My God, I thought, I miss those days.

Summer was quickly coming to a close. I was slowly making progress in my new found responsibilities as Mom, housekeeper, and do-it-all Dad. Yes, half the houseplants were dead from not being watered. The remaining half died from being over watered, and the artificial houseplants died from dust inhalation, but I was inching forward. I needed time. Even diamonds have flaws, I thought.

Claudine was due home from France and I welcomed her arrival, although I knew that with a third child in the house my job would become harder and not easier. There was one more skill that I wanted to develop before her arrival. It was now time for me to conquer the iron and ironing board. My daily attire was one of pressed wrinkles. I was taking most of our clothing to the dry cleaners and knew that I would have to come up with an alternative plan. It was becoming too expensive to continue to use dry cleaning services for everyday articles. There wasn't a choice. I had to learn how to iron.

The iron and ironing board quickly became my enemies- I hated them and they hated me. It didn't take long for me come to the realization that there would never be peace between us. I treated them as though they were living, breathing, evil entities. To me, they were real and out to inflict a great deal of punishment on me. This was war at its most sadistic state.

Technologically speaking, mankind has made great strides, and yet, look at this thing: Two X's with a board on top that gets repeatedly run over by a steam engine. How this antique slipped the ingenuity of modern man was beyond me. Perhaps, because it's kept in a closet, and well, it should be kept in a closet away from children, pets, and single fathers.

Regardless of where I placed the iron on the board, I somehow managed to brush against it with my hand causing me to shout a bombardment of curse words throughout the house. The children were wise in affording me plenty of berth while ironing. Not only could I not iron, but watching me attempt to raise and lower the ironing board was a sight to behold. Observing me ironing a shirt on a board that could either be two feet, or four feet above the ground, had to make for great conversation. In a rage of anger, I would pick up the board, flip it on its back, and throw it to the floor. The only visual comparison would be a man wrestling an alligator. During several of these encounters, I could swear that I heard the ironing board laughing at me saying, "Is this the best you can give?" "Keep it up," I would yell, "and you're going back in your closet."

My hands were slowly becoming a mass of scars. It was beyond my wildest comprehension how anyone could iron anything. All I seemed to accomplish was to create more wrinkles. Only now they were more permanent in nature.

One day I was sitting in the kitchen when I suddenly became aware of the cause of my problems. It was indisputably the ironing board cover. Obviously, it was flawed with wrinkles. This made it impossible for anything to be ironed with any degree of success.

After all, if I placed something on a wrinkled cover, and pressed on it, it too would become wrinkled. At first I tried to loosen the pad by untying the string under the ironing board. But in spite of how much I jostled the cover, it always seemed to return to its original position. I was left with no choice but to cut the string, remove the cover, and toss it away. I believed this had to be an improvement over my prior predicament.

However, there was something I did not realize. The ironing board, in its naked stage, had holes in it. Not one hole but a multitude of holes resembling an elongated piece of Swiss cheese. I might as well make the attempt anyway, I thought.

I placed a shirt on the ironing board in preparation for the next step. After putting water in the iron I waited for it to make the familiar hissing sound that I always heard irons make. A few seconds passed without a sound. Disappointed, I added a little more water, and then some more. I decided to iron anyway assuming that the hissing sound would catch up with me somewhere along the way. Tilting the iron in a horizontal position I began to glide it back and forth over my shirt.

Steamy hot water began to pour out of the iron soaking my shirt. The water continued to pour out onto the floor. I was amazed at the amount of water coming out of this little iron. I thought that I had punctured a water main. Quickly unplugging the iron, I ran to the sink and poured out the remaining water. I could tell the iron was angry that I had unplugged it because it was now hissing wildly at me.

I knew there had to be a better way to iron clothes. Using my masculine intellect I reasoned, why not dry iron? Who needs water? Instead of water I could use spray starch. I would simply have to use a lot of it. This had to be the secret to successful ironing. It would certainly be better than going through this whole fiasco again. I sprayed the shirt until it was good and wet and then sprayed it again. Now before me was a perfect candidate for ironing, or so I thought. As I worked the iron up and down the shirt, I was startled at what was taking place. My shirt was taking on the form, look, and shape of the ironing board. Numerous little round holes started to appear, and with every stroke, more seemed to surface. It was becoming so stiff that it looked as if it could walk out the door without me. "Enough, I would much rather pay the dry cleaning fee." I said.

Chapter 6

I PICKED CLAUDINE up at the airport. Her summer in France was a wonderful opportunity any young girl would treasure. I was glad to have her home to keep Tammy company and delighted that she wasn't here to witness the events of the last few months. It was nice to be a family again; even if a somewhat shattered family.

Claudine was the most aggressive and intellectually brightest of my children. She was beautiful and possessed a high level of what I called, "street smart." She also possessed a lust for life. Trying to accommodate her intellectual thirst was a never-ending job. Her needs were many.

As a child she entered the first grade on a high school reading level. By the time she was in the second grade, she memorized the entire edition of the Children's World Book Encyclopedia. One could turn to any page, in any volume, and ask her a question on a particular subject. The correct answer would come forth within seconds. Claudine had decided to go the route of a parochial education by entering The Academy Of Saint Joseph, a very prestigious girls high school on Long Island. It had one of the best educational programs offered anywhere in the United States. Here, she would be able to play mental volleyball with nuns who, I hoped, were her equal. The only issue that concerned me was discipline and her dislike of it.

As the new school year was about to begin, I ran around with each of the children making certain that they had the necessary school supplies. I also had to update their wardrobe by purchasing clothes, shoes, sneakers, and whatever additional items they might need. The girls were wondering if I would ever catch on to the how of doing a wash. Everything was either pink or reduced to postage size. I never realized how complicated this laundry thing was: whites required bleach but you couldn't pour bleach directly on the clothes for fear of burning holes in them or causing blotches. I always thought the more bleach, the cleaner the item until I noticed the fabric falling apart at the slightest touch. Cottons should not go in the dryer with the heat cycle on high. It caused shrinkage. Clothing made of linen had to go to the dry cleaners. Silk was a no-no. All said and done, I was beginning to wonder if there was anything that could be washed. With every article of clothing that I destroyed, I promised to buy a new one. Doing laundry was becoming very costly. I concluded it would have been less expensive to move to Florida where we could wear bathing suits all year round.

The job of becoming both mom and dad were gradually taxing my strength. I found myself food shopping in the wee hours of the morning then coming home and having to unpack all the groceries alone. One night, while carrying the groceries, I slipped on the icy walk leading to the house. Of course a bottle of cranberry juice met the pavement causing it to shatter. Standing there in the snow I asked, "Where is that other person in my life? The one with the extra X chromosome? The one that I had always relied on for help." Yes, I had joined "The Cult of Domesticity," and now knew why a feminist movement existed in our society. Anything was better than this.

The children were oblivious to everything around them. No matter how high I pilled the garbage at the front door that is where it remained until I carried it to the pail. Whenever I asked them why they didn't take out the trash, their answers were always the same, "We didn't see it!" How could they not see something that Sir Edmond Hillary would have trouble climbing over? Dirty dishes were never put into the dishwasher. I was happy if they found their way to the sink. As far as their rooms were concerned, I was nervous to go into any of them for fear of catching Legionnaire's disease or that some molded spirit might reach out and drag me under their bed into a different dimension, and the only way I could return would be through my television set. For some unknown reason, they thought leaving clothes and dirty dishes on dressers, in closets, and under beds was fine, a way of life. I was running a penicillin farm and didn't know it.

One day, realizing that my circuitry was beginning to fizzle, I picked up their clutter and threw it out the second floor bedroom window onto the lawn. It didn't faze them in the least. Whenever they needed a particular item, they would go out and retrieve it, but only that item. I wondered where had I gone wrong in raising them?

Whenever I tried to catch up on a little sleep, one of them would knock on my bedroom door to inform me that they missed the school bus. In Claudine's case, it meant driving her thirty miles to school. I learned to dread that knock on my bedroom door early in the morning. On weekends there were school dances to attend, sometimes two on the same night. It was my official job to serve as chauffeur and if I happened to be a few minutes late- heaven help me. I was beginning to learn that daughters were not a patient lot.

It was a Friday night. I just dropped Claudine off at her school to attend a dance. Tammy informed me that she was invited to a sleep over party at her girlfriend's house. The situation was improving by the second. Joey decided to go to bed early. I quickly searched through my private collections of videotapes looking for one of my favorite movies. Because our tastes differed, my tapes were one of my few possessions safe from pilferage by the children. Finding my movie I shoved it into the VCR, poured myself a glass of coke, grabbed a handful of munchies, leaned back, and let the good times roll.

I could tell that tonight everything was in my favor because I even managed to insert the tape into the VCR correctly. The last time I rammed it in wrong end first. Knowing that I did something improper I tried to remedy the situation by pushing all the buttons on the four remotes that operated the VCR, TV, stereo, CD and karaoke machine. A bright blue screen covered the TV that contained lots of mystery letters and numbers. I was left with no alternative except to yell, "Joey, help!"

Joey, coming to my aid, observed me sheepishly standing there with four remotes in my hand said, "You did it again! You just won't listen, will you! When will you ever learn how to use any of this equipment? And why can't you learn?"

"Joey, try to understand what I am about to tell you. Unlike you, I am one hundred percent Italian, worse, third generation Sicilian. You, on the other hand, are fifty percent German which means you can't sing a note but you do have this wonderful ability to put things back together again. True, you are genetically predisposed to put a turret on top of everything you touch, wear uniforms, and march instead of walk, but you can't help that. Furthermore, we didn't have these electronic gadgets when and where I grew up. In my neighborhood, people would have had tomatoes coming out of these things, and if that didn't work, they would have filled them with cement. Now, can you fix this or can't you?"

"Dad, if you leave me alone for about fifteen minutes I will have you up and running again. Go do something else while I work on this. Why don't you go dye something pink?"

"Good idea."

Well nothing like that was transpiring tonight. All systems were go. Enjoying the near extinct moments in my life known as quietness, I lapped up every morsel of it. I was alone, engrossed in my movie, and not paying attention to the time. Looking up at the clock I realized that I was running behind schedule picking Claudine up from her school dance. In an attempt to save time, I decided to drive there in my pajamas and of course I was pulled over by a State Trooper for speeding. I guess my attire, or lack of attire, aroused his curiosity because he looked at me as though I were a bit off center. Oh great, I thought, how in the world am I going to explain this? Pajamas, socks without shoes, and if he checks deep enough pink underwear. As I attempted to clarify my situation, I began to trip over my sentences, "Officer, for the first time in months they were all out of the house."

"Who was out of the house?"

"They were. The three of them. Actually, only two. One went to bed early and was sleeping. I was finally able to watch television undisturbed because I was caught up on my ironing, and washing. The dishwasher was empty and there wasn't any trash piled up at the front door and for the first time in a week I didn't bleach a hole in anything."

"Bleach? What hole are you talking about?"

"My daughter's blouse. Liquid bleach. Then, I remembered the dance..."

"Look," he interrupted, "Take it easy. (Sure, I thought, that's easy for him to say.) I don't have the heart to give you a summons. You already have too many problems." Well, at least we agreed on that issue. I could hear him laughing all the way back to his car.

There were little league games to attend. School functions and other related parent child events. Whether the event called for a father or mother, somehow. I was there.

One Saturday morning I dropped Joey off at church at 10:00 a.m. so that he could attend his scheduled confirmation class. Next, I rushed home to drop Claudine off at McDonald's where she was working part time. After dropping her off, I raced back to drive Tammy to a high school function. A short time later, or what felt like a short time, the girls returned home. At about 5:00p.m. I began to call Joey's name. Wondering why he wasn't answering I asked the girls, "When was the last time you saw your brother?"

"When you took him to church this morning," Tammy answered.

"Oh, my God!" I shouted. "I forgot your brother!" Racing back to the church I found Joey patiently sitting on the front steps.

"Hi, Dad," he called without registering a complaint.

I think that what upset me most was leaving Joey alone for long periods of time. I was worried that he might wake up in the middle of the night looking for me, or that a fire would occur in my absence. All this weighed heavily on my mind but did I have a choice? I was doing it by myself. However, this was the job that I had asked for. At times I would argue with myself. "Why don't you quit?" "I don't know." "Aren't you tired?" Exhausted." "Have you ever thought of packing your bags and running away?" "All the time. If I go would you go with me?" "No, I have to stay here to watch the kids." Hell, I couldn't even win an argument with myself so I might as well stay too, I thought.

The chaos and work were part of the package. What I didn't know was how exhausting it would get. I was learning that, regardless of how hard I tried, I still wasn't Mom. They missed her and I knew it.

The holidays were particularly difficult, especially the first Christmas. As the children placed each ornament on the tree that was made or purchased for them by their mother, they cried. It was Christmas, but emptiness filled our house. Memories were not always good. Sometimes they could be painful. In my case it was painful to watch, to remain helpless. I wondered how someone could inflict so much unhappiness on three beautiful children that any parent would be proud to call theirs.

I was about to leave for work one afternoon when the phone rang. It was my lawyer. He asked that I meet with him the next day. He had heard from my wife's attorney and wanted to discuss the divorce. I informed him that I would stop by his office at noon.

Chapter 7

CIRCLING THE CROWDED parking lot, I found a space near the entrance to the multi-suite office building. I entered and located the name of my attorney listed in the lobby directory. Although we had previously spoken on the phone we had not yet met. During my years in the New York City Police Department I had grown to view lawyers as a necessary evil. I believed the old adage that one lawyer in a small town would starve to death. Two lawyers in the same town would live very prosperous lives.

After all, if ethics and morals ruled their existence they would turn away fifty percent of their cases. I didn't want my current situation to deteriorate to a point where it would be financially beneficial to only the attorneys. My primary concern was the children and whatever it might take to retain custody.

I found my attorney's office with little difficulty. His name was listed first on the door followed by several other attorney's names. It immediately became apparent that he was the senior partner. I entered the office and was asked to take a seat in the waiting room. Seated around me were several men and women. Studying each of their faces, I wondered what their individual circumstances were. The first question that came to mind was who was the leaver? And, who was the leavee? A term I used to describe each party involved in a divorce. It wouldn't be hard to distinguish the difference. The leavee would be the one whose eyes were red from crying- the one possessing a bewildered look giving the appearance they had been struck by lightning. The leaver, in most cases, would be the one with a dream-like euphoric look symbolizing that they were now going to a far better place. A look that said, "Happiness is just around the corner." In my mind it was far better to be the leaver than the leavee. They were the ones who had a choice.

A few minutes had passed before a receptionist escorted me into my attorney's office, easily the largest of the surrounding offices. A man in his late forties walked out from behind a large dark maple desk and introduced himself. He was dressed in a dark tailored blue pinstriped suit, white shirt, and wore black expensive shoes. His beard was well groomed giving the appearance that he could very easily play King Arthur in Camelot. In his mouth was a long unlit cigar. I hoped that he wouldn't light it during our meeting. Most of the detectives I worked with in the police department smoked cigars. Something I had never developed a taste for and personally during my plain-clothes years I had inhaled enough cigar smoke to become a Cuban. He began his conversation by saying, "I heard from your wife's attorney and they want to proceed with the divorce as quickly as possible."

"What's the rush?"

"What's the rush? She's in love, or so she thinks and by the way, she wants custody of the children."

"She, what? After all these months, now she wants custody?"

"That's right. Now lean back and let me give you some advice," he said.

With some apprehension I did as he asked. He recommended that I let her take custody of the children- that if the case went to court I would not be awarded possession of three kids, especially two girls. A judge, he contended, was not going to believe that I could do the job. At least not the way it should be done. He said that what I was really doing was asking him to cast his vote against motherhood. Judges, he insisted, were also politicians and rarely sided against mothers in custody cases. Rolling his eyes to accentuate his point he said, "God forbid you made some terrible mistake. The press would trace it back to him as the one who granted you custody."

By the way he positioned himself in the soft leather chair I could tell that I was about to be placed on the receiving end of a philosophical lecture. He began by telling me how senior citizens were driving around killing the youth of America by signaling left and turning right.

How they failed to observe stop signs and operated vehicles in the left lanes of highways doing forty-five miles an hour. And no matter what statistics insurance companies may quote about their safe driving habits, they left a lot of bodies in their wake. Some poor teenager, he insisted, would never be able to reach the age of the senior who killed him because that senior's reflexes slowed to a point where he had no right to be behind the wheel of an automobile. Shaking his head in disbelief he told me that a ninety-year-old man stopped by his office the other day. It was his third accident this year. He said that this man's osteoporosis was so bad that when he operated his vehicle his nose was wedged in-between the steering wheel. He looked as if he never had a glass of milk in his life. "I pleaded with him to stop driving before he killed someone," he shouted. The elderly man told him that when he returned from driving to Maine he would give it some thought.

Deciding that I finally had enough of his endless bantering I interrupted, "Do you mind telling me what all this has to do with my divorce?"

"What I am trying to make clear to you is that in this society there are sacred cows. Women raising children and seniors are two of them. Let her raise them. It's too big a job for one person to do, especially a man. You can't do it, and you won't be successful at it."

"So," I laughed, "when are you going to tell me what's on your mind?" I appreciated his thoughts and advice but he was wrong. I was going to do this job and I was going to succeed at it. I had to.

I questioned if he or anyone knew how difficult it was for me to visualize my soon to-be ex-wife in a demonic light. I had to fight every second of every day trying to keep my guard up, trying to remember that she was not the same person that I knew and loved. While she was relentlessly tearing the heart out of this family, I felt sorry for her. I anticipated that any moment she was going to wake up, come to her senses, and return to her role as mother and wife. Not a day went by that I did not think these thoughts and not a day went by that her impenetrable hardness did not snap me from my trance with a strong dose of reality. It was hard for me to fight this fight. If it wasn't for the children, I'm not sure I could, or would want to fight.

Still, I explained, I was smart enough to know that when a parent abandoned their children for a stranger, the children were no longer their number one concern. Their priorities had changed. Number one on the hit parade was now the new person in their life and they were compelled to make their new relationship work at all costs. There wasn't any room for failure. The children, and their needs, were placed on a back burner.

In a woman's situation, time was also against her. Society has made it harder for women to start a second and third relationship. A man could date, and marry, a woman ten or fifteen years his junior. I tried to make it clear that I was not arguing with him or anyone else about the fairness of this situation. It wasn't fair and it never would be fair. All I was stating was an objective view clarifying the logical reason why my children would be second in their mother's life. Time simply would not allow her to start over again. She had to make this realtionship work at any cost.

This was contrary to my situation. There wasn't anyone that I had to appease, or answer to, just myself. I may have lacked the skills but I hadn't been confronted with the need to develop certain child-rearing abilities, but that wasn't an insolvable issue. None of this was my choice. I wasn't looking to test my paternal or, in this case, maternal capabilities. It was all dropped in my lap. I wasn't in my present situation because of any willful decision on my part. I was lucky that I was able to drag myself out of bed every morning. All this was so much more than I had bargained for. I was waiting for someone to count to three, snap their fingers, and bring me out of my trance but I didn't hear anyone counting. Believe me I was listening.

I asked him if he was eluding that because someone wore a skirt and lipstick that they were automatically qualified to raise children? That success was guaranteed? Well, then, I disagreed. I suggested that he take a good look at what was going on around him because I saw both fathers and mothers asking four-year-olds for their opinions and views on all sorts of issues. Five-year-olds were getting an equal say in how a household should be run. Six-year-olds were disrupting dinner and dismantling pews during Sunday mass while their parents sat idly by, unwilling, and unable to control the little devils. I also suggested that he take a walk into his local supermarket and let me know the next time he heard a child say, "Please" or "Excuse me." Or for that matter hold a door opened for a senior citizen. I reminded him that teenagers today had more ornamental rings protruding from their bodies then a merry-go-round and that both mothers and fathers were failing in the basics of child-rearing. If this was my competition then all I wanted was the opportunity to compete. He started to interrupt me.

"Excuse me I'm not done," I said. "You got the juices flowing and I want to finish." He sat quietly allowing me to vent.

I went on to say that most men did not want to assume the burden and responsibilities of another man's children. This man walked out on his own children, left them hundreds of miles away without a father, and I was supposed to believe that he would take care of mine. They would never be paramount in his life. He would never be able to love them as though they were his. How could he? They would always remind him of me, their father. In time, he might even take his frustrations out on them. I could not allow that to happen.

There was another strange metamorphosis taking place today that frightened me. There have been too many instances where mothers have allowed step-fathers, and boyfriends, to abuse their children. Mothers were allowing men to perpetrate some heinous crimes against their children in order to start life over again with a new love. I could not risk that happening to my children. I could read the handwriting on the wall and it was telling me to be very careful. The little voice that we all have inside us was shouting at me to fight to keep my children safe. How could I ever forgive myself if something happened to them because I remained sitting passively on the sidelines? The answer to that question was, I couldn't. My children had to be first in somebody's life and unfortunately I could no longer trust their mother because I no longer knew that person, she died and who this stranger was that had emerged was beyond me. I wasn't saying that all my decisions would be the right ones. I was simply implying that it was going to be easier for me to make a decision. I had to rely on who I was, and what I was about, and what I learned from my parents, family, and life in general. My bet was on me. I was going to do this job and I was going to succeed at it because if I failed my children would never have any self-worth. The race would be lost at the starting gate. I couldn't and wouldn't allow that to happen. I couldn't go on knowing that they weren't first in somebody's life. They deserved that. I would rather sell my soul than compromise my children. They were and always would be first here. I pointed to my heart. He leaned back in his black leather chair and did what I hoped he wouldn't do. He lit his cigar.

"There is one chance."

Not saying a word I waited for him to continue.

He told me that all three of the children would have to want to remain with me. If they insisted upon staying and not going with their mother we could win custody. They were old enough to make up their own minds, at least the two oldest girls were.

"And my son?"

He said that if the girls insisted upon remaining with me, the judge would most likely allow my son to stay too. "He wouldn't want to be the one to divide children between parents. The system doesn't work that way. He wouldn't look good to any Child Protective Agency that might be watching." However, he emphasized that the longer I had custody of the children, before the case came to court, the more unlikely they wouldn't want to remain with me.

"Why?" I naively asked.

He explained that the *out of house parent* always looked better to children because they never said no. "That's what women have been complaining about all these years. Dad shows up once a week to take the kids to the park, zoo, and movies. He brings a car full of gifts, and in their eyes he's Mr. Wonderful. Meanwhile, Mom is the one who says no to a whole host of issues."

I realized that this time it would be my turn to say no, that Mom would now become Mrs. Wonderful. I was afraid that sooner or later I would lose my temper and, at that moment, she was going to look awfully good to them.

He was right. Everything he said made sense to me. Still, I had to try my best and hope that our love for each other would overcome any temporary setbacks in our relationship. I thanked him for his advice and asked that he keep me informed as the case progressed.

"One more thing before you go. If she gains custody of the children she also gains custody of the house. The house goes with the children. No judge would ask that children be forced from their home."

"So, the house I worked so hard for all my life is gone overnight along with my family?"

"That's right. Your future ex and her new love move right in."

"And me?"

"You? Make sure that you have enough charcoal for them to light the barbecue and then see if you have a friend with a fold out sofa because that's as good as its going to get for you."

"You're coming in loud and clear." Starting to walk away, I turned to say one last thing. "Maybe she deserves part of this house, and perhaps I do too, but there is one thing I am certain of, her new boyfriend doesn't deserve any of it. Not one nail."

"You're right. Life can get pretty lousy at times. Can't it?" "That's, an understatement."

On the way home I wondered how everything got this bad so quickly. The person that I loved most in my life would now be seated opposite me in a court of law fighting me for what we had created together. I was numb.

I drove home thinking that I didn't have a chance in winning a custody battle. I hoped that I might be able to persuade the court to award me custody of Joey. After all, I was the one who raised him. He was my little pal. He meant more to me than life itself.

After Joey was born, my wife had decided to pursue her graduate degree. I rearranged my work schedule so that I could remain home during the day to care for him. I was the one who fed him and changed his diapers. During the afternoon I took him to the park and pushed him on the swing. Wherever I'd go, Joey was always with me. We were inseparable. I needed him to help me do minor repairs on my car. My mechanical ability was close to nil. When I attempted to put something back together, I would observe Joey standing there shaking his head inside his fur-lined blue parka. I would stop whatever I was attempting to do and ask, "Joey, am I doing this the wrong way?" He would shake his little head yes. "So, Joey, in other words you think the other part should go on first?" A nod enlightened me to my mistake. He was always right. It progressed to a point that if I wanted to take something apart I would ask one of his sisters to fetch him before I began. He would stand there watching my every move. It was the only way I was able to put anything back together. I couldn't lose him. He was my right arm. With time we became even closer. However, I knew the reality of the situation. Judges would never separate siblings. My thoughts of keeping Joey were wishful at best.

I had never dreamed that my children might not be an everyday part of my life. I wondered why I had wasted so much time pursuing life's other interests. It was too late to roll back the clock. Despair was here, and the way it was looking it was here to stay.

Chapter 8

I WAS GETTING little help from the girls with household chores. Like most teenagers they were entirely absorbed with their own personal issues. With the crisis that was taking place in their lives, I wondered how they ever made it through the day. It's a difficult job for a single man to raise a daughter. A single man raising two daughters, they might as well be aliens. I quickly learned to stay out of their personal conflicts knowing that they would resolve their issues without my help. The few times I tried to mediate their arguments it boomeranged on me. They would quickly make up and somehow I became their mutual enemy. At times like these, I would walk away whispering to myself, "get ready to rumble." A wiser choice was to lock myself in my room while mumbling some incoherent sounds through the door hoping that they would go away. When incidents of this nature occurred, I would reflect into my childhood comparing the difference between the way I was raised and the way I was raising my children.

Whenever my brothers and I misbehaved in public, in front of relatives, or family friends my mother would give us what she referred to as, "The evil eye." Seeing, "The evil eye," we knew we were in trouble beyond the point of no return. "The evil eye," was usually followed by one of two threats. The first, "Come here, I'm not going to hit you." The second, the more dangerous of the two, "Wait until we get home." I hated number two because it ruined the rest of my day. This was not an idle threat on my mother's part. She intended to deliver the goods, and for a five-foot one-inch lady I was amazed at the velocity of her swing- why the Yankees never signed her up was beyond me. Of course when she was finished dispensing her idea of frontier justice she would always say, "and wait until your father comes home." As though I didn't already have enough. I mean, what more could he possibly do, lynch me?

Whenever possible I always opted for the first choice. It was definitely the better of the two alternatives. Number one had its drawbacks but the survival rate was much higher. I could see my mother winding up as she lured me into her den with the false promise of, "I'm not going to hit you." Approaching her, I would whisper, sure she's not, my head is just returning to its normal size from the last time she promised that she wasn't going to hit me.

However, there was an answer to this predicament that would satisfy her and increase the probability of my survival. It was all in the reach. From having gone through this same scenario in the past, like a seasoned prizefighter, I knew the exact length of my mother's reach. My technique required that I allow her to graze me. Then pretending to be hurt, more than I was, I would beg for mercy. For some reason this seemed to return the situation to "Pre-evil eye status." Yes, my kids were lucky that I locked myself in my room rather than giving them, "The evil eye."

Growing up, because of the close proximity of neighborhood friends and family, whenever my brothers or I engaged in some type of deceitful behavior, my mother instantly became aware of mischievous conduct. She had a better spy network than the CIA and the KGB combined.

One day while I was walking home, I borrowed, for lack of a better word, an apple from Mr. Catalano's fruit stand. Prior to entering our apartment, I found a new home for the core by throwing it down the corner sewer. Knowing that I properly disposed of all the evidence I climbed the stairs to our tenement. As I closed the door behind me, my mother immediately approached me.

"So, why did you steal the apple from Mr. Catalano's fruit stand?" She accusingly asked.

Still tasting the apple nectar I thought for a second before deciding to try my, "what apple Mom?" Approach.

"You know what apple," she snapped. "No I...."

"Don't interrupt me when I'm speaking, or you'll really be sorry," she threatened. "The Macintosh apple- the one with the missing stem and the bruise on the side. That's what apple, Mr. wise guy."

Startled, I wondered, how did she know so much about this apple? Next, she is going to tell me the exact day it fell from the tree. There were only three possibilities. She either had the goods on me, she was trying to intimidate me, or she was this apple's guardian angel. I now had a choice. Should I continue pursuing my lie? Did I want to risk encountering the wrath of a woman that made me dry every drop of water from the sink when I was done washing my hands? A lady that covered everything in the house with plastic? A woman that would not allow me to wear shoes in the house? The person I watched for years cutting the tinsel on the Christmas tree with a scissors to make sure that each strand was perfectly even? If she could have found a way, she would have cleaned the angel's ears on top of the tree with a QT tip. She was obsessive and I was about to become her compulsion.

Suddenly, with the pressure mounting, I was overcome with a sense of panic. I was running out of time. Any moment could be wooden spoon time. With that in mind, I blurted out, "Mom, I promise I'll never steal another apple." Later, when my swelling went down I asked her how she knew that I had stolen the apple. Protecting her source her answer was always the same, "A little birdie told me."

Of course I was smart enough to realize that in my neighborhood the bird assisting my mother had to be a pigeon. No respectable bird of any worth would setup residence in Brooklyn.

The old neighborhood housing consisted mostly of small apartments commonly know as railroad flats. All buildings were attached, not deviating in height or width, and ran the length of a city block. Each building contained six apartments. If one elected to enter any apartment on the block, other than a slight difference in decorating style, all were exactly the same in size and shape. The design consisted of two continuous parallel lines divided into four equal parts. A Frank Lloyd Wright influence was definitely lacking.

Except for a refrigerator, stove, and one family television, modern conveniences were non-existent. Clothes were washed in the kitchen sink, and dried on clotheslines. These lines ran from the kitchen window attaching to a pole in the back yard. Of course, hanging out the laundry was the perfect time for mothers to jabber with neighbors engaging in the same activity. I could hear them shouting news of family weddings, births, deaths, and just plain old trivial gossip for all to hear. It was little wonder why neighborhood residents knew everyone else's business.

The streets were the children's playgrounds. Most children were able to maneuver between parked cars with the adroitness of a gazelle. Every sporting activity had a season that blended into another. Stickball, basketball, and punch ball were played with fervid enthusiasm and competitiveness. If one had the ability to punch a ball from sewer to sewer, he was highly sought after when choosing up sides.

As dinnertime approached, regardless of what sport I was engaged in, I immediately halted play. Dinnertime in our household was 5:00p.m. My father would not tolerate a late arrival. On many occasions, I would glance down at my watch and, to my dismay, discover I had four minutes to cover the distance from the local playground to the dinner table. In his prime, I would have given Roger Bannister a run for his money. Huffing and puffing I took the stairs three steps at a time to our top floor apartment. As I opened the door, I prayed that my father wasn't putting down his fork indicating dinner was over.

I was expected to attend church every Sunday and did until my teenage years. Starting out in the direction of our parish, along the way, my trip was detoured to the local poolroom, or bowling alley. Aware of the possibility that my mother might grill me about the context of the Sunday gospel, I was careful to elicit the correct information from a church-going friend. Putting the information to memory, I returned home to enjoy the five-course family Sunday dinner. If I failed to acquire this information, I would mumble that it had to do something with fish and bread.

Confession was also a required part of my life. I always wondered why I had to attend confession every Saturday to confess the same sins I had unburdened myself of during my prior visit. Why not simply walk in say, "ditto"and be on my way.

What I remember most were the holidays. Families would gather together to share the joy, love, and of course, food at the apartment of one relative or another.

It was all special back then- two parents striving through good times and bad times to provide a life for their children. When life became harder so did the resolve not to quit. Dreams were uncomplicated with wanting more. Yes, it was a time of simplicity that, in many ways, tasted sweeter than today.

Chapter 9

CLAUDINE'S HOUSEHOLD RELATIONSHIP with her brother and sister was particularly difficult. As the oldest child she tried to assume the roll of mother, and although she possessed the intellectual capacity, she lacked the maturity a person needs to be a parent. Her way of accomplishing any task was by intimidation. Most situations were remedied on their own. Sometimes in order for me to regain control, I pretended to be angrier than I actually was, and at other times, I was angrier than I should have been. Sorting out their issues was a tiring job that required daily attention. Usually, preoccupied with my own thoughts, I spent a lifetime saying yes to the children's many requests without paying much attention to what they were asking.

"Dad, is it okay if I go out and play in traffic?" "Sure, have a good time."

"Dad, I started the chain saw, would you mind if I saw the garage in half?" "Take a couple of aspirins."

I was beginning to learn that when you are a single parent there aren't any checks and balances. I came to the realization that I would have to start paying attention to everything my beauties were saying and that, I concluded, was too much to ask of any man. Everything was going rather smoothly until Claudine asked me if she could purchase a sun lamp. My answer was a firm no. "Claudine, when summer comes you can develop a natural tan. Until that time you may not purchase a sun lamp of any type." Not waiting for her to answer I said, "Am I coming in loud and clear?"

"Yes, Dad." "Good."

I was so proud of the fact that I was listening. However, listening wasn't enough with Claudine. It must have been a moment of insanity on my part, because I forgot to say that she could not borrow, lease, rent, steal, or by any other means possess a sun lamp. I left the door opened for her to squeeze through.

The next night Claudine borrowed a sun lamp from her girlfriend. Taking it up to her bedroom, she convinced her brother and sister to join her in pursuing a tan. A few hours later the three of them approached me in the den. I could not believe what was taking place. Within minutes their faces started to bubble and blister. They soon became unrecognizable. I quickly rushed all three children to the local emergency room. A doctor informed me that they had severely damaged their skin. Claudine suffered the most because she was reading under the sun lamp and the possibility existed that she may have injured the retina of her eyes. Her eyes were packed with gauze and bandaged. I was instructed not to remove the bandages for several days, which meant that I would have to serve as her guide dog. I was also given medication to apply to the children's facial burns with orders to scrub it off to prevent infection. After spending several hours in the hospital, I loaded my mummies into the car and drove home making one stop along the way to purchase straws for them to drink: through.

"What a fun night this was," I whispered, as I assisted them out of the car.

Tired, I collapsed in bed, drained physically and emotionally and my body twitching. I fell asleep. In a few weeks, the three children were like new and I was ten years older.

There was very little personal time for myself. The children's needs were many. Prospective colleges and meetings with guidance counselors required my attention along with a never-ending barrage of paperwork. I opened three checking accounts because I didn't have time to balance my checkbook. Oh, how I wanted help, somebody, anybody I could tag off to for a rest- someone that would jump into the ring and wrestle in my place. All I wanted was to sleep. Even while lying in bed, there was always a variety of household and adolescent related issues resounding in my head.

Many times I found myself in arguments with each of the children. Quite often, I was the one who was wrong. Attempting to deal with my own emotional problems and of course with my world looking so bleak, I took my frustrations out on those closest to me. I felt like a train out of control. It was even more difficult to deal with the guilt that followed.

Drifting into a comatose state, I would fall into a deep sleep. Whenever that occurred I knew that I had reached my emotional limits. The tears were many, but so were the hugs and laughs. Then there was that awful dream.

During the night I started to have a dream, a nightmare. It was so frightening that it would wake me from a sound sleep. I'd wake up in a cold sweat unable to shake myself free from its hold. I dreamed that Joey was going to be afflicted with cancer. Not just cancer, but bone cancer, and in my dream I was driving over a bridge with Joey and someone else in the car. Terrified, I would rush into his room to reassure myself that he was okay, that it was only a dream. Opening his bedroom door, I'd stand in the doorway listening to him breath while he was sleeping. Satisfied that he was fine, I'd return to my bed.

Regardless of how hard I attempted to shake the effects of my dream, it was impossible for me to fall back to sleep. I would remain awake and I would pray, "Please God, don't let anything happen to him, he's my life, he's everything to me." Finally, the dawn would shake the chill of my nightmare away. A few weeks would go by and then the same dream would once again show its ugly face. I kept asking myself why is this happening?

Financially, matters were becoming more difficult. I had lost their mother's income, a Long Island schoolteacher making a decent salary. Nine months had gone by, and I had not received a penny in child support. I guess it was a form of pressure, or selfishness on her part. Maybe she was wishing life would become so difficult that I would quit and give up the job of being a single Dad. After all those years she really didn't know me very well, I thought.

Once a week the children would visit with their mother. During the week they would communicate daily over the phone. The conversations were superficial, mostly small talk about the weather and daily news occurrences. I could not help but think that here I was killing myself with the daily pressure of raising three children and the only pressure she was talking about was barometric.

I was sitting in the den one afternoon when my lawyer called informing me that he was arranging a meeting with my wife and her attorney. He asked if I would attend. He also requested that I be there at least a half hour early to discuss my case. It was time for me to sit down with the children to present them with their options. I was aware that this decision was going to be painful for them to make. It was a choice that children should not have to make. It should never have been part of their lives. Instead, they should be attempting to decide what movie they wanted to see, or which dress they wanted to wear. This was way out of the ordinary and so unfair.

Joey, I realized, was a non-entity. He was too young to influence his sisters and the court. I reflected on what my lawyer had mentioned earlier, that judges do not divide children in custody cases. I knew that if any one of the children decided to live with their mother, all would be lost.

I was aware that Tammy would follow her sister's lead. She always looked to her older sister for guidance. Claudine and I never agreed on many issues and during the last few months our relationship had become even more strained. She was a lot to handle and in my present state of mind, I was more impatient than at any other time in my life. We were so much alike that we constantly bumped heads. Both of us were strong willed, and adamant in many ways. Even as a child, her mother would constantly beckon me to discipline her knowing that she was too much for her to handle. To Claudine, I was the guy who wore black.

My main concern was the children's welfare. By this time I was certain that each of them would not do well if they elected to live with their mother. I needed them, but they were too young to realize how much they needed me, and the possible detrimental effects of choosing otherwise. If they decided to live with their mother, and this male stranger, the course of their lives would be altered forever. They weren't old enough to see the whole picture, to visualize the future. They only knew what life was like living with me. Perhaps it would have been better had they experienced living with their mother for a while. After all, the only tangible memories they had of her were good ones. I was the one who had opened all sides of me for viewing. My lawyer was right. The out of house parent had a big advantage.

My advantage was that my children were able to determine right from wrong. In Claudine's mind, and heart, I knew that she had a strong sense of fairness. She disliked what her mother had done and totally disliked the new person in her life. She did not intend to let anyone get away with that. My presence and influence lived in each of my children. I counted on that.

I knew that the children loved their mother. Unfortunately, they were left with no choice. A decision had to be made. While I was thinking these thoughts Claudine interrupted me, "I'm not going. I'm staying here with you."

"Are you sure?"

"Yes, I'm sure. What Mom did, and the way that she did it, was wrong."

I wondered if she knew what she was bargaining for. I wasn't too good at this single fathering thing and I had a tendency to carry on at times. Certainly, I wasn't the easiest person to live with.

"Tammy, it's your turn. What do you want to do?"

"If Claudine's not going, then I'm not going."

I was aware that this was an exceptionally trying decision for Tammy. Her relationship with her mother was similar to mine with Joey. The two of them would get up early each morning and jog several miles before breakfast. They spent endless hours shopping together and shared the same artistic hobbies, each extremely talented in their own right. Tammy was hurt deeply by her mother's actions, a perfect love now blemished. Taken from Tammy was the belief that she meant as much to her mother as her mother meant to her. What she needed most was to know that there was still someone that she could believe in, someone who would never betray her love. I was the one person that she would let into her private world. I made up my mind to put the pieces of her shattered heart back together again. It would take time.

"That leaves you, Joey. How do you feel, do you want to go?"

A simple shaking of his head answered my question. Now, here's a boy who has a lot to say about this issue, I thought. Joey simply shaking his head didn't mean that he had not given this matter a lot of consideration. In fact, he might have given it a lot more attention than anyone else in the room. His decision wasn't simply based on his toys and the comfort of his bed. He was my son. We both knew that I could always rely on him. He wasn't going anywhere without me. To think of life without my children was beyond my comprehension. I was delighted with their choice. If the decision were left solely to the courts, I wouldn't have had a chance. The only question that remained was could I do the job?

I put on my shirt and left the house for my attorney's office. As I arrived at my appointed time, I was once again asked to take a seat in the waiting area. It wasn't long before I was escorted into his office. He walked over to greet me. He was dressed in his usual dapper attire, except this time he was wearing a pair of old dirty worn-out shoes. I thought it was unusual that a person dressed to perfection would wear shoes in this condition. I laughed, thinking that perhaps this was his way of encouraging me to pay my bill. Pulling back his black leather chair he took his seat and began to adoringly lick his huge cigar. "You're not going to light that thing are you?"

"Not now."

"Good. Just from that answer I can tell that this is going to be a productive meeting."

"Well, here's the scoop my boy. I called your wife's attorney yesterday and he spoke to Mrs." I stopped him in his tracks.

"There is no Mrs. anything anymore. Don't ever put my last name after her first name again. She gave that privilege up when she walked out on me and her children. That little fringe benefit is a thing of the past. I may not have a lot of rights but I have the right to determine who is going to use my last name. Somewhere in me there's a little Sicilian left. Do we have time for a fast story?"

"Go ahead. I'm all ears."

Chapter 10

MY FATHER'S FATHER was a huge man in stature. He immigrated to the United States when he was sixteen years old. Arriving alone, he was processed through the immigration bureaucracy at Ellis Island along with millions of other emigrants.

Not knowing anyone in this country, he ventured over to the Little Italy section of Manhattan. Once there, he was able to recognize a few names from his small village in Sicily. He approached them hoping they would offer some advice and assistance in getting started in this new world, this promised land he heard so much about in Italy. It wasn't long before he found work as a laborer building the subway system of New York City. It was a physically demanding job. His nights were short, barely allowing him time to rest before starting another grueling day of work. It was during those years that he lost two fingers from his right hand from a machinery accident. Not once did he complain about the accident. He had too much pride. It came with the turf and he considered it no more than an unfortunate part of his job and life. My grandfather understood the hardships of life, and complaining was not the Sicilian way.

When my grandfather was a young boy, his father was shot in the arm. It became infected. Finally the arm had to be amputated to save his life. He told me that his father wore a chain around his neck. Attached to the chain was the bullet that had been removed from his arm. One day he asked his father why he wore it about his neck. He replied, "Because someday I am going to give it back to the man who gave it to me."

As preponderant as my grandfather was, he was equally as kind. Above all else he loved his wife, children, and grandchildren. He had rules and his dominance remained uncontested but I never saw him walking down the street without holding my grandmother's hand. He was an emotional man who, upon hearing good news or bad, was capable of shedding a tear.

One of the most difficult tasks I ever had to undertake was to inform him of the breaking up of my brother's marriage. The family tried to keep him in the dark for as long as possible hoping to spare him the pain and anguish of hearing this rather sad event. We knew it would not set well with him. However, there came a time when he had to be told the truth.

In my grandfather's world, you married forever. For a man to leave his wife was totally irresponsible. A man had an obligation to his wife and children to be there for all time. In his mind, there was no compromising this responsibility. The thought of a woman leaving her husband and children was even less conceivable to him. This was the gravest sin of all. It did not happen in his world. He could not begin to perceive something so nonexistent to him. Yet, he understood a woman wanting to go if her husband violated certain rules, the rules that governed his life. My brother Tony and I decided to inform him of what we knew would be a catastrophic occurrence in his life.

I rang the brass-plated doorbell of his apartment house and waited for the return buzzer to sound allowing us to open the vestibule door. We entered the first floor hallway and began to climb the stairs leading to my grandfather's second floor apartment. With every step we could smell the aroma permeating throughout the building of some special meal that he was preparing. My grandfather was the best Italian cook, bar none, anywhere. He possessed the knack of turning a very simple dish into a gourmet delight. A culinary artist of the old school and in spite of how hard anyone attempted to duplicate his recipes, the food never tasted the same as when he prepared it.

Upon reaching the second floor, we found the door slightly ajar leading to his apartment. Making our way through a narrow foyer we found him sitting at the kitchen table awaiting our arrival. My grandmother had passed away a few years ago. I believed that he had never gotten over her loss.

The sounds of canaries were singing non-stop in the background. I turned to my brother and asked, "how does he get them to sing so much." He replied, "he puts a little hot pepper flakes in their food." I mumbled, "this is like the island of Dr.Moreau." We walked over, gave him a kiss, pulled out two chairs and sat down opposite him at the kitchen table. At his left foot I could see a gallon of homemade red wine.

As young boys, regardless of what activities we were engaged in, during the month of September everything came to a halt. It was time to assist my grandfather in his traditional ritual of making his home-made wine. This was serious business and he would not tolerate the slightest bit of horseplay. He wanted every drop he could squeeze out of each grape. Sometimes he squeezed them so hard that I thought I could hear the grapes screaming.

Weeks before making his wine he made a daily trek to his local grape supplier where he carefully picked out the cases of grapes that he thought would produce the best wine. Proclaiming to be making enough wine to last until the next year, he usually ran out months before his target date and had to resort to purchasing several gallons from a local liquor store.

As we started our conversation he interrupted us. "Would you like a glass of wine?"

"Yes, thank you," the two of us politely responded.

To say no would insult him and it wasn't near the end of his batch where he was counting every glass. If it had been, I would not have deprived him of his heavenly nectar. He picked the gallon up from the floor and poured three glasses of wine, then he sliced a peach allowing a wedge to fall into each glass that at one time must have contained jelly.

While visiting, one could have as much wine as they wanted as long as they didn't touch the gallon. To pour yourself a glass of wine would be an insult of the highest order a very disrespectful act that might cause an unusual reaction by my grandfather. It would be better not to test his temper. We toasted to our health, followed by some small talk. "It's a nicea to see the two of you. This is a nicea surprise," he said in' broken English.

I could tell he knew that we had something on our mind, but allowed us to present whatever we had to say in the manner of our choice.

"Grandpa," my brother Tony began, "we have bad news to tell you."

He put down his glass and looked up. With my grandfather's attention now undivided, my brother continued. "Our brother Sal, is getting a divorce." Still, there was no response. At this point, I said, "his wife is leaving him. She doesn't love him." With that remark his face became cold and hard. I could see he was assimilating all the facts and wanting more. I knew that his primary concern was my brother and my brother's children. Looking at him, I wondered where all this was leading. Finally, he asked.

"Your brother, he fool around on his wife?"

"No."

"Your brother, he gamble his pay check away?" Again, we both answered, "No."

"Your brother he no lovea his wife and children?"

"Yes, grandpa, he loves them very much. He spends most of his time at work and when he's not there he's at home with his family. Grandpa he's an accountant. That's what he went to college for. He's working very hard at giving his family a better life. They mean everything to him," I said.

His questions were not complicated. None of them derived from the Jung school of psychology. They were unostentatious questions coming from a modest, proud man. Sitting there, listening to him, I thought about the simplicity of his logic and of his world. He had a code that governed the way all men should live. A wife could have cause to leave her husband for a violation of any of the above rules; that the failure of a man to meet certain family responsibilities could be met with marital retribution on his wife's part.

We all sat there in silence for a few seconds. Then with one motion he stood straight up causing his chair to screech along the linoleum floor. For a man his age, I was startled by the quickness of his move. I watched as he disappeared into the kitchen. I could hear the sound of a kitchen draw being opened, then closed. It wasn't long before he returned. As he paused in the doorway, the old Sicilian's frame left little room for light to filter through. I looked at his formidable figure standing there wearing his hat. Defined by his father's genes and forged by what he witnessed as child growing up in his little village in Sicily, left him no choice in what he was about to do.

Squinting, I could see that there was something in his hand. I focused my eyes on his right hand. He was holding a large kitchen knife. My only thought was, Oh God! Here we go! He turned to us demanding that we bring the car around to the front of his apartment house. ·

"Why? (As though I didn't already know the answer to that question.) Grandpa, would you mind telling me where we are going?" I asked.

"You are going to take me to her house," he demanded.

"And what are you going to do when you get there?" Stuttering, I continued, "and what is the knife in your hand for?" The next answer, and the matter of fact way in which he presented it, shocked me.

"I am going to cut her into little pieces and flush her down the bowl."

I looked at my brother as though to say, "Is this guy kidding?" My brother, standing there, with his mouth wide opened, was frozen in his tracks. By the look on his face, I knew that we were having similar thoughts of how do we handle this? And how do we get the hell out of here? Leaning against my brother I whispered, "I can see tomorrow's Daily News headlines, "Two of New York City's Finest Involved In One Of The Most Gruesome Crimes Of The Century."

Finally able to speak, I said, "Grandpa, we would love to take you to her house but neither of us have our cars, we walked here instead of driving." Continuing to whisper so that he couldn't hear me, I said, "Yeah, grandpa, maybe we could do this some other time, perhaps after church some Sunday morning." With that said we both kissed him goodnight and left."So, when I tell you that she can no longer continue to use my last name it's because there is a little Sicilian still residing inside me and I like it there."

"I think I understand," said my attorney, in a somewhat subdued voice. He then asked me if I would like a cup of coffee and I accepted. I had a feeling that I was going to need it. He began telling me that he was aware of my emotional pain and how I must be spending many hours wondering why I didn't see any signs of betrayal. He was of the opinion that most men failed to see any double-dealing until it was too late, that deceit was never easy to detect. He also felt that men's egos had a tendency to get in the way of reality. They never believe that a woman, especially their wife, would dare perpetrate this type of personal insult upon them. Women, on the other hand, seemed to be able to spot collusion a mile away. After all, men had given them cause to develop this odoriferous scent.

With as much compassion as one could expect from a divorce lawyer he said that I wasn't the first guy this happened to and I wouldn't be the last, that treachery and trust both started with a T. "So, go easy on yourself. This is the 21st century and what do you expect?" he asked.

I told him that I expected solar warming, blight, locust, and maybe an alien invasion. What I didn't expect was to see mothers walking out on their children. Children deserved more from them; more than I or any man could ever give. They should be able to call out her name and hear the music of their mother's voice.

"Don't you understand that there isn't a more beautiful word than mother?

Abbreviating it should not be allowed."

"You made your point but now we have to talk business."

"Let's."

He told me that he spoke to my wife's attorney and informed him of the children's decision to remain with me. Sometime later her lawyer called to explain that my wife was blaming me for the children leaving her.

"She's what!" I shouted. None of this made sense to me but it didn't have to. Lately, very little in my life made sense.

I wondered how any mother could admit to leaving three children to survive without her. In her case, she may have needed to justify leaving, therefore, she didn't leave them, they left her. Nonetheless, she was in pursuit of happiness and not about to let anything get in her way.

My attorney's advice was to settle the case -to let her have the children and to get on with my life. I could see that he wanted to light his cigar. "Go ahead," I said. He lit it then proceeded to take a long drag, inhaling most of the smoke.

"I thought you weren't supposed to inhale those things?" I foolishly asked. He rolled back his eyes as though to say, "so what."

He explained that he was an attorney for hire and if my wife had walked in the door first he would have represented her. In child custody cases, he would much rather be on the mother's side. "It is so much easier," he said.

However, under the facade that everyone in this world deserves legal counsel, he represented whoever paid his bill. At his beck and call, he had this wonderful excuse that allowed him to make money while defending the dreg of society. He went on to say that some people called him a shyster, crook, and a million other names, none of which bothered him. Regardless of what people thought of him he insisted that he hadn't lost his ability to distinguish right from wrong, or his sense of fairness. He asserted that parity did not exist for men in child custody cases and, although the odds were stacked against them, some men elected to fight.

"The last time you were here I briefly explained that judges do not treat men and women equally in these types of cases," he said. "What makes that so?" He paused to take another drag on his cigar. "Look at you sitting here in my office wearing a suit and tie. By the way, where did you get that nice pink shirt?"

He went on to tell me that I looked successful, and that in a judge's eyes a successful person should always share his wealth, or at the very least, should not be in much need of assistance. He also contended that women were organized in divorce and child support cases and asked when was the last time I saw a television talk show, hosted by single fathers, complaining about the negligence of their ex-wives. Yet, he said it was impossible to turn the channel without seeing women, on a stage, and in the audience, wanting to tar and feather their ex-husbands. He also affirmed that there weren't any newspapers or magazine articles referring to the plight of the single father and that rarely did single fathers received credit for doing an excellent job. If they did, society would have to acknowledge the fact that some mothers were leaving their children and that, he assured, was an untouchable reality. "Remember, he said, "men abandon children, women leave them and just in case you're not aware of it, 'Blackstonian Law' is a thing of the past."

I appreciated his insight but I didn't have time to analyze philosophical theories concerning females verses males in custody issues. Nor did I have the time, or the inclination, to cure the ills of society. As far as I was concerned, this was as close to purgatory as I wanted to get. My hat was off to all single parents. Gender wise, I was slowly becoming androgynous. I wasn't certain if I should urinate standing up or sitting down, and at times, I even felt a little pre-menstrual. I only knew that I was tired. All I wanted was to be able to afford my children a fair opportunity in life. I was hoping that he would show me how to accomplish that. However, I realized that it would be useless for me to ask him any questions. He was a lawyer doing what lawyers do best: turning a molehill into a mountain.

Not quite finished, he went on to say that in spite of how painful this ordeal had been for me, he was proud that I wanted to assume the burden of raising my children and that he sometimes threw prospective clients out of his office with instructions not to return until they were no longer in love, and were willing to defend themselves. Trying to accentuate his point, to make sure that I knew his lecture was directed at me, he waved his finger in my direction like some irate schoolteacher. I sat there quietly, aware that he recognized my sensitivity, my vulnerability. Coiled from hurt, I remained naked, each nerve exposed. He had me pegged.

Finally reeling himself in, cognizant that his conversation was starting to drift, he said, "I'm off on a tangent again. Let's get back to your case. If you do not want a court battle then you are going to have to pay her half the value of your house."

"I refuse to drag my children into court. If I have to buy the house that I'm already living in, so be it, and I'm not touching the children's college money. Look, let's stop bantering. Give me the whole deal." I insisted.

"You get ninety dollars per month per child." "Ninety dollars, that's it?"

"You heard me. Plus, she wants to be reimbursed for your daughter's trip to Europe. She said that it was your idea to send her to study in France so you should be the one to pay for it."

"Continue, let me have the rest." I demanded.

"She also gets unlimited visitation rites. But, I wouldn't worry about that." "Why not?"

He smirked saying that she wouldn't be around very long, that in her delusional state both she and her traveling boyfriend were bolting. He had a ring in her nose and was about to pull it in any direction that he wanted. He was certain that the one person she would never blame for any of her grief was this worthless refuse that she was taking off with, this *angus in herba*. In her eyes, he was the Holy Grail and more. I should never believe, not for one second, that she might one day wake up from her mediumistic state and come to terms with what she had done.

He also believed that the two of them were about to jettison their parental and moral responsibilities and would soon be out of everybody's lives, and that if I didn't take this deal, once she moved out of state, I would never receive a penny in child support.

"Look, Joe, I have been practicing divorce law for a long time. You're going to have to trust me on this. The two of them are going," he insisted.

I started to calculate the figures. I would receive ninety dollars per month per child. The total for one year would come to three thousand, two hundred and forty dollars. That didn't pay for the children's school lunch. This amount would be paid until they were emancipated, or they reached the age of twenty-one.

She also wanted a stipulation stating that I would not move outside of the New York Tri-State area. When my lawyer asked her attorney if she would make the same stipulation, even he laughed. He paused, looking at me to study my expression.

"In my opinion this whole deal is extremely unfair."

"You're right. It is unfair. The only way to make it fair is for you to take the money and leave the children for her to raise."

"No, I won't do that. Don't bring that up again."

"Let me give you an example of unfairness at the highest level," he said.

I could see he was winding up for another long dissertation. I hoped that it would be a good one; since I was being billed by the hour I had no choice but to sit and listen.

He told me that one night he walked into his kitchen and there making a television speech was Christi Whitman, the Governor of New Jersey. The subject of her speech was the effort being made in New Jersey, and in the United States, to pursue fathers who failed to pay child support. Over and over again she reiterated that fathers would be brought to justice to force them to meet their legal responsibilities. What she did not say, not one time, was that mothers who failed to pay child support would also be brought to justice. Not one person in that audience questioned her improper use of gender. "Why shouldn't all parents be forced to meet their legal responsibilities?"

Governor Whitman, according to him, was prejudice and bias against men. Worse, she got away with it. Had the situation been reversed, he insisted, Christi Whitman and every woman in that audience would have cried foul play.

He asked if I knew that in some states they now had police officers, escorted by a bus, whose sole jobs were to apprehend deadbeat

Dads. "Do you know what you are never going to find on that bus?" Without waiting for me to reply he answered, "a deadbeat Mom." Not that there weren't any deadbeat moms but, he contended, that the bus would roll right by a deadbeat Mom's house to arrest the man next door. He believed that our society has recognized and supported the efforts of every minority except single fathers and I can tell you, just by what walks in here every day, they are on the increase.

He agreed with societies contention that men have principally been the ones negligent in their court ordered family obligations, but he also felt that politicians and judges shouldn't focus their attention solely on men, that the law should be the issue and not the sex of the person who violated it. He insisted that fair was not always fair. At the conclusion of his narration he said, "The first time your ex violates her divorce agreement and short changes you on your child support check; let me know how you feel about Governor Whitman's speech?"

"Hold on a second," I interjected. "Let me make myself clear. I'm not anti-female. I'm anti any parent that abdicates their duty and responsibility when it comes to raising children regardless if they are male, female, or android."

After listening to him rant and rave for the last forty minutes, I knew that some of his points were valid but I was viewing the world through a parent's glasses and I was contemptuous of any parent that sentenced their children to exist in a world comprised of weekly phone calls. Sure, everyone deserved some degree of happiness but not at the misery of children?

"Now listen to me," he said, drawing me back to why I was sitting in his office in the first place, "I want to give you some final advice."

"I'm still listening."

He told me that if I wanted to make my soon-to-be ex-wife miserable the best way for me to achieve this was by being happy and successful. He was certain that whatever malignant characteristic, in a parent's personality, that allows them to flee their children would also guarantee them an existence of misery and unhappiness. With a sadistic sneer on his face he insisted that life had a way of taking care of all such matters, that it was the ultimate avenger.

"Presently you may have a very difficult time trying to comprehend what I am telling you, but someday it will make sense," he said

"Thanks for the advice and if I ever experience happiness again you'll be the first one I'll call."

A short time later my soon-to-be ex-spouse and her attorney arrived. The Sicilian in me would not allow me to look at her. My attorney leaned back in his leather chair and placed his feet on top of his desk. Facing the two of them he exposed a huge hole in the soles of both shoes. He then proceeded to blow smoke rings in their direction until they both started to cough. Now I knew the reason for his tattered shoes. That was simply a form of agitation. Perhaps this was an indication of where he believed their life was heading. Whatever his reasons were for his behavior strictly belonged to him. Sitting there had to be the strangest feeling in the world. A lifetime of love and closeness summed up with no more feeling than an ordinary house closing.

Two months later, I found myself standing before a judge. I raised my right hand, and because of the legal statute governing the reasons a divorce can be granted in New York State, I lied and said that I wanted the divorce. Seconds later, for the first time in more than eighteen years, I was divorced and single. I didn't feel single because I didn't know what it was like to be single. I had spent too many years being one of two.

Driving home I wondered if people would be able to determine that I was single by looking at me? When I dropped the dry cleaning off tomorrow morning, would the clerk behind the counter say, "Good morning, and oh by the way, how does it feel to be single?" Could people tell? All I knew was that it felt as though my right arm had been amputated. I felt empty, lost, adrift at sea with no land in sight. God how I wanted these feelings to pass, the nausea to stop, to be whole again, but they wouldn't. They stayed with me throughout the day, every day. My only reprieve was in the little sleep my body demanded, then I would open my eyes and all these feelings would rush back in chanting, "Where have you been? We're not finished with you yet."

It was time for all of us to grow up, especially me. I was now on my own trying to complete the impossible. I wondered, what I had gotten myself into?

A couple of weeks later my ex-wife moved to Missouri, a place she had never visited in her life. She asked the children to relocate with her. They refused and she blamed them for leaving her. I thought, what wonderful mechanisms rationalization and projection are. If Freud hadn't discovered them, some divorced parent would have. I knew that her offer was no more than a perfunctory gesture. It wasn't followed by a statement saying, "If you children decide not to accompany me, I'm not going." A mother should never leave her children for a man promising a life of bliss. Instead, she should remain taking on all comers that would dare harm one single hair on their head. That is not what was happening here. She was making a choice and selected her new life over her children. In this case, motherhood was AWOL.

There was a positive side about my ex moving out of town. It reduced the interference and conflict that parents create while sharing custody. Doing it alone, I would stand or fall on my own merits. There was no one to help and no one to blame. Time would be my judge. It would tell the tale of success or failure. I had a strange feeling that the odds were stacked against me.

Chapter 11

AT 9:00 A.M. the next morning I received a phone call from the school secretary informing me that Mother Superior wanted to have a meeting with me. Hanging up the phone I screamed, "What has Claudine done this time? Just what I needed to start my week, another Claudine fiasco." It was only last night that I told her to stop causing so much chaos because of her, "show me," religious beliefs.

As I drove through the one hundred and seventy acres of The Academy, I admired the beautiful landscape. Nestled within these grounds existed a world of religion, tradition, and pride. I parked my car in an area designated for visitors, and walked up a row of never ending senior marble steps until I came to two huge wooden doors. It felt like I was visiting City Hall and not a Catholic school of learning. A ring of the doorbell brought a nun to greet me. She directed me to a small desk and asked that I sign the visitor's log.

We then proceeded up a second row of steps, similar in style, but somewhat smaller than the first. At the top of the stairs I entered a small hallway and, after being announced, I was escorted into Mother Superior's inner office.

It had not been my first meeting with the Mother Superior. I was hoping that the last visit would have been just that, my last visit. But far be it for Claudine to give me some peace. Even though I believed that I had accomplished some good with our recent talk, Claudine's contemptuous behavior continued to upset her instructors.

This time Sister Maria Stapleton did not greet me with a smile as she had several times in the past. Instead, I was offered a seat in the middle of the room opposite her desk. I now knew what a prairie dog felt like several hundred yards from its den with an eagle soaring overhead. I cursed for having been placed in such a vulnerable position.

Sitting in silence, waiting for Claudine's arrival, I glanced at the army of crucifixes, nailed at even intervals, on the wall behind Sister Maria Stapelton. I was certain that had she given the order they would have all dismounted and preceded to flog me with palms. Even her letter opener had a crucifix on it. I wondered why none of this registered on Claudine's Richter Scale.

Finally looking up, Mother Superior said, "good morning." Before I could return the amenities she went on to ask, "Have you seen Claudine this morning?"

"No, I haven't sister, I arrived home late last night and I was still sleeping when she left for school this morning," I said. While thinking, at least she made the bus today, things couldn't be that bad. That was a positive, wasn't it?

"Well perhaps I'll call her to my office so you can see her," she said.

Oh, oh, I thought. I smell set-up. I waited while Claudine was summoned. A few minutes later Claudine entered. I looked up not believing my eyes. She was dressed as an Indian: her garb, face, and everything else about her indicated Sioux.

Fascinated, I asked, "How did you get your face so red? And what happened to your uniform?" No answer.

Finally, Mother Superior turned to and asked, "Well?" Still no answer?

"Look, Claudine, at least tell us what tribe you belong too?" I said. What I really wanted to do was laugh but that wouldn't have gone over too well with the Mother Superior, and if I started, there would have been no stopping me. At that point Sister Maria Stapleton would have been left with no choice except to have us both excommunicated. Instead, pretending to be angrier than I really was, I explained that the divorce and her mother's departure created quite a bit of turbulence in all of our lives. With no other alternative at my disposal, I promised to address the situation and guaranteed there would be no reoccurrence of this type of behavior. Knowing that I would not be able to keep my word I said my farewell and fled. I decided that I would not worry myself about the perils of Claudine until I, once again, took my first step up the never ending row of marble steps, leading to the two huge wooden doors of her school. All this was no more than another day in the life of a single parent. Or what I referred to as, "a thrill a minute." I wondered why everyone was so upset? I was growing accustomed to the chaos in my life. All single parents were used to turmoil.

A week later Claudine played a wonderful piano recital for the senior class and their parents. Possessed of so much natural talent, if I could harness her abilities, her potential would be boundless.

Along with my other parental duties, I managed to find time to teach Claudine how to drive. She was by far the worst driver I had ever observed. Although extremely intelligent, she had a difficult time distinguishing her right from her left. She hadn't experienced any trouble when it came to using a credit card, but right and left were another issue. Plus, her mind was somewhere else. Where? I had no idea.

The volume on her car radio was loud, usually blaring an aria from some unrecognizable opera. This fact in itself was very strange. I had to wonder what seventeen-year-old listened to this type of music?

The only possible benefit for subjecting myself to the risks of her bizarre driving habits was that she would be able to drive herself to school whenever she missed the morning bus, which was much too often as far as I was concerned. The concept of this idea was tantalizing enough to lure me into placing my life on the line.

Two years ago, I purchased an MGB sports car. It was in near perfect condition. I guess it was an attempt on my part to recapture my youth. To keep it out of harms way, I parked it in the garage and even went so far as to place a blanket over the top of it. The children were asked to be careful when taking their bicycles out of the garage because I didn't want it scratched. Once a week, whether it needed it or not, I would find the time to wax my little pride and joy.

One day I was walking through the garage when I noticed

something different about my MGB. Investigating it further, I discovered the front of the MGB protruding through the dining room wall. Mangled under the front tire was the new bicycle that I had recently purchased. Of course Claudine was the perpetrator of this horrific act and now she was about to venture out onto the highways where normal people operated their vehicles.

Much to my surprise she passed her first driving test. One day I was puttering in the back yard when I heard the phone ring. It was Claudine.

"Dad, is that you?"

"Yes," I could tell by the sound of her voice that something was wrong. "Claudine, calm down and tell me what's wrong?"

"I got into an accident but I'm okay. However, the car is a little damaged. Can you meet me? I'm only a few blocks from the house."

"Fine, stay put. I'll hop into my car and I'll be there in a few minutes." "Dad," and then a pause, "I'm in your car," she meekly said.

"You're in my car! Where is your lime green Volkswagen?"

"It's in the driveway. I decided to take your car instead of mine."

"My new car! The one with two thousand miles on the odometer?"

"Yes, but I didn't see the other driver! I was crossing this main intersection and I haven't the slightest idea where he came from." "Okay, okay, I'll be right there."

Within minutes I arrived at the scene of Claudine's accident. Parked off to the side of the road was my new cougar. The right rear side was completely demolished. Looking around I didn't see another car. I turned to Claudine and asked, "Where is the other car? The one that you didn't see?" Slowly she raised her arm pointing her index finger in the direction of the other vehicle. Following her line of path I observed a big yellow school bus.

"Claudine, is that the other vehicle?"

A squeamish nod of her head answered my question. Excited, I said, "You didn't see that! It's bright yellow and takes up half a city block! Look, don't answer, I've heard enough."

I exchanged the necessary legal documents with the bus driver and sadly watched as my new car was towed away to a local repair shop. The final result: I was still driving Claudine to school in the morning only now I was driving a lime green Volkswagen.

A month later Claudine graduated. The commencement ceremony was a special event. The graduates all wore white gowns. As they entered the chapel, they were handed a bouquet of red roses. Her disappointment at not having her mother attend her graduation must have been heartbreaking. What a terrible hand she was dealt. Not to attend such a special occasion had to be extremely hurtful. I was learning, starting to realize that we have to love our children today, not tomorrow, because every moment we allow slipping by in their lives could never be repeated. No matter what relationship the future may hold between Claudine and her mother, this day could never be duplicated.

Prior to Claudine's graduation, we began to investigate numerous colleges she considered attending. My children were raised with the idea that they would attend college. The discussion was limited to which college they would attend and future graduate work. Claudine had decided to attend Fordham University. I was surprised at her choice, thinking that she might have had her fill of a parochial education. I asked her if she was certain concerning her decision? "Yes, Dad, I'm sure."

"Have you selected a major?"

"I think that I might major in art history." "If that's your choice, then go for it."

Throughout time, Jesuits have been the cause of more wars than almost any other religious sect. Now one of the world's biggest antagonist was about to enter their midst. Given enough time she would make the crusades look like a trip to Disney World. It was time for me to go out, buy my popcorn, sit back, and enjoy the show.

I blinked and a year passed by. During the course of the year, we all had to make many adjustments. It had not been easy on any of us. The emotional healing process from being divorced seemed endless. Whenever I thought that I was advancing an inch, I took a step backwards. Most people I spoke to managed to conjure up their own theory concerning the period of time it takes one to heal from a divorce. I came to the realization that you are healed when you stop thinking about how long it's going to take you to heal.

The children were trying to make a go of a difficult situation but they were scarred. At times, we tested teach other's nerves. My privacy was gone. Everything I owned, from little items to larger ones, was up for grabs. Anything that I wanted to keep for myself required a secret hiding place. It wasn't unusual for me to comb my hair with my fingers. Where my hairbrushes had gone was an insolvable mystery. Wherever they were, I was certain that my pens, deodorant, talcum powder, and various articles of my clothing were keeping them company. My secret hiding places had to be changed on a regular basis for fear of discovery. Big clothing seemed to be the attire of the day and at 6ft, 185 pounds I fit the model of what the girls liked. Sweatshirts, jackets, and tee shirts were all disappearing from my closet and draws. Not only did they borrow my clothes but they also exchanged them with their girlfriends. I was in the supermarket one day when I noticed a girl walking by wearing my new shirt. I didn't know her, but I recognized my shirt. I was lost in a sea of subterfuge.

When one of the girls was home, I could get away with the luxury of orally communicating my directives without hearing who did what last, and what felt like the outbreak of world war three. When both girls were home, and I wanted them to perform a few household chores, the best method of accomplishing my goals was by leaving them a written note. This saved me a lot of grief. I learned the secret to minimum aggravation was to turn myself into a non-entity. If they wanted to argue they could argue with a piece of paper. It was around this time Joey came to me expressing that he was experiencing some pain in his left leg.

"Joey tell me exactly where it hurts you?"

"It hurts me in my back and goes right into my leg." "Does it hurt a lot?"

"Not a lot, only a little."

"Well, if it keeps on causing you any degree of discomfort let me know and we'll have it looked at."

"Okay, dad."

A few weeks later he approached me saying that he didn't feel well. He started to run a fever. I took his temperature and noticed it was slightly higher than normal. "Alright pal, you're not going out to play today. Make yourself comfortable on the couch. Today is an inside day."

Joey just turned thirteen and the thought of not being allowed to go outside to play after school met with a great deal of unhappiness on his part. As he began his protest, I cut him short, "Joey, I don't care how much you pout, you're staying in the house until your fever subsides."

The next morning I drove him to my local HMO center for a checkup. It was just before noon when we arrived at the doctor's office. A few minutes after our arrival we managed to locate the pediatric department. The waiting room was extremely crowded with children suffering from the usual coughs and colds. I watched as most mothers met with little success in trying to comfort their young tikes. A few of the children had a preconceived idea that they were here to receive an injection of some type and weren't about to conform to any behavior other than screaming.

I tried to joke with Joey hoping to alleviate any concern that he might have about his leg. It wasn't long before they called Joey's name and directed us to an unoccupied room. Joey sat on an examination table while I remained standing at his side. Soon a nurse entered.

"Good morning."

"Good morning." I politely returned her greeting. She proceeded to ask a few preliminary examination questions which I answered.

"Joey, please undress down to your shorts. The doctor will be here shortly," she said. It wasn't long before a doctor entered the room. She was in her mid-thirties and appeared to be in a rush. She asked me about Joey's medical problems. I explained that he was running a low-grade fever and experiencing pain in his pelvis, back, and leg. When I finished speaking, she asked, "Would you mind waiting in the hall while I examine him?"

"I'll wait," I said. What I really wanted to say was, "Yes, I mind, I want to be here with my son to see what's going on." Instead, I gave in to her authoritative request.

When she was finished with her examination she instructed Joey to dress and asked that we both join her in her office located down the hall. She was already seated at her desk when we walked in. I guess by the look on my face she knew that I was somewhat anxious.

"Nothing to worry about." Without missing a beat she continued, "what your son has been experiencing, for lack of a better choice of words, are growing pains. It's not uncommon for boys his age to experience this type of pain in their joints and legs. Their bodies simply can't keep up with such a fast rate of growth. With time, it will pass."

Her answer seemed logical. Then why did I have this sense of uneasiness, this knot in the pit of my stomach that something was terribly wrong? However, my feelings were so abstract that I couldn't put a label on them, at least not at this stage. I pushed aside any bad thoughts that I might have. After all, she was a doctor. She saw hundreds of children every week and would know if anything was wrong and why argue with good news?

"Joey, do you have any questions for the doctor?"

"Yes, can I go home now?"

"Yes, you can go home."

On the way home I tried to explain to Joey what the doctor had told us. He appeared satisfied with my explanation.

For the next few days, I kept a close eye on him as he mowed the lawn and went about his other chores. Joey would never say no to any household job that he was assigned. He knew I needed help and didn't want to see me overburdened with work. If he thought he did something wrong, or caused me to become angry, it would cause him a great deal of unhappiness. Simply expressing disappointment in his behavior would be enough to remedy any problems. He wasn't a tough boy, but gentle and kind, a special boy that few parents were lucky to have. Joey was my whole life and he knew it because I told him so.

His mother left him when he was ten years old and his memories of her were fading.

We had a bond between us that, with the passing of time, brought us closer together. One night I asked if his leg was still hurting him.

"Not a lot daddy. Only sometimes."

"Well, if it keeps up let me know and we'll go back and pay the doctor another visit."

A week went by and Joey again started to run a low-grade fever and once again I confined him to the house. I noticed that every time he exerted himself, even moderately, the pain in his leg would reoccur forcing him to stop whatever activity he was engaged in.

He would then come into the house, fall down on the sofa, and rest. I found it disturbing looking at him reclining on the couch so discouraged. After remaining in the house for a while he would venture outside and continue his previous activity. But, his spark was gone.

It was also becoming obvious that he was gradually starting to lose weight. It was so subtle at first that I didn't notice it. He was a growing boy and I thought that he was simply taking on the look that many young boys his age do.

I asked him, "Joey, are you okay? Is there anything I can do for you to pick up your spirits? You look so sad."

I had a feeling that he might be depressed because he hadn't seen his mother in quite some time. I asked myself, could it be that a part of his life was lacking something that only a mother could give? "Joey, would you like to go and visit your mother for a few days?"

"Dad, do you think that Mom is mad at me for not spending part of my summer vacation with her?"

"Joey, why don't you call her and ask if you could spend a week or two with her." Excited, he said, "thanks Dad, I think I will."

He picked up the phone and dialed his mother's number. I left the room to afford him a little privacy. As he hung up the phone I heard him say, "I love you Mom." A few minutes later he walked into the den. Looking at his sad face I knew that something was wrong.

"So are you going to Missouri."

"I don't think so. Mom told me if I wanted to visit her that I would have to pay for my own ticket." Anger started to build up inside me. I waited a few minutes until I was able to regain my composure before continuing our conversation.

"Hey, is that all that's bothering you? Listen to daddy. I'll pay for the ticket. Let me worry about that part of it. All you have to do is board the plane and don't forget to remind the pilot about the flaps. Is that okay with you?"

"Dad, you don't mind doing that?" "Not at all. Now go outside and play."

I sat on the sofa wondering how a mother, who had not seen her child in over a year, a person who owned two horses, could be so unkind to renounce his gesture of love. I asked myself, what could possibly be going on in her mind to make her behave like this? Does her affliction have a name? And, would it someday pass? In spite of her rejection, I knew that each of the children loved her very much. She was a lucky woman who, somewhere along the way misplaced her values, and now she had constructed an impenetrable wall around her, not allowing her children's pain or love to enter. She had left herself no choice but to remain in her dungeon of solitude because if she had emerged she would have had to reconcile not her truth, but God's truth.

I could only pray that the children didn't blame me for their mother leaving, or worse, blame themselves. I could live with the first thought but not the second. Slowly a grin came across my face and then a smile. I started to laugh thinking that what she really needed was a visit from my grandfather. I was glad that he had passed away so he didn't have to witness or be subjected to what had transpired in my life. It would have broken his heart. But I thanked him for the smile anyway.

The next morning I booked Joey's flight to Louisana. A couple of days later I drove him to Islip Mac Arthur Airport. During the drive we hardly spoke. I could tell that he wasn't enthusiastic about leaving, but I also knew that he didn't want to hurt his mother by not visiting. I respected him for his decision. He was placing his mother ahead of himself. This was his nature. I knew I would have trouble handling his absence. He had never been away from me before and the fact that he wasn't feeling well caused me some concern. I asked him to call me when he landed in Missouri to let me know that he arrived safely.

Sometime later that evening the phone rang. It was good to hear Joey's voice.

"How are you feeling?"

"My leg is still hurting."

"Did you do anything to re-injure it or make it worse?"

"I went down a water slide the other day and I think that made it worse."

"Joey," I interrupted, "tell your mother to take you to a doctor and do it as soon as you hang up the phone."

"Okay, Dad, I will."

"Fine, call me tomorrow and let me know the outcome. Take care. I love you."

The next day I was just about to leave the house when I heard the phone ring. It was

Joey, "Hi buddy, how are you doing? You're not going to come back home with a mid-western accent are you?"

"No, Dad, I don't think so."

"Tell me about your leg, how is it feeling?" "Mom brought me to her doctor."

"And what did the doctor have to say?"

"He said the same thing that the other doctor said, that I was growing too fast." "Well, I guess two doctors can't be wrong. Just try to slow down a little bit. You know what I mean. Try to curb your running around and give your leg a chance to rest, okay?"

"I will."

"Remember, I love you and you'll be home soon. Bye Joey." "Bye Dad, I love you too."

Before I knew it a week had gone by. I was excited that he was coming home and looked forward to seeing him. The girls had missed him too. They didn't have a little brother to tease, or a slave at their beck and call.

With thoughts of Joey on my mind I found it difficult to sleep. The next morning I was up early. I decided rather than pace about the house I would keep myself busy by driving to the airport. I found a parking space and walked to the scheduled arrival gate stopping along the way to purchase a newspaper. Finding an available seat, I made myself somewhat comfortable. Periodically, I glanced up to check on the arrival time of Joey's flight.

As the plane rolled up, I attempted to position myself to get a clearer view of the passengers walking up the ramp. What I saw next frightened me. It was Joey. He was void of color, appeared frail, and had lost a great deal of weight. He was limping, dragging his leg behind him. I rushed to his side and put my arms around him afraid to let go for fear that he might fall. Plus, I didn't want to let go. I didn't know what to think. I felt sick and in shock. Most of all I was scared.

Once inside the car I made a feeble attempt at some small talk. I tried not to make my concern and dismay too obvious for fear of frightening him. Finally, I asked, "How did you enjoy your trip?"

"I had a great time."

"I'm glad that you enjoyed yourself." Not really paying attention to what I was saying my eyes kept darting in his direction examining his thin body. Afraid to ask the question but no longer able to avoid the issue I said, "So tell me about your back and leg, what's going on?"

"I think that I made it worse by going down the water slide because up until that time it wasn't hurting me too much."

"I'm sure that the slide didn't do your leg any good. Why don't you recline your seat and rest a bit."

"I think I will."

I reached over to touch his forehead. By this time in my nurturing career I could tell the children's temperature to within a half a degree simply by touching their foreheads. I was very rarely wrong. He was a little warm, running a low-grade fever. No matter how many times I asked myself why, I couldn't come up with an answer to this mysterious affliction. What I did know was that my son was home where he belonged and I was going to get to the bottom of his problem.

Over the next few days I tried to prepare all his favorite dishes. I was going to put the weight back on him that he lost while he was away. I would make it my mission in life. I made cakes, pies, and puddings. If he had a craving for a particular food it was going to be available for him to eat. Regardless of the hour I arrived home, I forced myself to get up early the next morning to make certain that he had a good breakfast before leaving for school. Pancakes, French toast, eggs, bacon, and a malted milkshake to wash it down weren't a problem.

If Joey was too tired to join us for breakfast, I would carry his breakfast up to his room. Joey's appetite was pretty good. He usually ate whatever was placed in front of him. At the end of his meal he would say, "Boy, Dad, you really went through a lot of trouble making all that food."

"No trouble at all. Don't worry about the work that's my job. Your job is to put some weight back on."

Within a few days his fever was gone. He was looking a little better until one afternoon when he started to roughhouse with me on the floor. I accidentally pushed on his leg causing him to let out a scream. "What's wrong; Joey? Are you okay?" "It hurts," he cried.

"What hurts?"

"My leg, daddy, my leg."

"Joey, I didn't push that hard on your leg to cause you to scream like this." I realized that this was all wrong. No one I ever knew had this type of reaction from growing pains. He remained on the floor crying. I felt helpless standing there watching him sob. Knowing that I hurt him made me feel even worse.

I sat with him until his pain subsided. When he felt well enough he managed to climb to his feet. I watched him as he limped out of the room. Right about now I had enough of this growing pain nonsense. "Joey, I think that we are going back to the doctor," I said.

That night I stayed awake rehashing anything in the past that may have caused an injury to Joey. I even tried to work backwards by attempting to identify any illness that would fit his symptoms. I kept purging my memory trying to put together the pieces to Joey's problem. What was I missing? Was it obvious to others? Why couldn't I solve this puzzle? I wished that my knowledge of medicine wasn't so limited. What I didn't lack was common sense and common sense told me that something was terribly wrong.

During the course of my life I had always been very assertive. However, my emotional melt down during and after my divorce had drained me of energy and fight. But now the old me was back, and I was angry and frustrated. I was determined to get to the bottom of Joey's ailment or turn the town upside down trying.

Chapter 12

I WENT INTO Joey's room several times during the night to check on how he was feeling. He kept repeating, "Daddy, my back is hurting me."

"I know, just be patient a little longer," I pleaded. "Tomorrow we are going to the doctor's office and we'll take care of your problem."

The next morning, before leaving the house, I asked him if he wanted anything for breakfast. He declined.

On the way to the doctor Joey asked, "Dad, do you think that my fever might be causing the pain in my leg and back?"

"No, I don't think so. Instead, I think that the pain in your leg and back might be causing your fever."

Meekly he asked, "So what do you think is wrong with me?"

I told him that I had been giving this matter a lot of thought and the only diagnosis I was able to come up with that made any sense was Lyme's disease. We lived in a tick infested area of the country and Lyme's disease in Long Island was hitting epidemic proportions. Giving me his full attention, he listened as I explained that the pain in his back, legs, and joints, as well as his fever, were all symptoms of Lyme's disease and that people contracted Lyme's disease after having been bitten by a deer tick carrying the disease. "You don't remember seeing a tick on you or being bitten by one do you?" He thought for a few seconds before answering, "no." I explained that most of the time the tick was so small that you couldn't see it.

"If I have Lyme's disease what can the doctors do for me?"

I informed him that in most cases Lyme's disease was treated with an antibiotic. Which antibiotic, I wasn't sure. I went on to say that after a few months he would feel as good as new, that I believed we had caught it early enough so that he would recover rather quickly. But instead of speculating, "Why don't we wait a few minutes, we're almost at the doctor's office."

Once again we took a seat in the pediatric reception area. Joey, in quite a bit of pain, was now noticeably limping. It was obvious that he was favoring his left leg and not capable of distributing his weight evenly. I was amazed at how quickly his physical condition was deteriorating. I was in a lot of pain too, only my pain was in my heart. I reached down and took his hand in mine. I wanted to touch and comfort him, to let him know that I was there, that everything would be fine.

It wasn't long after we arrived that they called Joey's name and directed us to an examination room. A nurse entered and the scenario of our first visit was repeated. I joked a little with Joey and he managed to deliver a smile. His temperature was taken and found to be normal. This didn't surprise me in the least because his temperature would go down as quickly as it would go up. I wanted to believe that this was the last time Joey would run a low-grade fever, that simply being in a doctor's office would have some magical healing affect. I hoped that the air possessed some medicinal quality, and that by inhaling it Joey might start to feel better.

A young doctor walked in. "Good morning. My name is Dr. Morgan," he said. He appeared to be in his late twenties, had a full manicured beard and a warm smile. He asked me the nature of Joey's problems. I took my time describing Joey's complaints and all that I had observed over the last few weeks. I also explained my theory of Lyme's disease to him. He paid close attention to what I was saying and suggested that Joey take a blood test to determine if he had Lyme's disease, but before doing that he wanted to examine him. While speaking in a soft gentle voice, Dr. Morgan took his time concentrating on the business at hand and not rushing to his next patient. I liked him.

"Joey, would you mind lying down on the examination table for me so I can take a look at what's hurting you?" Joey did as Dr. Morgan asked.

This time I did not leave the room. I wanted to be there to see what was going on. I wanted to be there for him. As Doctor Morgan began his examination I started to become impatient. Wanting an immediate diagnosis I began feeding him questions hoping to lead him in the direction that I wanted to take him. He wouldn't fall for it. He wouldn't play my game. As he rotated Joey's left leg, Joey let out a scream, "It hurts me. It hurts me a lot." With some concern, Dr. Morgan said that he wanted to take a picture of Joey's leg. He then directed us to the X-ray department.

In route to the X-ray department, Joey was still showing the painful signs of his examination. Again I held his hand. My poor little boy, what are they putting you through? I thought. Unfortunately there wasn't anything I could do to help him. All I could do was hold his hand. After arriving at the X-ray department, Joey's name was called and within minutes his X-rays were taken. I was pleased to see that we were moving along rather quickly. Hoping that we would soon have an answer, I kept thinking just give me a prescription for tetracycline or amoxicillin or whatever is used to treat Lyme's disease and let me take my son home.

A half an hour later we returned to Dr. Morgan's office. I found him sitting behind his desk waiting for us. A terrible feeling began to dampen my hopes. Dr. Morgan was no longer smiling. I didn't know what to think. It felt like a year had past before he uttered his first word.

"Dr. Carter, our orthopedic physician, is in today and I would like him to take a look at Joey." I knew that Dr. Morgan wasn't about to answer any questions until Dr. Carter had an opportunity to examine Joey and so I refrained from asking any until that time.

We walked to the orthopedic department located in a different area of the building. I signed in, and we waited. A tall distinguished black man walked out of his office and introduced himself. "Hello, I'm Dr. Carter. I understand that Joey is experiencing a little problem, would you mind if I examined him?"

"Not at all."

Dr. Carter turned to Joey asking, "Is it okay with you?"

Joey nodded his approval.

Pointing to an empty examination room Dr. Carter said, "You can follow me into this room over here." As we entered the room, I made up my mind that I would not leave Joey's side. Dr. Carter asked Joey if he wouldn't mind stripping to his shorts. It was becoming difficult for him to take off his jeans unassisted. Any movement of his leg caused him a great deal of pain. Gently lifting his leg I helped him take off his jeans.

Dr. Carter began to examine Joey's left leg in the same manner that Dr. Morgan had done only a few minutes before and again Joey screamed. A few other twists and turns of his leg met with the same response.

"Can you lift your leg off the table?" Dr. Carter asked. Joey could only raise his leg an inch.

Next, Dr. Carter proceeded to examine his good leg. This time there was no indication of pain. Asked to raise his right leg, he raised it straight up with very little effort.

"What do you think?" I impatiently asked.

"I haven't had a chance to review his X-rays. Why don't you and Joey take a seat in the waiting room while I take a look at them? I'll only be a few minutes."

I helped Joey into the waiting room and remained there with him nervously waiting for Dr. Carter to call us. Ten minutes had gone by before Dr. Carter emerged asking that we step inside his office. Before sitting I studied his face looking for a sign of concern on his part, something that might indicate the seriousness of Joey's condition. I did not like what I saw. Dr. Carter cleared his throat.

"There's a problem with the X-rays, not with the X-rays but with what I saw in the X-rays that will require further intervention." I quickly interrupted him then turning to Joey I said, "Daddy would like to be alone with the doctor for a few minutes. Would you mind sitting in the waiting room?" Before Joey was able to answer I added, "I promise I won't be long." I took a deep breath and watched as Joey hobbled out of the room closing the door behind him. Uneasiness was coming over me, a horrible feeling that something was terribly wrong.

Dr. Carter resumed his conversation by saying, "Let me show you the X-rays so you can get a better understanding of what I am talking about, and why in all hell wasn't he X-rayed before today?" I didn't have the answer to that question. Perhaps it was my fault. I knew Joey was in pain, that something was wrong, was I so caught up in the chaos of my life that I didn't give his problem the attention it deserved?

Dr. Carter proceeded to show me Joey's X-rays. Even though I had no medical training, it was easy to see the difference between the X-rays of the left side of his body and those of the right side. Joey's right pelvic area was bright and clear with definitive lines of demarcation; while the left appeared gray, cloudy, finely marked, and kind of scaly looking. I didn't know which side was abnormal; I only knew that they were obviously different in appearance.

"You know they can do a lot with this today," Dr. Carter solemnly said.

Somehow I managed to gather up the courage to ask the question that I had been feeling down deep in the pit of my stomach. The question that I immediately ushered away exiling it from my thoughts and life.

"Are we talking cancer?" As my words left my lips, they rocked me. Cancer was a word that I thought I would never use, at least in reference to one of my children. I wanted to find a way to withdraw my question to siphon back every syllable but it was too late, he had already heard me.

Dr. Carter took a deep breath before answering my question. "Yes, I think: so." Chills ran through my body. My knees buckled. I felt sick and had the urge to vomit. I did not want to hear anymore. All I wanted to do was run out into the waiting room. To put my arms around my son where I knew he would be safe and to never let him go. These things didn't happen in my family. They occurred in other families, to other people's children. This cannot be true, I thought. It can't be happening to my little boy. I wanted to scream, "You don't understand how much I love him." My eyes filled with tears as I sat there in complete shock. It took me a long time to regain my composure, until I was once again able to speak.

"Are you sure that he has cancer?"

"No, in my opinion there is a small possibility that it could be an infection, but I don't think so." Dr. Carter paused.

As he looked into my eyes, I had the feeling that he wished he wasn't the bearer of this sad news. I knew that he wanted to be wrong, but he had been at his job too long to disagree with his training and past experiences. He continued, "What I would like you to do is take Joey to a small Nassau County Hospital for a bone scan. Would tomorrow be too soon?"

"Not at all. Let's get it over with. The sooner the better." I was about to leave when I asked Dr. Carter if it would it be possible to give Joey something to ease his pain. I was beginning to get a feeling that the next twenty-four hours would be a living hell for Joey and, at the very least, purgatory for me.

Dr. Carter said that he didn't want any of Joey's symptoms to subside, possibly masking the cause of his illness, until Joey completed his bone scan. He suggested that I give him Tylenol. I didn't like what he had to say but I understood his intentions.

Hesitating, attempting to gather my thoughts, I told Dr. Carter that I wanted Joey to see the best doctor in this field, that I wasn't going to settle for anyone less. I didn't care where he was located or how busy his schedule. It had always amazed me that people, with potentially terminal illnesses, sought help here at some small Community Hospital, and according to them, their doctor was always the best. I viewed the situation differently. There were no great doctors in small Community Hospitals, only good ones. I knew that when it came to dying there was no second chance, that when you're dead, you're dead for a long time. There was no saying, "Next time I'll get off my proverbial lazy ass and make the trip to a renowned hospital in

Manhattan." I also knew that the doctor who pronounced you dead on a Tuesday would still play golf on a Wednesday. This was my son and I was taking him to New York City where they had the best doctors and hospitals in the world. To prove my point I asked Dr. Carter, "If Joey was the President's son, or the son of a Sheik, where would he go for treatment?" He thought before answering.

"He would go to one of the better hospitals in New York City?"

"Right, and that's where I'm taking my son." Trying to take control of a worsening situation I said, "Now give me the name of the very best doctor in this field?" Without hesitation he answered, "That would be Dr. Cole, there isn't any better."

"What hospital is he affiliated with?" "He has privleges at several major NewYork City Hospitals."

"Can we arrange that?"

"We have an affiliation with them and I know Dr. Cole. I'll work on it." "Thank you."

"Are you aware of what it is going to entail making that trip on a daily basis?"

"Doctor, keep my son alive."

Chapter 13

JOEY WAS STILL sitting in the waiting room when I concluded my meeting with Dr. Carter. As I approached him, I made an all out effort to conceal my emotions, it wasn't easy, but somehow I managed to pull it off.

"Daddy, what did you and the doctor talk about?"

I told him that Dr. Carter wanted him to take a bone scan because he believed that there might be an infection in his bone, and once the test was completed Dr. Carter would decide what medication to give him to make him feel better. "Is it okay with you if we go for that test tomorrow?"

"Okay, if I have too."

During the ride home, I made up my mind not to inform anyone of my conversation with Dr. Carter. At this point in time I did not want to unnecessarily alarm any family members. Claudine had left for a summer tour of Egypt and wasn't due home for a few days. Tammy was home but frightening her wouldn't serve any purpose: Joey was her pal and if she thought there was anything seriously wrong with her little brother it would devastate her.

I decided to stay home for a few days and not wander too far from the house. I thought it best to devote myself entirely to Joey's medical problem. Plus, I didn't want to be away from him, not even for one second. Everything else in my life would be placed on hold. Nothing else mattered. My son was the only one I could think about. He consumed my every thought.

That night I couldn't sleep a wink I sat in a chair trying to recapture the events of the day but all I could hear were Dr. Carter's words reverberating in my head. I entered Joey's room several times during the night. The pain in his back and leg would not allow him to sleep.

YOU CAN'T TAKE MY SON

Sitting on the edge of his bed, I caressed his head while he tried to assume a comfortable position. In an attempt to reassure him I told him not to worry, that we would get to the bottom of what was hurting him and whatever it was could be fixed. I promised him that before he knew it he would feel like his old self again. I begged him to be a little patient for a few more days.

The next morning I was up early. Joey took a few bites of breakfast but refused the rest.

"I'm not hungry. I can't eat."

"That's fine you don't have to eat. It's really fine. Maybe after you take your bone scan you might want something? We'll wait until then."

Our appointment was scheduled for 10:00 a.m. However the bone scan department called asking that we arrive there a little earlier. The test required that Joey be injected with a nuclear dye that required an hour lead time. After the dye circulated throughout his system the bone scan would be taken. Not wanting to be late I left the house at 7:30a.m.

North Nassau Hospital was located forty-five minutes from where we lived. For us to get there, we would have to travel westbound on the Long Island Expressway. Joey was experiencing moderate pains in his back and leg. I could see that he was having a difficult time trying to maneuver his body into a position that would reduce his discomfort. I talked him into reclining his car seat hoping that would help make him a little more comfortable.

Traffic was heavy causing me to curse the other drivers that were delaying us. Didn't they know that my son was sick and in pain, that I wanted to get him to the hospital and back home as quickly as possible? Looking at my watch I knew that we were running behind schedule. With Joey's pain intensifying, I decided to ride the shoulder of the expressway. What other drivers thought of me was their problem. We arrived at the hospital on time.

Not being familiar with North Nassau Hospital, a small local hospital on the north shore of Long Island, I hoped that we wouldn't experience any difficulty locating the bone scan department. Fortunately, we found it rather quickly. Within minutes Joey was injected with some form of dye. An hour later, for the first time in his young life, he underwent a bone scan. I prayed that it would be his first and last one.

The drive home was much faster. The eastbound traffic was relatively light. With the day's events draining Joey of his strength he went directly to his room to rest. Now, all I had to do was wait for the results of his test.

Unable to concentrate on anything but Joey's bone scan, I once again paced about the house. As the day progressed I began to wonder when somebody would call with Joey's test results. Not that I wanted to know what was going on but that I had to know. I thought about calling Dr. Carter at our HMO center. I kept picking up the phone to dial but talked myself out of it thinking that no news was good news. I reasoned that if something were seriously wrong with Joey they would have called me. Yes, that's it, I thought, nothing was wrong, they're taking care of more important issues; then the phone rang. It was Dr. Carter. The tests were positive. My breathing became labored and my hands started to shake. I couldn't speak a word. Dr. Carter spoke first.

He informed me that he was making arrangements for Joey's admission to a New York City Hospital, that he would work on it today and over the weekend and, with any luck, I might be able to take him Monday morning. Understanding my concern, he reminded me that the possibility exists that we may still be dealing with a serious infection and not cancer.

"I am sending you to see the experts. Let them handle it. If you have any questions call me," he said. I thanked him. Shaking my head, I wondered how does one appropriately thank someone for this type of news?

It was several hours later when an administrative aid finally called from the HMO office to inform me that Joey had an appointment to see Dr. Cole Monday morning. Not fully aware of the day of the week, I looked at my calendar- it was Friday. I asked if we could see him tomorrow. She informed me that Dr. Cole was away on vacation and would not return until Monday. She also asked that I stop by the HMO office to pick up Joey's X-rays.

I wondered why everything of an emergency nature takes place on Friday; leaving people to be tormented by, what must feel like, the longest weekend of their lives. I wished that I were more important. Important people never have to wait.

Claudine's flight was due to arrive from Egypt and I promised to pick her up at the airport. Tammy volunteered to keep her brother company in my absence. I was hesitant about leaving him, but the drive to Kennedy might allow me to clear the cobwebs from my head helping me to think and focus my thoughts. I decided to go. Driving to the airport, I opened the car windows. The cool night air felt good as it whipped about the car. For the first time in days I was able to breathe deeply.

During the trip to the airport, I made up my mind to downplay Joey's condition. I didn't want to frighten Claudine. I would be honest in presenting the facts to her, because I have always been honest with my children. Plus, she was mature enough to cope with the reality of the situation. However, I decided to emphasize the infection issue rather than the cancer aspect.

Claudine's flight was on time. I greeted her with a big hug. I carried several of her suitcases to the short-term parking lot. I questioned why women traveled with so much luggage. By the time I reached the car, my shoulder felt as though it had been dislodged from its socket. I opened the car door and we positioned ourselves in the front seat for the long ride home. Claudine gave me another hug and kiss. We weren't in the car five minutes when she asked, "When are you going to tell me what's wrong?" For a second I forgot with whom I was dealing. "C'mon Dad, let's have it all. Don't play games with me."

"Wow! Does it show that much?" "Yes. It does."

I updated her on the events of the last couple of days. Quietly she soaked up every morsel of information that I was telling her. I could smell the smoke emanating from her brain as it worked overtime assimilating and analyzing all the pertinent facts. When I finished speaking I knew that I was in for a barrage of questions and suggestions. She didn't disappointment me. To the best of my ability, utilizing the little bit of information and knowledge that I had at my disposal, I answered her questions.

Arriving home we raced into the house and up the stairs to check on Joey, Claudine's expression said it all. This was not the little brother that she had left behind several weeks ago. That brother was young, spry and full of life. This was a different boy, one who was frail and in terrible pain. Feeling their sadness and worry about Joey, whom they always referred to as, "their little guy," I placed my arms around my daughters. I wanted to hug them but I needed one too.

During my absence, Tammy explained that Joey was experiencing a lot of pain. I gave him some Motrin and a few minutes later he fell asleep. I was aware that his sleep would be momentary at best. The girls went downstairs to the kitchen. A few minutes later I joined them. I was grateful that they had each other to lean on. I needed them to be able to comfort one another because I knew that I wouldn't have much time to devote to them. I was very proud of the fine young women they were becoming. It was now three years since their mother absconded. They were doing it all without her. As hard as it was for them, they were succeeding in becoming the type of daughters that would make any man feel proud. I was.

That evening I returned to Joey's room. I pulled out a chair and sat next to his bed. I was feeling very tired, craving sleep, I wanted to close my eyes but fought it off. I remained next to Joey until I was no longer able to fight the urge to sleep, then I went into my bedroom and gave in to my exhaustion. I had purposely left my door open hoping that I would hear Joey if he called out during the night. It was in the early hours of the morning when Joey entered my bedroom.

"Daddy, my back is killing me, it really hurts a lot." His face looked so sad. I put the television on in my room and suggested that he climb into bed with me thinking that he might be a little more comfortable. Without saying a word he climbed in.

Next, in an attempt to take some pressure off his back I tried to position a few pillows under his leg. I hoped that it might afford him a little relief from his pain, then I went downstairs to prepare something for him to eat. He took a few nibbles and fell asleep. I was glad that he was able to sleep. I tried but couldn't.

Saturday morning rolled around. Joey remained downstairs on the couch watching television. The simplest tasks were becoming more difficult. In order for him to stand it became necessary for me to lift him to his feet. As the day went on his limping increased. The degree that he was favoring his good leg was more apparent than ever. No longer able to climb the flight of stairs to his bedroom I put my arm around his waist and together we slowly climbed one step at a time. Joey's pain was becoming intolerable. I wanted to give him something a little stronger than Tylenol or Motrin but instead, I followed Dr. Carter's directions.

With early evening approaching, Joey had reached a point where he no longer wanted to move from his bed. Searching the house, I found an old heating pad and placed it under the area that was causing him the most pain hoping that it might ease his discomfort.

"Dad, would you rub my back? Rubbing it makes it feel better."

I sat on his bed and rubbed his back. I prayed that he would fall asleep for a few hours. If he did, at least when he awakened it would be that much closer to Monday. Plus, when he slept he wasn't suffering. But his sleep was sporadic at best. His pain was now severe enough to wake him from the little sleep he was getting. I asked him if he would like some dessert thinking that if he was busy eating it might distract him, but he had no interest in food.

As the night progressed Joey began to cry. Soon, he was screaming. I sat next to him wiping away his tears. I made an effort to engage him in some small talk trying to calm him. I knew that he enjoyed baseball, and cars, so I steered the conversation in that direction. It worked, but briefly. By Sunday, he digressed even more. The gravity of the situation was worsening. I was amazed at how fast his condition was deteriorating. His pain now seemed uncompromising. By this time, I was totally exhausted. It had been two days since I last slept. I wanted to take a nap but wouldn't dare. If Joey called it was important that I be there. Looking at him made me feel even more helpless.

He asked if he could watch television downstairs in the den. The only way for him to go down the stairs was for me to carry him. I picked him up and carried him to the couch. A few minutes went by before I heard him cry, "Daddy, would you carry me upstairs to my bedroom? I want to go back to bed."

"Sure I'll carry you up to your bed."

Once again I carried him up the stairs. It was impossible for him to find even a small degree of comfort regardless of where he was in the house. His physical condition was quickly declining. The pain was becoming too much for him to tolerate. I could no longer touch his leg without him wailing. Each time I touched it I felt as though I was the one causing his agony. He began to cry uncontrollably. There wasn't a thing I could do except sit and watch him cry. My heart was broken. I was looking at the person I loved most in this world slowly being taken from me. I was always able to fix whatever was wrong in his life. I was his daddy, the one he came to for help, love, and just about everything else. My little boy was begging for help and there wasn't anything I could do except hold him. I past being scared a while back. I was terrified.

Supporting all of Joey's weight, I carried him into my bed wishing that he would fall asleep next to me. Fighting exhaustion, I closed my eyes. It was 3:00a.m. Later that night I stretched my arms out to touch him, but he wasn't there. It was now 4:00a.m. I slept longer than I should have. Startled, I jumped out of bed. Nearby, I could hear crying. Only the sound wasn't coming from Joey's bedroom. It was coming from somewhere else in the house. Still half asleep, I was having a difficult time gathering my thoughts. Staggering into the hallway I managed to pinpoint Joey's location. He was in the upstairs bathroom just outside my bedroom. I walked in and found him sitting in a bathtub filled with hot water.

"Daddy, I can't take the pain."

Tears were running down his face. My heart broke looking at his body, now less than thin. "Joey what are you doing in here?"

He repeated, "Daddy, I can't take the pain. I thought that the hot water might help me."

"It's alright. Sit here. I'll keep you company. Stay as long as you like." I sat with him for some time, and then reaching down I picked him up and carried him to my bed making every attempt to be careful not to touch his leg.

While I was carrying him I made him a promise- a promise I had no right to make. Trying to hold back my tears I said, "Joey, you have to hang in there a little bit longer. Daddy has never lied to you before and I'm not going to lie to you now. I promise that you are going to get through this. You are going to get better. It may take some time but you'll be as good as you were before you became sick. I promise to never quit on you and I will keep you informed about everything that takes place. I won't keep you in the dark. You have to promise me that you are going to fight, to fight hard, and to never stop fighting. You can't quit on yourself and you can't quit on me. Together we are going to get through this. Joey you are my partner, my buddy. You have to trust daddy." He finally fell asleep. I cried, and I prayed.

This had to be his worst night. His pain now progressed to a point where it was unyielding. All that I had to cling to was the hope that Joey was suffering from a very serious bone infection. The bone scan was able to determine that something was abnormal in the pelvic area. It did not identify the exact cause of the abnormality. I was determined not to think virulent thoughts of cancer. The connotations associated with cancer had to be eradicated from my mind. I couldn't travel down that road.

Tammy sat with me until she was too tired to keep her eyes opened. She had to attend school the next day and I thought it important for her to catch a little sleep. I felt guilty for ignoring her the past few days but single parents carry a knapsack full of guilt with them wherever they go. At least that's how the home base parent feels. The other, I wasn't qualified to voice an opinion on.

Monday morning finally languored in. I was up early and not a bit tired. I was functioning on pure adrenaline and fear. Positioning myself near the telephone I awaited procedural instructions from Dr. Carter. Unable to restrain myself I called the HMO center at 9:00a.m. Hell, I thought, someone had to take the initiative. A receptionist answered the phone. I asked for Dr. Carter and was informed that he was seeing patients. I was told that he would call me when visiting hours were finished. At 11:00 a.m. the phone rang. It was Dr. Carter.

"Good morning. I'm sorry that it has taken me so long to get back to you. I had quite a few patients to see and I was waiting for the hospital to notify me concerning Joey's medical agenda." I cut his conversation short.

"That's alright. Please update me on what I am supposed to do. Joey is crying with pain. He is in dire need of help. He can't go on in his present condition. Something has to be done and now."

"I understand."

"Have you heard from the hospital?"

"Yes, they are expecting him but first stop by my office and pick up his X-rays. Once you have the X-rays, bring Joey to the admitting office at Mt. Sinai. Again, I want to remind you that nothing is conclusive. Before an accurate diagnosis can be made he is going to have to undergo additional testing. It still could be a serious infection that is causing his problems. Try to remain calm. Let's take this one day at a time and keep me posted," he said, before hanging up the phone.

I had to remain optimistic. I had to cling to my faith and my hope. I convinced myself that Joey was going to be fine. I repeated over and over again that nothing like this had ever happened in my family.

That cancer was genetic by nature. It could be a non malignant tumor placing pressure on sensitive cells and ligaments. If that were the case then surgical intervention was a viable alternative. Even I knew that X-rays, by themselves, could not indicate cancer with any degree of certainty. I still had hope and I wasn't about to abandon my hope.

I decided to apprise my brother Tony and his wife Mary. Mary loved Joey very much. She always thought he was a wonderful boy. So did everyone who knew him.

Mary volunteered to accompany me to Mt. Sinai. I welcomed her company. I was quite aware that any medical decisions concerning Joey would have to be made by me but I welcomed any thoughts and opinions that she might offer. At this time I needed an adult to bounce my feelings and thoughts off of. I shook my head wondering how could anybody do this alone? I was barely able to function. I knew that one wrong decision on my part could cost Joey his life. If I had believed that up until now being a single parent was draining, I knew that I was about to enter a higher plateau; one that would require every ounce of strength I had and more. I asked myself, "Could this be my test in life?" If so, my only wish was that Joey was not being used as the test vehicle.

I attempted to situate Joey in a comfortable position in the rear of the car. Then I placed a pillow under his head and legs. He was racked with pain. Walking had become impossible. "Joey, try to sleep, I will wake you when we arrive at the hospital."

Joey's pain wouldn't allow him to sleep. Every bump and pothole in the road caused him to bellow leaving little doubt as to how much he was suffering. For years I traveled the Long Island Expressway never realizing the poor condition of the roadway until today. My only thoughts were of getting Joey to the hospital as quickly as possible. Hoping, once there, something could be done to at least lessen his pain.

While I was driving I didn't want to look over my shoulder. I wanted to make believe that none of this was taking place, that we were going to Manhattan to see a Broadway play, or to engage in some other pleasantry. Too frightened to look behind me, I fixed my eyes on the road making every attempt to avoid hitting any protuberance that might cause Joey to cry out with agony.

No longer able to tune out his suffering I glanced over my shoulder. Trying to pacify him I said, "We're almost there. Hold on a little bit longer." My remarks went unheard. Mary attempted to keep me occupied by talking about anything and everything that came to mind. Her small talk bounced off me, unable to penetrate my concern for Joey.

I was driving over the Triboro Bridge when suddenly I became overwhelmed by my emotions and the verity of my dream. My nightmare was real. Joey might be afflicted with cancer and I was driving over a bridge heading into Manhattan with Mary. Yes, now I knew. Now it was clear. She was the other person in my dream. My body jolted. Mary's look said, "What's wrong?" I shook my head unable to speak. If I explained, she would not have believed me. Yet, it was true. My worse premonition was becoming a reality. There were so many questions that remained unanswered. Why did I repeatedly have that dream? What was the purpose behind it? Who was trying to tell me something? And, Why? Why? Why?

A lifetime later, we arrived at Mt. Sinai Hospital. I found an empty parking space, parked my car, and deposited a few coins in the meter. I leaned over carefully lifting him out of the back seat. What little strength he had was now diminished to a whisper. Mary walked ahead to find the admitting office located somewhere inside the entrance to the Klingenstein Pavilion. Dodging traffic, I carried Joey across the street.

Maneuvering our way through the lobby we managed to catch up to Mary who was holding the door open for us. I gingerly lowered Joey into a chair. He looked so frail and pathetic. I wished that there was something I could do to stop his crying but I was helpless.

"Daddy the pain in my back and leg won't stop," he cried.

Tears were streaming his face. Trying to calm him proved futile. I asked Mary to keep him company while I tried to speed up the admission process. Approaching the receptionist's window, I said, "My son needs help and he needs it quickly."

"I can't help you until you have properly filled out the admission forms," she said without looking up. She appeared indifferent and insensitive.

"Give me the forms," I sarcastically snapped.

Not paying any attention to detail, I quickly filled out the required information, thinking that if I made a mistake I would rectify it later. I returned the completed forms to the receptionist and asked, "What now?"

"Now we have to locate a wheelchair and have him transported upstairs to his room."

Three minutes later I was standing in front of her with a wheelchair. "Okay lady, here's a wheelchair, now tell me where to take him?"

"You can't take him anywhere. Someone from patient transport has to take him to his room."

"I want you to listen to me," I said. She raised her head to make eye contact with me. My lips taunt with anger; the inflection in my voice caught her attention. With my eyes piercing through hers, I told her that right about now I had my fill of administrative bullshit. I asked her if she saw the little boy over there, the one in pain who couldn't stop crying? I said that he has been like that for three days and that I did not want any more delays. "If you do not get me someone from transport to push his wheelchair then I am going to wheel him around this hospital until I find a compassionate person that will help him," I threatened.

It wasn't long before a transport aid showed up. Wiping the tears from Joey's face, I assisted him into a wheelchair being careful not to touch his leg any more than necessary. Merely attempting to place his foot on the footpad caused him to scream.

"Where are we taking him?" I asked the aid. "Falk 2," he answered.

Falk 2 was quite a distance from the admitting office. To get there required that we take an elevator to the basement, then walk underground to the Fifth Avenue side of the hospital. Once there we entered a second elevator that serviced the Falk building of the hospital. The transport clerk pushed button number 2 and seconds later we emerged onto Falk 2. The three of us were left standing near the elevator entrance while the aid submitted our paperwork to the unit clerk.

It quickly became obvious that Falk 2 was a floor consisting mostly of adolescent children that were being treated for a variety of illnesses. I found it disheartening as I looked around me. Some children were in wheelchairs, while others were walking about with only one leg, using crutches for support. Many were attached to IV's. What I was observing was definitely not an encouraging sign.

Falk 2 was in extensive need of repair. The only thing about it that wasn't old was the age of the patients. The corridors were exceptionally wide. The ceilings were high, giving a different appearance than most modern hospitals. This place was a step back in time. Even the paint on the walls was peeling and chipping. This austerity did not fit the rich reputation of Mt. Sinai. Later I learned that Falk 2 was scheduled for demolition.

We waited for a nurse to take us to an unoccupied room. The room mirrored the rest of Falk 2. The windows were huge. They opened and closed by means of old fashion sash weights. Covering the windows were beige pull down shades that, at one time, must have been white. Actually, it was difficult to determine what their original color was because of the graffiti names of former patients and visitors that adorned all but a few inches of available space. So, this is the place where sick children travel to from all over the world, I thought. This dilapidation is where they hope to find the knowledge and treatment to keep them alive. So far, all that it was showing me was that I might have made the biggest mistake of my life, or Joey's life, by coming here.

Helping Joey onto his bed was quite an effort as I sat him on the extreme edge of the mattress. I supported his head while Mary manually cranked his bed lower until Joey was lying flat. Now came the hard part; his leg could only be manipulated fractionally. As I gently touched his leg he shrieked, "Please daddy, don't touch it, it hurts too much."

"Okay, I'll try to be careful. Just a few more inches and you're almost there. All you have to do is try to hold out a little bit longer and a doctor will be here to take care of your pain. I'm sure they will give you something so it won't hurt you anymore. It won't be long now."

I could not believe that this was the same boy who, just a few weeks ago, looked so healthy and happy. He was so dispirited. I kept asking myself, "What happened to my son? Can somebody please tell me what's going on here?"

While I was talking to Mary, several staff members entered Joey's room. Some were attired in white hospital jackets while others were dressed in everyday street clothes. A woman introduced herself. "Hello, I'm Dr. Granowetter from the hematology/oncology department. Please call me Dr. G."

I immediately attempted to size her up. She was in her late thirties, slight of stature, and had short black hair that gave the appearance that she was constantly running her fingers through it. As she walked towards Joey's room it was apparent that she was not easily distracted. Wasted motion was nonexistent to this lady. Without openly professing her authority I recognized that she was a no-nonsense doctor and in charge. Her work was her life. These young ailing children were her reason for getting up in the morning and going to bed at night. They were her reason for living.

I summed up my thoughts by thinking: if this were a high school geometry class she would be the one that I would want to be sitting behind. She was all business. I was hoping that she would smile but as I glanced about me I realized that there was little to smile about here. An immediate question came to my mind. How many children has she lost? And how many has she saved? If something was seriously wrong with Joey, did she possess the knowledge and the resolve to save one more? That's all that mattered to me. We needed her on our side. We were at her mercy.

I wanted to say to her, "I know who you are but you're in the wrong room; we have no need for your services. Please go elsewhere where you can do some good."

At that moment she introduced her colleague, Dr. Lipton, as the physician in charge of the pediatric hematology/oncology department. I thought what a strange word oncology was. There was nothing soft or warm about it. It intimidated me.

Dr. Lipton, presented a completely different image than Dr. G. A nice looking man in his late thirties with salt and pepper hair, he gave the appearance that if he had not chosen the medical profession he would have made an excellent politician. Although he was making patient rounds along with the other members of the oncology team, it was obvious that he was preoccupied with administrative issues. He was warm, personable, and seemed well liked by the patients and staff.

Accompanying them were two clinical nurses assigned to the hematology/oncology department. They introduced themselves as Carol and Laurie. Both looked to be in their late twenties, were friendly, and appeared devoted to their work. Carol was the jokester of the two, teasing and playing with each patient that she came in contact with. Laurie demeanor was more serious and reserved as she concentrated on the business before her.

Their personalities complimented each other. Dr. G would be Joey's physician.

She also told Joey rather than pronounce her whole name it might be easier for him to refer to her as Dr. G.

She began her conversation with Joey in a comforting, reassuring, voice. "So, Joey, I hear that you're not feeling well. Why don't you tell me how you're feeling and what's Hurting you?" With his voice barely audible, Joey tried to communicate the location and magnitude of his pain. Dr. G. listened carefully. She then asked that I wait in the hall while she conducted her examination. I did not object knowing that Joey would howl as she moved his leg. I refused to remain there helpless watching him cry.

What I really wanted to do was close my eyes, wake up, and be someplace else. Anyplace would do, I wasn't too particular. After all I had to be dreaming. I've had bad dreams before, ones that seemed real and terrifying at the time but upon waking up were so distant from reality that I would laugh at the ludicrousness of it all. But, this wasn't a dream and there wasn't anything remotely foolish about it. This was real, touching a part of me that had never been touched before. It was reaching way down into my soul tearing at my essence, at my very being.

Once in the hall, I joined Mary who was now accompanied by my brother. It felt good to have family nearby. They asked what was taking place and I updated them explaining what little I knew. Without any further conversation the three of us entered the visitor's lounge. Our total concentration was on Joey and what was transpiring in his room. Anticipating that his door might open at any moment I couldn't tear my eyes away from it. I wanted someone to walk out and give me some answers. I had the questions. I needed the answers.

My anticipation and nerves were starting to get the better of me when Joey's door opened. Dr. G. emerged from Joey's room with the rest of her entourage. Spotting the three of us sitting in the lounge she entered, closing the door behind her.

The silence was deafening as we waited for her to commence speaking. I wanted her to say something, anything. What I really wanted were fast answers like, "Joey is fine. There is nothing really wrong with him that some handful of pills won't be able to cure. His infection will be gone in a couple of weeks." At which time we would thank her for all the trouble that we had put her through, apologize for taking time away from her busy schedule, and be on our way.

As Dr. G. began to speak I clung to her every word.

"Joey is in extreme pain. I want you to know that we will be able to control his pain, but not yet. He has very little lateral movement of his left leg,"

Fine, I thought, we know all that, get on with it, give me more, and do it quickly before I burst. She continued, "We cannot make an accurate diagnosis as to the cause of his pain without him undergoing several tests. I am going to schedule him for some X rays, blood work and most likely a biopsy." Then, to my surprise, she told us that Dr. Morgan had not yet returned from his vacation and that she had made arrangements for Joey to be seen by Dr. Sherry. She assured us that Dr. Sherry was an excellent pediatric orthopedic surgeon and would be in shortly to examine Joey.

Searching for the right words, I somehow found the nerve to ask my question, "What's all this talk about cancer? Does my son have cancer or does he not have cancer?"

She said that she understood how we felt but that she was going to have to take it one step at a time. "If you are asking me if I am ruling out cancer, I must answer, I am not. If you are asking me if I am ruling out an infection, again I must answer, I am not." Pausing for a moment to allow us to assimilate some of what she had just said, she set aside her Hippocratic demeanor allowing compassion to speak, "I know how much you have all been through and how concerned all of you are, but please be patient until I can I give you an accurate diagnosis. Do you have any additional questions?"

"What other tests do you intend to give Joey?" Mary asked. "First, I would like him to be X-rayed."

"I brought a copy of his X-rays with me," I interjected.

"I know, however we would prefer to take our own X-rays. Once they are taken I want to send him for a CT scan, MRI and another bone scan. But before we proceed with those tests I would like to draw a little blood, test his urine and get him hydrated." She paused for a few seconds and then continued in her matter of fact dialogue. "I will explain the purpose of each test as we move along."

"I understand that you will explain the purpose of each test and I thank you for doing that, but I am more interested in the results than the purpose," I said.

"When I get the results I will pass them on to you, I promise." "Fair enough."

"By the way," she said, "Joey is dehydrated. He needs fluids. If he does not replace his body fluids on his own, then we are going to have to accomplish it by means of an IV. Perhaps you can convince him to take some fluids?"

"I will talk to him and try to get him to drink. Now what about his pain?"

She told me that his pain could not be addressed at this moment, not until Dr. Sherry had a chance to examine him and Joey had completed a few tests. Until that time she felt it best not to administer any medication. However, she would give him a little codeine and if that didn't reduce his pain she would give him something stronger later that evening.

"Codeine! My God, with his pain that's no better than aspirin. He's in need of a lot more than codeine. Well, I guess he has no choice," Trying to hold back my tears I said, "You must promise me one thing- that if you can't make him better you will not allow him to suffer. I couldn't endure that."

"I promise you he will not be allowed to suffer."

I looked at my brother Tony and Mary to see if they had any questions. "When do these tests begin?" Mary asked.

"Right now."

It was now Tony's turn to ask a question. I knew the question he was going to ask before it left his lips.

"So let me get this clear. There is still a very good chance Joey is suffering from a bone infection. Is that right?" He urged.

"Yes, there is that possibility."

Tony cut her short not allowing her the opportunity to continue. He received the answer he wanted and that was all he was going allow her to say.

No longer able to control my emotions I found an empty room, walked inside and began punching the wall. I couldn't stop crying. Looking out the window and staring up at the sky, I pleaded that he was mine and I loved him. I made him and you can't have him. I taught him how to play catch and how to build a snowman. I waited with him at the bus stop when he left for school in the morning and

I was there when he came home. You can't give me something this beautiful and take it back. You can't take him from me. You can't leave me here to spend the rest of my life wondering where he is and what he's doing. Who was going to tell him to put on a jacket when he went outside to play in the cold? Who was going to tell him that he had to be home in time for dinner? Was anyone going to remind him to do his homework? Was anyone going to give him his cough medicine when he got sick? Can't you understand that I don't want to be here without him, that this was never about him or me, but us. I can't spend the rest of my life waiting to see him again. I won't let you take him because he's mine. Exhausted, I leaned on the wall begging, "Please God let me keep him. Take me. I'll go now without a complaint. Take me, but let my son live."

Not wanting anyone to see me in my present emotional state, I waited until I was able to regain my composure before returning to join Tony and Mary in the visitor's lounge. The three of us, trying to absorb what Dr. G. had just told us, sat quietly looking for something reassuring to say. Several minutes passed before I was able to say anything at all. Forcing a question I asked Tony and Mary what they thought.

Mary, speaking first, was unconvinced that something was seriously wrong with Joey. She believed that we should not be concerned about Joey having some serious illness. "After all between you and your brothers you have ten children, and none of them have had a child-related serious illness." With certainty, she went on to say that Joey had a serious bone infection and that was it. That was how she felt and that was how she was going to handle this situation. It felt good to hear her speak so assuringly. I admired her resolve, that she would not allow a splinter of doubt to enter her mind.

Tony sat there shaking his head, indicating that he agreed with Mary. I ate up their positive attitude. It gave me the hope that I needed and longed for. I asked that they excuse me for a few minutes while I checked on Joey.

I walked into Joey's room and managed to fake a smile and a

warm hello. "So, Joey, are you through fooling around here? Don't you think that you have received enough attention for one day?" Joey didn't answer he was trying to make himself comfortable but his pain prevented him from settling in. "Hey, let me help you," I said. I gingerly placed two pillows under his bad leg hoping to mollify a little of the painful pressure that he was obviously experiencing. I made every effort to be careful but he screamed nonetheless.

Joey had now gone several days without food. Physically, he was beginning to disappear. Beneath his clothing he was being transformed into a living skeleton. His bones were starting to protrude through his skin. He was slowly taking on the look of a holocaust victim. "Please, Joey, eat a little something, anything at all, but eat," I pleaded. With his pain suppressing his desire for food, he shook his head no. A nurse standing next to his bed informed me that it was more important for him to drink. His body was becoming seriously dehydrated. He needed fluids.

I poured a glass of water and touched his lips with the rim of the glass. He took a few sips before waving me off. I respected his wishes and backed away, trying not to force the issue. At that moment his door opened. A distinguished looking man in his fifties walked in. My instincts told me who he was.

"Hello, I'm Dr. Sherry," he said in a deep baritone voice.

"Yes, I know who you are. We've been waiting for you." He wasted little time in getting to the point. He quickly began asking me questions related to Joey's past and present health. To the best of my ability I attempted to answer him. When we were finished conversing, he turned his attention to Joey. He asked him to describe his pain. Joey, tired and weak, made a valiant attempt to answer Dr. Sherry's questions.

"How about a quick examination?" Not waiting for a reply, Dr. Sherry's went right to work. I stood their quietly trying to become part of the room. I watched as Dr. Sherry's examination, identical to Dr. Carter's, brought about the same painful reaction from Joey.

As Dr. Sherry proceeded with his examination. I wished that

anyone and everyone, who wanted to probe and examine Joey, would all do it at the same time. That way he wouldn't have to endure the agony that these repeated explorations brought with them. Joey's ability to move his leg had decreased while his pain had amplified. Not only could he not move his leg, but he could not tolerate the agony that touching it brought about. If this was an infection, I had never witnessed any infection like this during my life- leaving me to wonder, who was this intruder that had violated my son's body maurauding freely trying to deprive him of his youth? Dr. Sherry completed his examination. He looked at me and nodded his head in the direction of the hall. Taking his cue I followed him into the hallway.

Carefully choosing his words, he began to speak, "I'm certain that we can all agree that there is something present causing Joey's pain." I held my breath as he explained that the only way to find the cause of Joey's pain was to do a biopsy of the area of his discomfort. But, before he removed a piece of tissue it would be necessary to pinpoint the exact location that needed to be tested. He informed us that he and Dr. G. had already ordered several tests. He was also aware that Dr. G. had already informed us of the various tests that were to be performed. He told us that each test served a specific purpose and that the combined results of these tests would afford Joey the best treatment possible. Reluctantly, he said, "he has no choice."

"How long before all the tests are completed?"

"No longer than two days. I promise we will move quickly." Tony, standing at my side, asked, "What about his pain?" "His pain will be dealt with later today."

"If this is an infection, then why can't we give him some type of antibiotic? Can't we go that route first?" I asked.

"That's not the way it works. Allow us to give Joey the proper medical treatment he deserves. That's all we ask."

"Fine, but to the best of your ability answer this question." Searching for the correct words, I hesitated before continuing to speak. "I'm certain that in the past you have treated patients with the exact symptoms Joey is presently experiencing." Not believing that I was on my way to properly structuring the rest of my question, and feeling somewhat frustrated with my lack of medical terminology, I resorted to my street personality. "In other words, give it your best shot and tell me what in all hell do you think he has?" Although I knew it was futile, I tried to manipulate him into giving me an answer. It didn't work. He wouldn't speculate. They had their game down pat better than my good guy, bad guy, police routine, I thought. Next, I played a courtroom diversion.

"Could it be an infection playing havoc with his system?" "Yes."

"Thank you," I said before shaking his hand. "See you tomorrow."

Dr. G.'s team was moving quickly. Within minutes after saying good-bye to Dr. Sherry, Joey's tests began.

The codeine wasn't affording Joey any relief. His pain now elevated to a degree where Dr. G. finally decided to give him morphine. Thank God, perhaps the morphine will offer him some comfort, I thought. Each dose of morphine should have relieved his pain for several hours. One half hour after Joey's first morphine injection, he was again tormented with pain. No longer able to tolerate its constant onslaught he began to cry and scream. Looking at my little boy lying in this place, helpless, in pain, and being injected with morphine, tears started to run down my face. "God," I asked, "where are you?"

Chapter 14

MT. SINAI IS a huge private hospital consisting of numerous medical departments. Each department is connected by color codes- painted striped colors that run along the floor and walls. Where one color stops, another begins. To find a specific department all one needs to know is the designated color, then walk aimlessly around hoping that somewhere in your travels you might get lucky and spot the color of the department you're looking for. To me, the complexity of this system seemed incomprehensible. I wondered how anyone would be able to locate anything in this huge place, in this city within a city, with its basements and sub-basements. Seeing what looked like the world's oldest man passing me in a corridor, I thought, he probably came here as a boy for his measles shot, and has been walking these halls ever since trying to find his way out. There was little doubt in my mind that this place could give the cloisters a run for its money.

Joey was assisted onto a gurney and transported to the X-ray department. Lifting him onto the transport table took quite an effort by the hospital staff. I danced around trying to assist them in moving him. It soon became apparent that I was making matters worse by getting in the way of people who were skilled in this sort of procedure. Unwillingly, I took a step back allowing them to accomplish what they had been trained to do.

Although Joey was under the influence of morphine, he continued to cry at the slightest jarring of his gurney. The trip to the X-ray department, located in the subbasement, only took a few minutes. An X-ray technician was awaiting his arrival. He immediately wheeled him through a door located near the entrance. A few minutes later I heard a blood-curdling scream stemming from the opposite end of the X-ray department. I looked at Mary and said, "My God, I wonder what they're doing to that poor person to make him scream like that?" Then I recognized his voice. It was Joey's. His gurney had been wheeled, out of view, along an inside corridor to the far end of the room.

"Mary, that's Joey crying," I said. I wanted to run to his side but Mary talked me out of it.

"Let them do what they have to do. It won't be long. Please don't interfere."

I acquiesced to Mary's wishes but continued to pace up and down the corridor. Ten minutes later Joey emerged in a cold sweat. He looked battered and beaten from being moved about in the X-ray room. The X-ray technician did not move him as gingerly as he could have. To him, Joey was just another patient on a long list of patients that he would see today.

With the morphine wearing off, I called Falk 2 and asked for Dr. G. She immediatley came to the phone. I explained Joey's condition and she promised to remedy the situation. Soon, Laurie was at his side with more morphine. A needle was inserted into his arm and a few minutes later the morphine took effect. With Joey's pain starting to ease, I asked Laurie how long the morphine would remain in his system before he required another dose.

"Actually, the prior injection should have lasted him a lot longer than it did. The dose he's receiving should have lasted three hours."

"It's not lasting a half an hour. What else can we do?"

"In his weakened condition, it would be difficult to tolerate any more morphine than he is presently receiving." Her comment upset me. It opened the door for a world of assumptions on my part.

The morphine allowed Joey to sleep until he was taken back to his room. No sooner had he returned to his bed when I was informed that he would have to undergo a bone scan identical to the one he had received only a few days ago. I sat on the edge of his bed, shaking my head, not knowing when and if all this would end. I picked up his hand and held it. I wanted to touch him, to feel his hand in mine. I needed that. It wasn't a lot, but it was enough.

An hour went by before he opened his eyes. "Dad, the smell of the hospital food is making me sick," he said, as he began to vomit. There wasn't anything I could do to remedy the problem. I told him that in a few minutes he would be going for a bone scan.

"Close your eyes and try to get a little more sleep." I pleaded.

I was hoping that he might want to eat once his bone scan was completed. I asked Mary to keep an eye on him while I left the hospital in search of some food that he might find palatable. I found a local grocery store and purchased some ice cream and fresh fruit. When I returned to the hospital, I placed the food in a refrigerator and crossed my fingers hoping that he would eat later that night.

Hours later Joey underwent the second bone scan of his young life. It was a long day. We were all extremely tired. I told Mary and Tony to go home and I would stay a little while longer. Mary agreed to leave because she wanted to be back early the next morning. I thanked them for all they had done and promised to meet them in the morning.

My intention was to remain with Joey until he received his next morphine injection. I wanted to make certain that he was sleeping before I left. Ten minutes passed before a nurse gave him his injection. Alone with my son, I shut the light in his room, sat in a chair, and watched over him as he slept. During my drive home, I wondered if the girls would be awake waiting to hear news concerning Joey and the events of the day. I made up my mind not to stress his failing health. As I walked in the house, they both registered their worry about their brother. I told them that nothing concrete had been determined, that tomorrow his medical agenda called for him to undergo an MRI and a CT scan. I suggested that we all try to get some sleep and kissed them goodnight.

I climbed the stairs and entered Joey's room. His bed was wedged in the corner of his room where he liked; it remained undone exactly as we had left it that morning. My eyes caught his display of baseball pennants, pictures of race cars, and other treasures that only a thirteen-year-old boy could cherish. I wondered why I had never really noticed them before.

A picture of Joey riding Black, the family's Tennessee Walking Horse, was lined up first in a series of photos standing at different angles on his pine dresser. A few inches to the right, I noticed a photograph that I had taken of him with his sisters at a local track meet. Emptiness filled my heart as I reminisced about the time I remained standing, screaming, cheering him on as he neared the finish line. Joey never really liked track, he said that it made him sick, that the nausea competitive running brought about wasn't worth it. How ironic, I thought, that what he hated most might soon become a daily part of his life.

Almost directly behind this picture was a framed photo that someone had taken of him at a Long Island field trial. A friend had asked Joey if he would like to run a puppy that he and his wife wanted to see get a little exercise. The grin across Joey's face, proudly touching both ears, said it all as he pushed his blue ribbon into the camera lens making sure that it caught every inch of it.

I thought about his first day of school and the difficulty he had climbing the steps of the huge school bus while carrying his little lunch pail. I remembered how he waved goodbye as the big yellow bus pulled away and I thought about that ten-year-old boy who ran to the window every time a car went by to see if his mommy was coming back. My son's room was exactly as it was this morning. Except for one thing, he wasn't in it. Instead, he was in another room, a strange room, where in place of pennants and pictures of race cars on the walls, there were oxygen connectors and other lifesaving instruments; none of which should be in a child's life. Yes, he was in another room, in some unfamiliar bed, lying in pain, far away from here, and me. I had to ask myself what kind of bad dream was I having? And when would it end? Sometime later I went to bed and I prayed.

I arrived at the hospital at 6:30 a.m. and elected not to wait for the Falk elevator. Hoping no one would be in my way to slow me down, I ascended the stairs two at a time. Entering Falk 2, rushing into Joey's room, I found him just as I left him the night before. I walked over and gave him a kiss.

It wasn't long before Mary and Tony arrived. Mary's smile lightened up the room. Joey returned her smile. I was amazed that he was still able to smile. Both Mary and Tony leaned over and gave him a kiss. "Italians," I said, "they never stop kissing." Joey smiled at my remark. A nurse entered and informed us that Joey managed to sleep through most of the night. We were glad to hear that his night had not gone too badly.

His next scheduled test was an MRI. Once again he was transported to the Annenberg Pavilion, on the Fifth Avenue side of the hospital, and once again he howled as he was moved. The morphine was not working. He would have to wait until after his test before he could receive another injection. The MRI machine, shaped similar to a torpedo tube, required that Joey remain perfectly still for the duration of the test. The purpose of the MRI was to project a detailed image of the inner workings of every part of his body. The significance of all these tests was to determine the nature of Joey's illness and the location of his problem. If he did have cancer, these tests were designed to determine the type of cancer, its stage of development, and how much it may have spread.

Add these ingredients together and you stand a good chance of receiving an accurate diagnosis. I was informed that the MRI test would last for one hour and forty-five minutes. Turning to Tony and Mary I said, "Who could remain perfectly still for that long?" I couldn't do it.

A receptionist informed us that another patient was using the MRI machine, and that we would have to wait forty-five minutes until it became available for Joey's use. "Why didn't you inform the nurse's station on Joey's floor about the wait? If you had, he could have remained in his room until the machine became available." She shrugged her shoulders as though to say, "Fine, you glad you said that, now wait anyway."

Some people are simply too ignorant to be sympathetic. If I wanted to be treated like in this manner, I could go over to the Motor Vehicle Department or some other government agency, I thought.

Forty-five minutes later Joey was assisted into the MRI machine.

Not moving a hair, lying there, listening to the roar of the machine, he remained perfectly still for his scheduled hour and forty-five minute test. As the technician assisted him out of the MRI, he began to rub his eyes, and then he shook his hands attempting to regain some circulation to his extremities. Finally looking up at me he said, "Daddy, I hate that machine."

"That's makes two of us and I wasn't in it."

He looked so sorrowful. His once tireless healthy frame now desecrated to a point where he was unable to hold himself up. As though he hadn't been through enough he now had to be beaten up by a machine that was designed to help him. Joey was taken back to his room and given a little more morphine. I was growing restless for an answer.

With all these machines probing the sanctity of his body, I wondered how long it would be until I received some conclusive information. Dr. Sherry arrived and asked to speak with me in the hall. I followed him to a quiet area of the corridor.

"I would like to perform a biopsy of Joey's pelvis tomorrow morning." Without allowing me to answer his question he continued, "I would also like to do a bone marrow aspiration. While I'm in there, I might as well do both."

"Doctor, I understand the biopsy of the pelvis but this is the first time that I'm hearing anything about a bone marrow aspiration. Would you mind explaining the purpose and what you hope to achieve, or disclose, by doing this?"

He informed me that it was not uncommon to perform both these procedures at the same time and that by doing a bone marrow aspiration he would be able to determine if there was anything that should concern us, that might be out of the ordinary. I didn't have to ask any more questions. Not that I didn't want to, but I knew where all this was leading. If I asked him are you looking for cancer? He would say, "yes". If I asked him are you looking for an infection? He would again say, "yes." I concluded that I was better off saving my breath.

I was wise enough to know that no one around here was about to make a speculative guess concerning Joey's illness. They were waiting until they had the backup of medical information at their disposal. No sense traveling down this road again. A dog accomplishes more chasing his tail, I thought. He was about to walk away when I said, "Doctor, I do have two questions for you." He gave me his full attention. "Who reads the biopsy? And is Joey physically strong enough to handle the anesthesia?" "Question number two first. Joey is plenty strong for the anesthesia and once his surgery is completed you can keep him company in the recovery room. Now for your first question. Mt. Sinai has the best pathologists in the United States, and to be certain there aren't any mistakes we require a second pathology test that will be done at an equally reputable hospital. Does that answer your question?"

"Yes, it does."

"Would you like me to discuss the surgery with Joey?"

"No thank you. I made him a promise that I would personally keep him informed concerning everything that was taking, or about to take place. I have to do this."

"If you need any help explaining anything, just ask. Otherwise I will see you in the morning."

I nodded my head and said, Good-bye."

Leaning against Joey's door, I prepared myself for our upcoming conversation. I entered his room and sat at the foot of his bed being extremely careful not to touch his leg. We had one more test scheduled: a CT scan with contrast. I wondered if I should wait for the conclusion of that test before informing him about his pending surgery. As I looked at Joey, he appeared alert. I decided to have my discussion with him.

Trying not to make the issue too complicated, I attempted to explain Dr. Sherry's intentions as simply as possible. I told Joey that I just bumped into Dr. Sherry in the hall and he said that he would like to take a closer look at what was causing his pain, and the only way for him to do that was by taking a little piece of tissue from the spot where his pain was coming from. "So, if it's okay with you, tomorrow morning, he will put you to sleep and do what he feels is necessary to make you better."

"Will it hurt?"

"No, you will be sleeping and when you wake up it will all be over. You won't feel a thing. I promise. You know that I wouldn't lie to you."

"What are they going to do with the piece of tissue after they take it out of me?" "They will put it under a microscope and take a closer look at it. This will help them decide which medicines to give you to make you feel better." "How will they put me to sleep?"

"Oh that's where I come in, for being such a pain all these years, I'm going to be the one to put you to sleep. You see, I get to use a big mallet and the longer I want you to sleep the harder I whack you on your head."

He started to laugh when a nurse and transport aid entered his room to tell us that he was expected in the CAT scan department. Without undue delay, he was wheeled into the Falk 2 elevator. The CAT scan department was located in the B-2 part of the building, known as the subbasement area. I was starting to become a little familiar with the location and layout of a small part of Mt. Sinai. I could, if necessary, find this department simply by memorizing the color schemes on the wall and floor.

Joey's CAT scan was scheduled to be taken with contrast, which meant that he would have to drink several glasses of a liquid that would illuminate a three dimensional picture of any problem areas in Joey's brain, head, and neck. Moving Joey from one table to another was becoming more difficult. Even though he had recently received an injection of morphine his pain wasn't subsiding. He cried at the thought of someone touching his leg. The CAT scan lasted forty-five minutes. Mary and my brother went home deciding to return early in the morning before Joeys scheduled biopsy. Given the late hour, and the fact that I was beyond exhaustion, I thought it wise to spend the night in the hospital. In Joey's room there was a fold out sofa that opened into a single bed. It matched the rest of his room. It too needed replacement. As I opened the sofa, I could see the metal support bars bulging through the thin mattress. I found a blanket, covered myself, and tried to sleep. Actually, I had little difficulty falling asleep. My problem was staying asleep.

During the night, I could hear young children crying out for their mommies. Funny, I thought, not once did I hear a child call for his daddy. I wondered why even incoherent old men lie on their deathbeds crying out for their mommies? Thinking the answer much too complicated I dismissed the thought. I could also hear the hospital staff talking, joking, and discussing the medical needs of various patients. With the phones constantly ringing, I knew that I had made a mistake by remaining here.

The next morning, nearly crippled, I made an attempt to climb out of my torture rack. I was certain that if I looked at the mattress label it would read, "Marquis de Sade Mattress Company." Hobbling about, I tried to regain a little circulation. For a brief second I thought of removing Joey's morphine line and sticking it in my arm. As I attempted to straighten up, I decided to never spend another night in this oppressive stretcher. To call it a bed would insult a bed of nails. I would have been better off driving home to catch a few hours of sleep in my own bed rather than sleeping here.

It was early in the morning when the hospital began to come alive with the sound of medical and breakfast carts being wheeled about. The phones were now ringing continuously. Parents and relatives started to trickle in for their day long vigil with their children. Hearing parents warmly greeting their children, I wondered what each child was afflicted with. What was the story behind every youngster on this floor and how were these parents able to cope with their children's misery as well as their own? Up until now I had not taken a walk around the floor. I did not want to know too much about these children and their families. Why should I subject myself to this type of pain and suffering? No good could come from knowing what was going on around me. There were no happy tales in this place. This wasn't a resort. This was a place where children entered whole and left missing a leg, arm, or worse. This was a dying place. I decided to keep my blinders on, to walk quickly to Joey's room and everywhere else in this hospital that I was going. It was bad enough that I didn't know what human tragedy was waiting to greet me each time the transport elevator door opened. Rather than view these poor pathetic souls I read the elevator capacity information posted above the floor number selection. I made up my mind to keep my head straight, talk out loud, hum, or do anything that I had to do in order to drain out the trepidation and pain around me.

While Joey was still sleeping, I decided to run down to the cafeteria to get a quick cup of coffee. When I returned to his room he was just beginning to rustle. I noticed that there wasn't any food brought to his room this morning, which confirmed the fact that he would soon be brought upstairs for his biopsy and bone marrow test. I kept repeating the word *marrow* and *cancer* thinking that I never heard anyone mention the word marrow without the word cancer either preceding it or following it. As far as I was concerned, they both frequented the same neighborhood. But, this infection thing could be plausible too. I was growing anxious knowing that in a short time we would have a diagnosis.

Soon, there would be no doubt remaining in our minds. Finally we would be able to head in the right direction leading to a cure. Surely I believed that in this world of modern science the appropriate medicine would be able to make fast work of whatever was draining Joey of his health.

Mary and Tony arrived just as a transport aid was entering Joey's room. I was informed that I could accompany him upstairs to the operating room where Dr. Sherry was already awaiting his arrival. I was also told that I would be allowed to be with Joey in the recovery room.

With the help of a nurse, Joey undressed and put on a surgical gown. As I looked a his naked body, I couldn't believe his frailty. His appearance resembled a starving child similar to one we view on a television fundraiser. He couldn't even be referred to as a walking skeleton because he was unable to walk. Or, for that matter, stand. How long had it been since he last had some food? Was it four days? Five? I didn't even know- I had lost count. I only knew it was a long time and the sight I was looking at was a shadow of the child I knew. Taking a picture of Joey from my wallet, I stared at it and then at him. This cannot be the same boy. Where did the healthy, happy boy in the picture go?

Gently holding his hand I walked alongside his transport table as it was wheeled up to surgery. I tried to reassure him by telling him that in a few minutes his surgery would be over and that he would wake up and ask, "Dad, when are they going to start?" At which time I would say, "It's all over." As we entered the surgical area of the hospital, I gave him a kiss. "Hang tough it will all be over in a few minutes and remember I'll be waiting for you in the recovery room. I promise I will be there when you wake up." As they wheeled him away I said, "I love you." Now all I had to do was wait. It felt like all I did was wait.

Across from the surgical area I entered a lounge. I sat there knowing that it wouldn't be long before I had the answers to all my questions. I prayed Joey would catch a break. I wanted my son back home where he belonged. He didn't belong in this place. No child did.

Sitting in the lounge, I longed for someone to talk to. I questioned if the parents of the sick children on Joey's floor knew how difficult it was to go through this alone. They were caught up in their children's problems, but at least they had a shoulder to lean on. They could console one another during the day and comfort each other at night when the pain of being alone was magnified. Did they know how hard this was on me? Then again, who could understand anything about anyone else's pain unless you have previously experienced it yourself? I realized that last week there was a person experiencing my present anguish, and up until a few days ago, I didn't know that this individual still existed. Yes, there was a world full of problems that I couldn't identify with. At that moment a nurse ended my pity party by informing me that Joey was being taken into the recovery room.

I pulled up a chair and sat next to him. It was apparent that he was still under the influence of the anesthesia. Reaching for his hand, I held it and caressed it gently while he slept. His skin was cold, not responding to my touch. I could feel each bone projecting, his blood pulsating; I was aware of his every breath. Holding his hand in my heart, I sat there quietly hoping that he could feel my presence and my prayers.

For the first time in days he looked at peace. At least I knew he wasn't experiencing any pain. Oh, how I wished he would open his eyes, smile at me and say, "Daddy let's go home, I'm okay now." He began to stir, drawing me back to reality. I could hear him starting to moan, mumbling incoherently. Trying to detect what he was saying, I placed my ear closer to his face. His voice became clearer. He was crying for his mommy. I could help him with whatever he asked of me but I had no control over this matter. There was nothing I could do. The girls had informed their mother of what was transpiring, but she did not reach out to him. I wished she had. He needed her.

I tried to comfort him by saying, "Daddy is here, you are going to be alright." I hoped that hearing my voice might break his thought pattern bringing him back to reality. I wanted him to know that someone was here who loved him. As the anesthesia started to wear off, he began tugging at his oxygen mask attempting to remove it from his face. I kept repeating, "You're okay." He opened his eyes; seeing my face he squeezed my hand, and fell back to sleep. He now knew that he wasn't alone. I remained at his side as he dozed in and out of reality.

Sometime later a doctor came in to examine him. He determined that Joey could return to his room. Joey looked up at me and said, "Daddy, I'm sick, I have to throw up."

I found a basin and held it close to his face allowing him to vomit. The anesthesia was hitting him harder than I had expected. Stopping several times in route to his room he continued to vomit. He was retching but nothing was coming up except bile. There simply wasn't any food in his system to bring up. This fact did not stop his body's natural reflexes.

"Daddy, I'll never let them give me anesthesia again. I didn't know that it would make me so sick. Did you know that it would make me this sick?"

"Joey, I didn't. It affects everybody in a different way. The anesthesia will wear off in a little while and you'll feel a lot better. The best thing that you can do is to try and go back to sleep."

Mary was nervously waiting for Joey in his room. While I was bringing her up to date, Joey fell back to sleep. We both remained sitting in his room not saying a word. An hour later Dr. G. entered.

"When will you be informed of the results of Joey's biopsy and bone marrow test?" I asked.

"I will have the pathologist view the biopsy as soon as possible but to be perfectly honest with you I don't think it will be done until tomorrow." With nothing else to say, I thanked her before she continued on her rounds.

That night I returned home to catch a little sleep. As I walked in the door, I noticed a pile of mail that I had not been able to attend to for the last few days. I thought that I should at least try to pay some bills before the electric company shuts off the power. Included with my bills was my monthly child support payment. I opened it and immediately noticed that Joey's child support payment was cut in half, an illegal deduction had been made by his mother because of his recent visit with her. So, instead of ninety-five dollars for the month he received forty-five. Too tired to do anything I cursed Christi Whitman, went to bed, and wondered what tomorrow would bring.

Joey was awake when I arrived at the hospital. With the anesthesia lingering in his system, he continued to vomit. As his breakfast was brought into his room, he complained that he couldn't tolerate the smell of his hospital food. I wasn't sure if it was the food that upset him or the aromatic odor of the steamed plastic trays. Regardless of the exact cause he directed that the tray, along with its contents, be taken out of his room.

The bone marrow test came back rather quickly. Dr. G. informed us that it was negative. There weren't any cancer cells in Joey's bone marrow. Both Mary and I hugged each other rejoicing at the news. Mary exclaimed, "You see, he doesn't have cancer. I told you that he had an infection."

For the first time in weeks, I was able to take a deep breath. I felt as though the weight of the world was taken off my shoulders. I wanted to call the girls to inform them of the good news and to apologize for not spending any time with them but decided to wait for the results of Joey's biopsy.

Chapter 15

IT WAS LATE morning when Dr. G. returned with the results of Joey's biopsy. She asked that we step into the lounge then locked the door behind her. She said, "I have the results of Joey's biopsy as well as the rest of his tests." I sat there attempting in some way to connect with her. I tried to read her expression, her moves, to do what I did best, to know what she already knew. However, she had the face of a seasoned poker player that left me no choice but to wait with nervous anticipation of what she was about to say.

Laden with fear and doubt, I could hear the sound of my breathing as she continued to speak, the results of Joey's biopsy were positive. My heart stopped. No, go back and say that again, I thought. They were supposed to be negative, not positive. Something is wrong here. He has an infection. I leaned over placing my face in my hands. I felt sick knowing that my prayers had gone unanswered. I no longer had hope. Without Joey, my life was no longer worth living. He made each day worthwhile. One word, cancer, was trying to take everything I loved away from me. I sat there unaware of what was going on around me. Suddenly everything had a haze about it. I was floating in a time capsule unable to open the hatch and climb out. I knew I was in a room with other people because I could hear their voices, but I had no idea what they were saying, or who was speaking. I couldn't concentrate. I couldn't even think. All these emotions were so new to me. I didn't understand any of them. I didn't know where to look, or how to stand up. Could I stand up? I wanted to rush these feelings away. I said to myself, "Okay that's enough.

Take control of yourself everybody is waiting." However, I was left with no choice except to sit stunned by what I had just heard. It took me a long time to digest it. Finally able to look up, I mechanically performed allowing everyone to think that I was part of the group.

Speaking calmly, Dr. G. continued her conversation. She said that Joey had Ewing's sarcoma. She explained that Ewing's sarcoma was cancer of the bone. Unlike osteosarcoma that was found in the extremities, such as the arms and legs, Ewing's sarcoma attacked the larger bones of the torso. In Joey's case, it was the pelvis. It afflicted children in their teenage years. The problem with Joey's sarcoma was that it was inoperable; there wasn't any way to remove a person's pelvis because the pelvis was needed to hold up the body. The only way Joey's cancer could be treated was with chemotherapy and radiation. I started to interrupt her.

"Please allow me to say this before I answer your questions. I want to make something very clear. No one knows where Ewing's sarcoma comes from so before you start blaming yourself for Joey's illness keep that in mind. I hope that all of you understand what I just said. Now I will answer your questions."

I didn't know what question to ask first. I had not prepared myself for this eventuality. I had so many questions but only a few came to my mind. I knew later, when I had enough time to sort things out, I would wonder why I had failed to ask so many pertinent questions that needed to be addressed.

"How are you going to treat Joey? Is he going to have to undergo much chemotherapy?" Mary asked.

She explained that Joey's protocol would not be an easy one and would be based on the best known treatment for his cancer. It seemed that each type of cancer was treated differently. A protocol that worked best for one cancer might not work for another. Her intention was to give Joey some of the most powerful chemotherapy drugs on the market. Not one drug, but several. Joey's treatments could last three years. At some point along the way, Dr. G. would halt his chemotherapy to begin radiation therapy. Joey would receive radiation treatments five days a week for a minimum of eight weeks. Upon completing radiation treatments he would again resume chemotherapy.

"Will he live?" I couldn't believe that I was asking this question.

For some reason unknown to me the words came flowing out of my mouth.

"To be honest with you, I don't know."

The only good news was that there wasn't an indication that Joey's cancer had spread to any other part of his body. Ewing's sarcoma had a history of moving into the lungs and bone marrow. Joey's tests indicate that this had not taken place. Dr. G. made it clear that he would have to be monitored very carefully, which meant that he was going have to undergo frequent MRI's, CAT scans, bone scans and a million other tests. "We would be living in the hospital," she said.

Tony interjected, "I know you said that you couldn't operate but I have to ask you again, is there any way anyone else could operate to remove his cancer?"

"I wish we could, but we can't." She explained that if it were osteosarcoma she could remove Joey's leg, or arm, fit him with a prosthesis and hope that it would never return. Sometimes she removed as much of the solid tumor as possible. At other times, treatment called for radiation therapy in conjunction with chemotherapy to shrink the size of the tumor making it small enough to be removed by surgery. "I know that you want to hear that we can surgically remove Joey's cancer but, because of the location of his cancer and the type of cancer he is afflicted with, we cannot surgically remove it and neither can anyone else."

"Kind of like a sick tree. You could remove a limb or a branch but not the trunk." I thought.

"How does chemotherapy work?" I asked.

I listened attentively as she explained that chemotherapy kills fast growing cells, that it kills just about everything that crossed its path. Cancer is composed of fast growing cells, and so it attacks cancer cells. "Oh, by the way, Joey will never be able to tolerate the numerous injections that he's going to receive. His veins will collapse," she informed us that Joey was going to be subjected to blood tests, nuclear medicine, dyes, pain killers, sedatives, and several types of chemotherapy- all that and more would have to be injected into his body. Pausing to make certain that she had our attention, Dr. G. said that Joey would need to undergo an operation to have a Broviac, a permanent IV line, implanted in his chest. A Broviac was a tube that surgically connected to a vein leading to Joey's heart. All injections would be given through his Broviac line including hydration which Dr. G. was going to order immediately. "He needs to be hydrated. We have waited long enough.

I will explain more about Joey's Broviac at a later time." "Anesthesia, again!" I said.

"Yes, the operation will last about an hour and a half. Believe me, there isn't any other choice. He needs a Broviac. A nurse will instruct the two of you on how to take care of it. It is imperative that it be kept clean. If Joey runs a fever he must be admitted to the hospital."

Briefly making eye contact with me she backed up her point. Dr. G. would not take a chance on Joey's Broviac becoming infected. After entering the hospital, a culture would be taken to determine the cause of his fever. The bottom line was that Joey would run constant fevers for any one of a million reasons. Add these admissions with his chemotherapy, radiation treatments, tests, and other reasons for coming here, I was getting the picture. Falk 2 would become our new home.

"Anything else we should know?" Mary asked. "Yes, a lot."

"Excuse me Doctor, but would you mind if we end this meeting until I'm able to think a little more clearly. All I want to know is when are we going to start Joey's chemotherapy?"

"We are prepared to start right away. Now I have to ask you a question." "What is it?"

"Do you want me to tell Joey or would you prefer to do it?"

Shaking my head in disbelief that this conversation was even taking place I said, "I'll do it."

Joey was my son and, although I trusted Dr. G.'s bedside manner, I knew him better than anyone else. I wanted to present this sad news without frightening him, in a way he would understand. Sitting alone

I wondered, how does one make sense of cancer? There is nothing about it that makes sense. Its simplicity is easy to understand. It starts with one rogue cell that feeds tirelessly and grows without objection until it no longer is a minority and even though destroying its host will terminate its existence, resulting in suicide, uncaring, it trudges forward. The dying is uncomplicated. The only complex part is the cure and trying to survive its wrath.

I asked myself how does a parent go about doing this? Is there any good way to tell a child that he or she has cancer? Is one way better than another? I knew how to tell him that he wasn't allowed to go outside to play unless he first did his homework. I knew how to tell him that he couldn't stay up too late on a school night. I even knew how to confine him to his room for misbehaving. But this, how do I begin to approach this? Where do I begin? Do I say, hey Joey, guess what? You have one of the worst cancers known to mankind. But don't worry because even though the odds are against you, if you can somehow find the strength in your anguished body to fight, you might make it. Of course only if you can tolerate vomiting until your insides are so raw that nothing comes out of you but bile and blood. And did I mention the part about being stuck with needles until your veins have collapsed? Also, you are going to have to tolerate a few other incidentals like radiation burns, urinating blood, and frequent diarrhea. Your heart, kidneys, bladder and teeth, along with the rest of your insides will be transformed into that of an old man. Oops, son, I'm sorry, I almost left out the fun part where you lose all your hair, and have to avoid sunlight. Darn! I just noticed that I'm running a little late for dinner, but before I go I wanted to mention that you are going to have to learn how to inject heparin into a tube that will protrude eighteen inches out of your chest. This bizarre apparatus connects to a vein in your heart that runs along the inside of your chest and neck. Yes, of course it's going to bulge under your skin. Did you foolishly think that it wouldn't? Not a *big* bulge, just enough for everyone to see. By the way Joey, don't forget to keep it clean, bandaged, and capped. After all, you wouldn't want it to clot with blood, or have your blood flowing out of it during the night. Well, there are a lot of other interesting little tidbits I could tell you but that is enough for one day. Wow! Now I'm really late for dinner. Joey, try to look at it this way, you've had thirteen good years haven't you? Didn't you think that you were due for something like this in your life? Sleep tight little pal. I'll see you tomorrow.

I knocked on Joey's door and entered his room. It was obvious that he had been crying. His pain, unwavering, was in complete control. The morphine wasn't doing its job. He looked distant. My composure regained, I said, "Hi creep. How are you?"

"Not so good."

"Well that's about to change. Pay attention to me because I'm going to bring you up to date on what's happening around here, and if you want to ask me any questions just fire away. Also, Dr. G. said that she would stop by in a few minutes to answer any medical questions that you might have."

Taking a deep breath, I looked into his hazel green eyes and began to speak, "Joey, do you remember some time back when I told you that I would be honest with you and always tell you the truth?"

"Yes, I do."

"That hasn't changed. That's exactly what I am going to do, but if you remember me saying that then you must also remember how we both made a promise not to quit on each other. You promised you would never stop trying and I promised I would always be there for you. Well, Joey, I am going to hold you to your promise and I am going to keep mine. Do you know what a tumor is?" Joey nodded his head signifying that he did.

"Well, just in case you don't fully understand it, in simple terms it's a growth inside a person's body. Now, some tumors are benign while others are cancerous. The cancerous ones give us the most trouble because they keep wanting to get bigger." Stopping for a moment, I asked him if he understood what I was saying, or if he wanted to ask a question. Once again he acknowledged that he understood. "Joey, as fate would have it you have a tumor and it's cancerous. This means it wants to keep getting bigger. Now, listen to daddy and listen carefully. The doctors in this hospital have medicine that will stop it from getting bigger and make it go away. They call this medicine chemotherapy. Dr. G. will come in here in a few minutes and explain how this medicine works. You see, Joey, there are some things in this world that I know a lot about. There are some things in this world that I know little about and there are some things in this world," Joey joined in, "that you know nothing about, and this is one of those things that you know nothing

Right Dad?" "Right."

I had used this phrase ever since he was a little boy and whenever I would start reciting it, he would shake his head and say, "Oh, no, here we go again." I was about to leave his room to ask Dr. G. to step inside when Joey asked, "Daddy, am I going to lose my hair like a lot of the children that I see around here?"

"Yes, you are, but at least yours will grow back. There are a lot of people out there who wished they had such a problem." The door opened, Dr. G. entered Joey's room and sat on his bed.

"Joey," she began, "in spite of anything you have heard about cancer you are not going to die. Our goal is to make you better." In simple terms, she went on to clarify some of Joey's questions.

"Why do I have to lose my hair?"

"Chemotherapy attacks the fastest growing cells in the body. Cancer is made up of fast growing cells. Do you know what other cells in your body are fast growing?"

"Hair cells?" "Good guess."

With Joey looking extremely tired, and experiencing a lot of pain, Dr. G. thought it wise to cut her conversation short. She asked to speak with me in the hall. Mary and Tony joined in the conversation.

"I don't know how to tell you this."

"What now?" I interjected, "How much bad news is going to flow our way in one day?" She told me that while I was in Joey's room she had received a phone call from my HMO informing her that they would not authorize Joey's treatment at Mt. Sinai and were refusing to pay for any medical expenses. They informed Dr. G. that Joey would have to be transferred to an affiliated hospital in Nassau County, Long Island.

"This must be some sort of joke. Who made this decision and why?"

Her face solemn, showing her concern, she said, "Your HMO said that they do not have an affiliation with Mt. Sinai."

"They sent me here!"

"I'm sorry, if it would make you feel any better I would waive my fee as would most of the doctors and staff assigned to the hem/onc team. You would never receive a bill for my services. But even if I were to eliminate my fee you would never be able to afford all the other related hospital treatment that is going to be required."

"Thank you for the gesture." My mind now racing, I asked, "If Joey were to be transferred to another hospital what would that entail?"

"Look, North Shore Hospital ia an excellent hospital. Some of our staff members also have privileges there as well. The only problem," her speech now slowing with concern, "all of Joey's tests will have to be repeated, including his biopsy."

"Why?"

She explained that because of medical liability issues most hospitals do not like to accept lab tests, especially a biopsy from another hospital. My HMO was not, in simple terms, practicing good medicine. It was not safe and did not have the welfare of the patient at heart. Dr G. was ready to begin Joey's first chemo treatment. "I will, however, put it off until tomorrow. I want to give you the opportunity to try to straighten out this problem with your health care provider."

Right about now I reached my tolerance level. All my frustrations and everything that had negatively affected my life over the last few weeks came to a climax. In the middle of the corridor I started yelling, "Tomorrow Joey is going to receive his chemotherapy right here at Mt. Sinai Hospital."

I wasn't about to let some bureaucratic, inhumane, pencil pusher cost my son his life. I had seen it happen all too often: one person's bad decision cost another person his life and then oblivious, the bad decision maker continued on his way undaunted, and unaffected. Some heartless fool, sitting at a desk miles away who didn't care that each test my child took sapped a little more life out of him, wasn't about to put the nails in my son's coffin. Joey couldn't fight for himself because there wasn't anything left for him to fight with. He couldn't possibly survive going through all this again. It would kill him and I could never find the words to tell him that he was going to have to be moved to another hospital, not after all he had been through. Tony tried to calm me but couldn't. As long as I had a breath left in me, this was not going to happen to my child.

Looking for a phone I found one outside the lounge. I dialed my local HMO center and after getting the usual run-around I was connected with someone from the subscriber relations department. Not allowing the individual a chance to speak, I bombarded her with one issue after another. When she was finally able to get a word in she informed me that these decisions were made at the corporate office in Manhattan. Good, at least the office is close by, I thought. At that moment I felt someone grab my arm. It was Tony. He said, "Please listen to me, you have to calm yourself. If you want to help Joey you have to remain calm."

Acknowledging him I proceeded to dial my HMO corporate office. I spoke to several subordinates before I was able to locate the individual responsible for making the decision to move Joey. After briefing him on Joey's medical condition I said that I wanted him to pay very close attention to what I was about to say. I informed him that it was not my idea to send my son to Mt. Sinai. I simply asked for the best pediatric department in New York City and I was informed that Mt. Sinai fit the bill. I was also informed that you, meaning my HMO, had an affiliation with Mt. Sinai and that's the reason Joey was taken here.

"Well you were given some bad information. Your son should have been sent to a hospital that we have a current affiliation with," he unemotionally responded.

"I don't give a fiddler's fuck about the should have's, I'm telling you that in my son's present condition he may not make it if you transfer him." Speaking a little slower, I told him if he did not allow Joey to remain in exactly where he is that I was going to sue all the physicians and everyone who misdiagnosed Joey's problems as growing pains, especially those who failed to take X-rays of his pelvis and leg. I would even include the janitor in my suit, and I would make it a point to sue him personally. His house, his car, his dog, and everything that he owned in this world would become mine. I would also subpoena each doctor that was treating Joey and have them testify that this decision was not in Joey's best interest, but detrimental to his life. Last of all, I said that sometime tomorrow I would stop by his office to pay him a visit. I asked him if during the course of his life he had heard people physically threaten other people and then cover up their threat by saying, 'I'm not threatening you but making you a promise.' "Well," I said, "I'm not making you a promise, I'm threatening you and by this time tomorrow if Joey is not allowed to remain here you will need hospitalization. The only question you will have to ask yourself is, which hospital will they take me to? An authorized one? Or an unauthorized one?" I then heard a click indicating that he had hung up the phone.

Tony approached me, "I'm glad that you took my advice and calmed yourself before making your phone call. Nice language too. And when you started yelling that you were going to sue all the doctors that treated Joey, you had every doctor in this place heading for the fire escapes. That was an exceptionally good move on your part."

"So, I have my flaws."

With Joey under the influence of a strong dose of morphine, I left the hospital. As I approached my car I could see that I had another parking ticket pasted to my windshield. The lightning bolts were flying and I was getting hit.

Life is fascinating, I thought. In addition to all their family and medical related problems, these poor people had to be subjected to an army of various law enforcement agencies swarming around their cars like sea gulls at a landfill. It wasn't fair. They didn't have a chance. With numerous "no parking" signs each displaying a different message, Einstein wouldn't be able to sort this mess out. Certainly these visitors, handicapped with worry, did not deserve this additional penalty.

Taking the side streets I decided to drive home through Harlem rather than taking the F.D.R. Drive. Sometimes when you feel you do not have enough, you need to experience less.

With my last impression of Joey still vivid in my mind and my anger starting to build, I asked God why he let me down? How he could have done this to me? I knew that Joey could not have done anything so vile in his thirteen years to deserve bone cancer so it must have been something I had done to make God angry. With my resentment building, I said, "If Joey had been okay, you would have expected me to thank you because people always give you credit for miracles. But now that Joey has cancer, I guess you have the benefit of executing your non-interference option. Well, God, that's not the way it works in my book. If you are willing to accept the plaudits when something good happens, then just like the rest of us, you have to accept the liability when it turns to crap.

Meandering in and out of Harlem's side streets, I stopped at a traffic light. While I was lost deep in my thoughts, a homeless man carrying a squeegee approached my car snapping me from my trance. Somehow I managed to place my indignation on the back burner for the time being. As he walked over to wash my car windows he said, "Good evening, officer." I laughed before returning his acknowledgment. Even though I had been off the force for a few years the smell and look of cop still lingered in my fabric. Street-smart people always knew who I was just as I always knew who they were and what they were up to.

With my ingrained police senses now alert and my adrenaline

flowing, I felt exhilarated and alive. Diagonally across the street, on the far corner, I spotted a prostitute trying to sell her goods to a man in a white Cadillac; only she wasn't a she, but a he. I hoped that the poor guy didn't have any intentions of bringing her home to meet momma.

Actually, she didn't look too bad in all her drag. Driving away my memory kicked in bringing me back to a place and time when I dressed like that.

Chapter 16

I WAS A young police officer assigned to the tactical patrol force decoy detail. Along with my partners, we had just finished our assignment posing as members of the Hasidim (commonly referred to as Rabbi duty) in the Williamsburg section of Brooklyn.

The job didn't require much ingenuity. All you had to do was grow a beard, wear a black coat and black hat, then walk around with your hands behind your back and wait for somebody to mug you. A real no brainer except for one thing, in the process of getting robbed you stood a chance of being stabbed or shot. We enjoyed this type of work and were very successful at our job. I hated to see the Rabbi detail end because I thought that I had looked particularly striking in my black fedora hat.

Next, we were assigned to the Bowery area of Manhattan. Several vagrants were being doused with lighter fluid and set ablaze. Somebody was having fun killing people in one of the most painful deaths imaginable. Our job: walk the Bowery, pretend to fall asleep on a park bench, and wake up at the slightest odor of lighter fluid. Wake up too late and the possibility existed that you might be turned into a human wick. It took us a few weeks before we managed to apprehend these sick individuals. With this situation remedied, I was assigned to drive a taxicab. Taxicab homicides were hitting an all time high in the city and the department needed several fast arrests in order to quell the bad press it was receiving. All these details met with little objection on our behalf. It was part of the job. Until!

One day while I was walking into a Brooklyn station house I was greeted by one of my partners.

"Guess what?" Bob said.

"I hate guessing games because I always guess wrong. Why don't you be a good guy and tell me what you have on your mind? And judging from the look on your face I don't think that I am going to be too fond of what you have to say."

"One of us has to be a female. A lot of women have been getting mugged around the lower end of Eastern Parkway and the department wants several teams out there, well you know the routine."

"Bill and Pat know."

"Yeah, and they say that you'd look great in white gingham."

"Okay, I can see where this is going. Let me be very clear on this one, we are all going to take a turn at this."

"But, Pat has a mustache!"

"Well, if any muggers ask him about his mustache he can tell them that he is up here from Brazil visiting his uncle Juan, but he and you are taking your turn."

Of course, when it was time to see who would be first to make the conversion, I lost the toss.

The next day I arrived as mentally prepared as one could be for my new assignment. I walked into the back room of the station house to join the other teams for our post briefings. It looked like a Christine Jorgenson convention. Talk about social deviance, I had never seen so many ugly looking whatever one might elect to call them in one place. Stopped in my tracks, I thought, they deserve to be mugged. This was an insult against nature itself. Changing into my female attire, I added to the group by making it one more ugly decoy. I turned to my partners and asked, "Do I look as bad as they do?" I waited for an answer but none came forth. "Well, that's not very encouraging," I said.

An hour later I was strutting my wares down Eastern Parkway making every effort to avoid looking into any storefront windows for fear of seeing my own reflection. I thanked God that at least it was nighttime. I was beginning to understand how a vampire felt.

I was walking along Eastern Parkway when through the corner of my eye I noticed a car driven by a single male occupant approaching. I never prayed so hard to be mugged, anything to get off the street.

The driver, now a few feet behind, managed to keep pace with my every step. Soon he was paralleling my stride. With his passenger window rolled down, he began to yell sexual propositions at me. I turned my head to get a good look at my new found boyfriend who just happened to be a member of the Hassidic community. Just what I needed, one of the Smith brothers with an out of control erection, I thought. I laughed, thinking that last week I was dressed like him and I didn't drive around trying to pick up ugly women. This guy was a disgrace to my fedora.

Hoping that he would get tired of the pursuit, I continued on my way. To my surprise, he persisted in following me. I guess I was too attractive for any man to resist. It wasn't long before I encountered another problem. I discovered that a six-foot man does not belong in leotards designed for a five foot, three inch person. This assignment came up so quickly that I had to borrow clothing from anywhere I could, and so, I was forced into my present embarrassing situation. Every few steps required that I reach down and yank this Rube Goldberg apparatus up in an effort to return them to waist high length. If I didn't, I ran the risk of tripping and breaking my neck. I kept asking myself over and over again, "Will this night never end?"

The second mistake I made was dressing too sexy. With my blond wig, heavy makeup, and dangling earrings, I looked like Betty Davis in, "Whatever Happened To Baby Jane." I was starting to realize that in spite of my size there were a lot of men out there who liked big women and they didn't care how ugly they looked. But then again, I did have dimples, and a pocketbook that glittered with sequins. I guess that was enough to make any man salivate.

Looking across the street I could see my partners enjoying themselves at my expense. Finally, reaching my waterloo and tired of my friend's advances I walked over to my pursuer's open window. Bending so that he could get a clear view of my face, I said in my normal voice, "Does your wife know what you're doing out here tonight? And further more, I'll have you know, I'm not that kind of girl, or guy. Well, whatever I am, I'm not that type." As the blood drained from his face, his eyes opened wide. He now realized that he was in way over his head. At this point, I decided to place the final stake in his heart. Showing him my shield I told him that I was going to drag him and his deflated manhood into the station house and notify his wife and family members to come down to bail him out. With the whole situation now way beyond his comprehension (and mine too) I thought he was going to have a heart attack. "Look," I said, "would you rather climb into my dress or go home?" As he peeled away from the sidewalk, I mumbled to myself, "The nerve of that guy, did he think that I was going to give away the store without being wined and dined. My mother raised me better than that."

With my would-be-suitor gone, Bob and Patty approached me. I knew I was in for a hard time.

"Hey, Bob," Patty said. "Personally I thought that the two of you would have made a nice looking couple. I'm not saying that it would have been easy going but you could ·have worked out your problems. You know, one year you spend Christmas at your house and the next year Chanukah at his place. Everything in this world is negotiable. Another thing that I want to mention, from where I was standing, it looked like you were having pantyhose problems."

"First of all, smart-ass, they're not pantyhose they're leotards. If you weren't so ignorant you would know the difference. A real man would never wear pantyhose."

"Well, whatever you call those things that you have on, I think that if you purchased a more expensive pair you wouldn't be experiencing all the problems that you're obviously having. Would you like me to go home tonight and ask my wife what brand she buys? Or better still, how about if I tell her to pick you up a couple of pairs in assorted colors?"

"I'll tell you what you can do, you can stop being a pain in the ass, go back across the street where you belong, and protect my rear end regardless of what it's wrapped in. Or guess where my pocket book is going to end up, sequins and all?"

"Touchy, aren't you? Come on Bob, let's go. I think that he's getting his period." Three days later Patty once again had some fun at my expense. We were working the Bushwick section of Brooklyn and decided to take some time off to catch a movie. While I was sitting with Bob, looking as beautiful as ever, Patty called 911 telling them that there was a prostitute working our movie theater. Of course he gave my description and before I knew what was going on I was approached by several precinct police officers and foricbly pulled from my seat and out of the theater. With Patty standing across the street laughing, watching me trying to explain who I was, and what I was doing, I knew that there had to be a better way of making a living.

The next sound I heard was the toll collector at the Triboro Bridge asking me for my bridge fare. It felt good to escape the reality of today for the memories of yesterday, if only for a little while. Arriving home I took a shower. Scrubbing harder than I usually do, I tried to wash away the smell of the hospital.

Chapter 17

MY PLANS FOR tomorrow were to check in on Joey. Then I would ask Tony and Mary to keep an eye on him while I delivered my threat, first hand, to the HMO administrator. I owed Joey that much. I guess I would have accomplished more had I told the administrator I was an upset postal employee. However, after today he would never forget me or be able to pass a death sentence on some other child.

Mary refused to leave Joey's side. She was taking care of him as though he were hers. I had decided that if anything should ever happen to me that she be assigned legal custody of Joey. It had been more than three years since his mother departed. Other than a weekly phone conversation about current events and the weather, the children's visits were limited to a yearly overnight encounter at their grandmother's house. A trip that required they travel five hours upstate.

I never experienced what life was like growing up without a mother to fulfill my every need. I wasn't living my children's life so it was difficult for me to empathize with their inner feelings. I wondered if they knew just how much they were missing. It must have been difficult for them to visit friends, seeing them nurtured and loved by their mothers. A single parent household is not the epitome of what life should be.

I hadn't spoken to their mother in several years. With the blessing of time, I relegated her existence to a rear compartment in my memory bank. I now had to make a decision whether to inform her of Joey's illness or to bypass the whole conversation. Concerning this decision, the 20th century me was in a fierce battle with the old genetic Sicilian that was always lurking about ready to add fuel to an already combustible situation.

The real question was, did she have a right to know anything that was transpiring within this family? Mary somehow convinced me to make the phone call.

A familiar voice, from out of my past, from a different life, answered the phone. I began my conversation by saying, "I have some bad news to tell you." Not affording her the opportunity to respond I continued. "If you recall, when Joey last visited he was complaining about pains in his leg and back." Choking with the reality of what I was about to say, I hesitated not wanting to compromise my dignity. I waited until I was again in control of my emotions before continuing. "Well, he has been diagnosed with bone cancer." Several seconds went by without a response. I began to grow curious as to what was taking place on the other end of the phone. I was about to speak when I heard in a flat, monotone voice, "That poor boy." I held the phone at arms length looking into the receiver. Unable to believe what I had just heard, I repeated her words, "That poor boy." I wondered could she have misunderstood what I had just said? Yes, that had to be it; she thought that I said Joey had a hangnail. After all, cancer and hangnail sound alike. I hung up the phone promising myself that I would never again argue with my grandfather's genes.

A few weeks before Joey showed any sign of his illness, I bumped into an old friend, a corporate lawyer who owned the stable where I had boarded the children's horse. I remembered how upset and distraught this man's wife was when the children's mother first abandoned them. The mother of three-year-old twin girls, and a ten-year-old daughter, she had ranted on unable to understand how a mother could even entertain the thought of leaving her children.

I asked him, "How is your wife and children?" "About two weeks after I last saw you she left us." "What do you mean she left you?"

"An artist asked me if he could paint a picture of our old barn. I told him why not. Two weeks later my wife took off with him for Florida leaving me with the children to raise."

I didn't know what to say. I was speechless. I wished I could have given him a few words of comfort or, at the very least, some encouragement but I could not. I wanted to say, "don't quit." Whatever happens, keep going forward because without you, your children will never be able to survive in this world. If you get tired, you'll get a second wind, I always have. But all I could say was good-bye, I wish you well. I would never forget that moment. From that day on, both he and his children would always be in my thoughts and my prayers. I had also learned that there were many forms of cancer. A parent abandoning a child was one of them.

I was growing tired of seeing and hearing about parents leaving their children; parents who painted a self-portrait of benevolent innocence as to why they left their children to be raised by their spouse. Many naive people might buy these fictitious lies, but not me. Parents who live far away from their children could save their window dressing for somebody else. There wasn't a good enough excuse, not in any language, for leaving a child to face life alone. I realized that selfishness was becoming synonymous with happiness and few observers were able to recognize the difference. My test was rather simple. You live here. Your children live there. Bingo... You failed.

With thoughts of Joey and the HMO quandary resonating in my head, I was unable to sleep. I also felt somewhat embarrassed at subjecting everyone to my rather unpleasant display of temper. I wondered if I could convince them that I was suffering from some form of Tourette's syndrome. Not wanting to linger about the house, I decided to drive to the hospital to be with Joey.

Joey was continuing to slide downhill. It was difficult looking at him without displaying my true feelings. He asked me to carry him to the bathroom. I was aware that he disliked using the bedpan. I picked him up, his weight now so light, it felt as though he floated into my arms. I was afraid to carry him, that I might accidentally injure him. As I began to move, he cried but insisted that I take him to the bathroom anyway. When he was finished, I carried him back to his bed. He looked as though he just went twelve rounds with the heavy weight champion of the world. Exhausted, and in pain, I gently placed him back in his bed. I wanted to shout, "How in the world is it going to be possible to move you to another hospital?" Having a feeling that I might have stepped on God's big toe it was time for me to have another talk with Him. We were doing a lot of conversing lately. I think that He knew I said a lot of things out of anger and frustration and that sometimes I could be a demanding son of a bitch.

"Dear God, I didn't mean anything I said last night please help him, he doesn't deserve this." Seconds later, Joey's door opened, it was Dr. G.

"Guess what?" Without waiting for me to answer she said, "an administrator from your HMO called and for some unknown reason they changed their mind. Joey is going to be allowed to receive his treatment here.

I said, "Wow, God, this is unbelievable service. You sure know how to move fast when you want to. Thanks, I owe you one. So, when do we start?"

"Right now."

I looked at Joey and said, "Hey, Joey."

"What, Dad?"

"The Marines have landed."

Chapter 18

IT WAS LATE morning when Laurie walked in to prep Joey for his first chemotherapy. Joey, overhearing my conversation with Dr. G. said, "I want to know everything that they are going to do to me before they do it." Looking at Laurie he asked, "Could you tell me what you call each medication?" Laurie assured him that she would.

This request by Joey didn't surprise me in the least. Even as a little boy, whenever we visited the doctor's office he always wanted to know what was going on. Most children turned their heads while receiving a needle, but Joey always wanted to watch. Over the last few days, while undergoing numerous tests, and in great pain, he still managed to ask each technician how the various machines worked. He wanted to see what everyone was looking at on the screens and monitors. This was Joey's way of assuming some control of what was about to take place. It was his body, and he would not relinquish his right to ask questions for as long as he was being forced to come here.

It was time for Joey to receive his first chemotherapy treatment. The first step was to inject Benadryl into his IV. Benadryl is an anti-emetic- its purpose is to help prevent vomiting, to relax the patient, and to prevent any allergic reactions from other medications. Within seconds after receiving his Benadryl Joey began to shake uncontrollably. Then he started to slap his face and head. With his fists clenched, he began to pound on his chest. I had no idea what was going on. It was all taking place too quickly. I couldn't believe the spectacle before me. I was certain that he was about to injure his already debilitated body. I made an attempt to hold his hands, to restrain him, but he forcibly pulled them away. Observing him barbarously clawing away at his face, I wondered where he found the strength to behave like this. Again I grabbed his hands only this time I pinned them to the mattress. Not letting go, I yelled for someone to get a doctor. The resident physician came running in. He made a quick determination that Joey was experiencing an adverse reaction to the Benadryl. It was being administered too quickly. The IV drip was immediately slowed and as quickly as his violent behavior began, it subsided. I looked at Mary and asked, "Enough excitement for one day?" "I think so."

Next, Joey was injected with Ativan to relax him in preparation for his chemotherapy. It wasn't long before he fell asleep.

Carol entered his room, carrying several vials of chemotherapy. She draped them from a metal ring connected to Joey's IV monitor and inserted a needle into his IV line.

Joey struggled to crack open his eyes, "What is that?" he asked. "It's your chemotherapy."

"Make sure you set it at a slow drip," he said before falling back to sleep. I looked at Mary and smiled.

I could see the chemotherapy casually starting to drip into his IV.

"Good," I said, "attack his cancer, rip it apart, dissolve it, and make it flee my son's body, every last son of a bitching morsel of it. I don't care where it goes just get it out of him."

I wanted to hold him in my arms but didn't. Instead, I allowed him to sleep and I prayed that God make him well. "Please God, give him back to me. I want my sweet healthy boy back. I want to see him smile and laugh again just like he used to. He has already cried too may tears and has endured enough pain. His life is just beginning. There is so much in this world for him to see and do. Everything is still so new to him and to be perfectly honest with you, I need him a lot more than he needs me. Please, I beg you, give me my son back."

I looked at Mary sitting next to Joey's bed. In her hand, she was holding something that was unnoticeable to most people. I could see her lips quivering ever so slightly. She was saying the rosary. With this team, I thought, we can't lose. Pray hard, Mary. Pray harder than you ever prayed before. Call in all the favors for all the wonderful things that you have done in your life. Right here, now, today, cash them in. This was the beginning of a war that was about to take place in Joey's body. I prayed that today was the day that my son started his slow walk home. That God made up his mind to return him to me.

While Joey slept I asked Dr. G., "Does the chemotherapy have an element that allows it to selectively kill cancer cells?"

She said that the chemotherapy Joey was receiving was anti-anything living. (I later learned that if these drugs were to accidentally drip on a patient they would burn a hole in their skin. They were called vesicants and that accidental leakage could vary in severity from mild to serious tissue damage requiring surgery).

"Before you leave today, I will supply you with some written information that will help you understand Ewing's sarcoma, cancer and related treatments," she said. Having learned about the intensity of Joey's medication, I thought, why not simply open his mouth and pour a gallon of liquid Drano down his throat. It would probably accomplish the same thing.

Mary and I remained at Joey's bedside until the early morning hours before deciding to leave. Mary elected to stay at a nearby hotel with Tony. I wanted to make the trip home to check in with Tammy. Our plan was to meet back at the hospital early the next morning. Before leaving the hospital, one of the oncology nurses handed me the literature that Dr. G. had promised me.

I arrived home but my main spring was wound too tight to allow me to sleep. I decided to thumb through the material I was given. I noticed that there were several books written by children with cancer for children with cancer. I read them like I was defusing a time bomb. I was afraid of what I might learn, of what was on each page, in each paragraph, the next sentence, the next word.

I made up my mind to quickly pass over any stories written by children who had not survived cancer, and concentrated on the stories written by those who did. I then moved on to the page making reference to Ewing's sarcoma. It said the following:

Ewing's sarcoma is a round cell tumor of the bone. It is the second most common bone tumor of children and young adults. Ewing's sarcoma accounts for 1% of all childhood cancers. It is slightly more common in boys than in girls. The disease is uncommon in black children. This bone cancer differs from Osteosarcoma in that it usually affects the weight bearing bones of the legs and the pelvis, the bone shaft, and ribs. It usually occurs between the ages of 10 and 25 and frequently spreads to other bones and the lungs. The cause is unknown. It is not inherited or contagious.

What You Can See or Feel

A young person with Ewing's sarcoma usually has pain and swelling with or without soft tissue mass. 25% of patients also have weight loss. An X-ray film of the involved bone usually shows a patchy moth-eaten pattern with defined edges. Other symptoms include fever, chills, and weakness.

Diagnosis

Definite diagnosis is made by a biopsy (surgical removal of a tiny piece of tumor tissue). The biopsy is looked at under a microscope to know the exact diagnosis. Once the tumor is spread. Other tests include: Chest X-rays; CT and or MRI of tumor area. Bone scan, bone marrow test, and liver scans.

Treatment Plan

The treatment plan usually includes: surgery, radiation therapy, chemotherapy, tests and physical exams. Progress in the treatment of Ewing's sarcoma has improved following the introduction of systemic chemotherapy. Surgery alone, or the use of radiation therapy to control the tumor, quite often results in a high incidence of spread to other parts of the body.

What Will Happen in the Future?

The prognosis for long-term survival has greatly improved since systemic chemotherapy has been added to the control of the local disease offered by surgery or radiation. The challenge remains in treating the disease that has spread.

Next I looked up Joey's chemotherapy medications:

- **Cytosine** - The main toxic effect, in bone marrow suppression, anemia, nausea, vomiting, diarrhea and abdominal pain, oral ulceration & hepatic dysfunction. Cytosine is most effective in treating tumors with a high growth rate fraction. Cytosine could cause pulmonary toxicity, coma, cerebella dysfunction including personality changes, gastro ulceration, liver abysses, pulmonary edema, liver damage, skin rash, sudden respiratory distress, anorexia, fever, bleeding (all sites), dizziness, jaundice, chest pain and shortness of breath.

- **Vincristine sulfate injection** - Prior to the use of this drug, patients and/or parents should be advised of the possibility of untoward symptoms, hypersensitivity, constipation, abdominal cramps, weight loss, nausea, vomiting, oral ulceration, diarrhea, intestinal necrosis, anorexia, impairment of fertility, hypertension, motor difficulties, paralysis, bone pain, convulsions and blindness.

- **Cytoxan (cyclophosphamide)-** Second malignancies have developed in some patients treated with cyclophosphamide. Most frequently they have been urinary bladder myeloproliferative, or lymphoproliferative malignancies. In some cases, the malignancies have developed several years after cyclophosphamide has been discontinued. In women, it can cause fetal harm. It can also interfere with oogensis and spermatogenesis. It may cause sterility in both cases and may be irreversible. Boys treated with cyclophosphamide may develop oligospermia or azoospermia associated with increased gonadotropin but normal testosterone secretion. Hemorrhagic cystitis may develop in some patients. Fibrosis of the urinary bladder, sometimes extensive, may also develop. Bladder injury is thought to be due to cycloposphamide metabolite excreted in the urine. In a few instances with high dosage cycloposphamide, severe and sometimes fatal, congestive heart failure occurred within a few days after the first dose. Cyclophosphamide has been reported to potentiate dororubic-induced cardiotoxicity. Infections- Treatment with cyclophosphamide may cause significant suppression of the immune responses. Serious, sometimes fatal, infections may develop in severely immunosuppressed patients. Cycloposphamide may interfere with normal wound healing. Hair loss will occur along with a change in the pigmentation and nails.

Closing the book, I sat in awe of what I had just read. Many people were unfortunate enough to receive one of these drugs in tablet form to treat their cancer. Others received one of them intramuscular, an injection into a muscle, usually in the arm, leg, or buttocks. Joey was receiving all intravenously through an IV, which meant that a needle was injected into a vein or a Broviac catheter allowing the chemotherapy to flow into his bloodstream. It didn't get more potent than that.

I learned that the basic idea behind chemotherapy was simple; it was a cancer fighting medication. To understand cancer requires no more knowledge than the ability to understand the difference between the ways normal cells function and the way cancer cells function. Normal healthy cells divide and grow in a controlled type of behavior.

Cancer cells keep dividing uncontrollably, without order. Chemotherapy is supposed to interfere with the way cancer cells grow and multiply. Each type of cancer is treated with a different type of chemotherapy that has previously proven to work best in fighting that specific type of cancer. The sad part is that chemotherapy affects normal cells as well as cancerous ones. What scared me most was discovering that chemotherapy could cause cancer. Which made me wonder how can cancer be conquered with a medication that causes cancer? To me, it sounded like a no win situation. Sometimes in later years, people come down with a different type of cancer, such as leukemia, because the healthy cells became mutated by the earlier chemotherapy.

Chemotherapy can be so terribly dreadful, in so many ways, that people have been known to quit, to stop fighting for life itself. The constant sickness that chemotherapy causes is so draining on the body and the human spirit that death sometimes becomes an alternative. Yes, sometimes even the strongest throw in the towel. Joey's cancer was an exceptionally rare and difficult cancer. I wondered if he would quit. Would the numerous courses of chemotherapy he required beat him into submission? And even if he could tolerate the dreadful effects of chemotherapy, would he be able to conquer his cancer, or would he be subjected to chemotherapy only to succumb to the inevitable? With Joey in his bed, fighting the inhumanity of this dastardly disease, and all these thoughts rambling through my mind, I allowed myself to place my male vanity aside. I cried until I had no tears left to cry. I remained awake staring at the ceiling I would have given anything to be able to fall asleep but I had forgotten how. The demons of the day were chasing me at night.

Chapter 19

IT WAS EARLY in the morning when I left the house. The sun behind me, rising in the eastern sky, hurt my half closed eyes. I was growing used to the sun at my back. It was there in the morning as my car placed each mile of road leading to Mt. Sinai in its computerized memory, and it was there in the evening when we retraced our morning route. Some mornings I welcomed the soft cover of clouds that allowed me to unhinge my eyes proving to me that my baby greens were still there. Glancing from the road to the rear view mirror, I was amazed at the sea of red corpuscles that I saw starring back at me. "I thought they were supposed to be white," I said.

Most nights I would leave the hospital, travel to work, and try to catch up on the business at hand. Accomplishing very little, my forehead would greet my desk with a thud. I would remain that way for a few hours; then startled, my eyes would open. Hoping that I didn't over sleep, I would rush back to Mt. Sinai and Joey.

This morning, not knowing what was awaiting me, I found the drive in exceptionally difficult. With great apprehension, I climbed the stairs to Falk 2. As I walked quickly through the corridors and down the hall, I passed several children all afflicted with cancer. Some looked perfectly healthy. If it weren't for their skin pigmentation being sallow, and the fact that they hadn't any hair, it would be difficult to detect that they had cancer. But the thought that cancer took up residence inside of them, eating away, feeding first and tirelessly on these children was inescapable. Others, missing arms and legs, hobbled by resembling war causalities. They were, in fact, war causalities. Each child was fighting a war with cancer- the nemesis of all that was good. I was beginning to understand where cancer had come from. The devil created it to perform his ungodly deeds. Who else would dare create something so putrid and evil?

I met Mary in the elevator and we both expressed our concern as to how we would find Joey after his first chemotherapy treatment. We entered his room and I walked over to give him a kiss. Sliding his head across his pillow, he waved me off as he reached for a basin. Unable to lift his head he placed it along side his face as close to his mouth as possible, and vomited. His basin was filled with bile and blood.

"Oh no, Joey, what are you doing? What's going on here?" I asked. At that moment Dr. G. walked into the room.

"Doctor; why is he vomiting so much? And why all this blood?"

"Joey has been vomiting so violently that he may have bruised some tissue. It will stop."

"When?"

"Within forty-eight hours or so. By the way, Joey, did you show your father what you can do?"

"Doctor, I think that I have already seen what he can do and I really do not want to see anymore of it."

"No, that's not it," Dr. G., said. She pulled down Joey's sheets exposing his pencil thin legs. And then it happened- Joey lifted his bad leg straight up in the air, then side to side.

"Oh, God!" I cried, "What happened? What took place while I was gone? Joey, your pain?"

"I have no pain."

"Son, say that again for daddy. Did you say that you have no pain?"

"I have no pain."

"Yes! Yes! Yes!" I screamed. Life was suddenly worth living again. From somewhere in the deepest depths of despair, the light of hope was now a glimmer. Dr. G. started to talk. As she began, I thought, please don't steal this moment from me, I need it. I need it! I don't want this feeling to end. Don't rain on my parade. If you want to bring me back to reality, can't you wait a few seconds longer? Let me feed on this morsel of hope. Let me bask in my optimism.

Turning to Mary, I could see a big smile across her face. My thoughts flashed back to her clutching her rosary beads. Whatever took place here last night was a sign that God was listening to our prayers, that he was touching me in some way. I didn't know how or why, but I felt his warmth. Maybe he was beginning to understand how much I loved my son. Dr. G. broke the silence and asked that we step out into the hallway to talk.

"Look," she said, "this is a very good news but,"

"But, what?" I interjected. Thinking why does a "but" always have to accompany good news?

"We have a long way to go. This is Ewing's sarcoma and it doesn't give up easily." What Dr. G. believed happened was that the chemotherapy forced the tumor to shrink enough to take a little pressure off some very sensitive tissues. She reminded us that Joey's tumor was large and embedded into his bone. Trying to soften the blow of what she just told us she said, "Now please try to understand that I am very happy with what I have seen here today. I have never seen this type of reaction before. It's good."

Dr. G. was right. Just when you thought cancer was on the retreat, it gave you the slip, parried, and stealthily reappeared somewhere else in your body, or it became immune to chemotherapy. I also knew the ambivalence that I was presently feeling was part of the protocol, the roller coaster ride. When someone you love has cancer, it could be sunny skies one minute and an F5 tornado the next.

Joey just completed his first course of chemotherapy. He had seventeen more to go and judging from what was going on in his room, and his physical deterioration, I had no idea where all this was leading. I just knew that I loved him.

Looking at Mary, I asked, "Was there ever a choice in any of this?"
"No, unfortunately not."

"You know, Mary, this might sound strange but Joey is going through with this program whether he wants to or not. I'm not giving him an alternative." I opened the door to Joey's room. He was still vomiting. Blood was dripping from his nose. "Well, that will teach you not to go out drinking with the boys on a school night."

"Please, you have to get me out of this place. I can't stay here. I hate it here. If you don't get me out of this place I'm going to die. I want to go home. Daddy, take me home.

I hate the smell of this place."

"Joey, I hear you. I just spoke to Dr. G in the hall. She told me that you can go home, but first you have to drink and eat a little something. You don't have to eat a lot, a little will do, and then I can get you out of here."

"Daddy, if you take me home I promise you that I will eat."

"I hear you. Now let me crank up your bed a little so that I can try feeding you some food. You know you don't have to eat this hospital food, anything you want I will go out and get for you, all you have to do is let me know what you would like." With that remark, I cranked up his bed to a forty-five degree angle.

"Please, daddy, lower the bed. It's making me dizzy. I can't stay like this." "Try it, Joey. Try to stay like this a little longer. You'll get used to it."

"No, I can't. Lower it. It's making me sick."

Listening to him cry was too painful for me. I lowered his bed. "Okay, as you wish, but I'm going to be back in a little while to raise it again so you might as well make up your mind to stop fighting me."

I knew that I had a significant problem on my hands. Dr. G. wouldn't allow Joey to go home unless he first drank and ate, and Joey wasn't about to concede to either request. I had to do what I do best. Negotiate a deal.

As far as I was concerned I had already negotiated with Joey. He promised that he would eat if I took him home. I decided to speak with Dr. G, "If you allow me to take Joey home he promises and I promise that he will eat. Doctor, if he remains here we are going to lose him. His spirit is already broken." She thought for a moment.

"I'll let you take him home on one condition, if Joey doesn't eat or drink within the next twenty-four hours you have to promise me that you will bring him back."

"Sounds like a deal to me."

I walked back into Joey's room to give him the good news. For the first time in days, a smile came across his face.

Mary remained with Joey while I pulled my car around to the Fifth Avenue side of the hospital. Being very careful not to injure him, I carried him from his wheelchair and gently helped him stretch out across the rear seat. I placed a pillow under his head, a blanket over him, and his basin next to his face.

Joey vomited, without pause, as we inched our way home in rush hour traffic. If I could have ridden on the hood of the car I would have. I would have done anything to drown out the ululation and horrible retching sounds emanating from the back seat.

The trip took us well over two hours. It felt good to pull into our driveway. I reached in the back seat of the car and lifted Joey out. As I carried him up the stairs, he meld into my arms as though we were one. "How does it feel to be home?"

"Good."

"Yeah, that was one hell of a vacation you picked. Do you think maybe next time we could try Aruba instead?"

Tammy, upon seeing her brother, started to cry. "Dad, I had no idea."

How could she possibly have any idea? How could anyone? Savaged by his cancer and medication I had difficulty believing that this was Joey myself. At this point he was unable to lift his head without assistance.

I carried Joey into his room and gently placed him on his bed. He looked up at me and asked, "Dad, do me a favor and pull all the shades in my room. I don't want any sunlight coming in, and then would you leave me alone. I want to be left alone, and leave the basin before you go."

Before leaving I placed the basin as close to his face as possible. I could hear him dry heaving as I walked down the stairs.

Tammy was sitting in the kitchen. Her eyes were still red from crying. I sat down next to her and said, "We are all in this battle together. It's the battle of our lives and somehow, I'm not sure how, we are going to get through this. We were a family before all this started and we will be a family when it's over." She looked at me as though to say, "Oh, Dad, I want to believe you, please make it come true."

With nothing to do and feeling completely helpless, I thought I would prepare several of Joey's favorite foods just in case he decided that he wanted something to eat. There was my promise to Dr. G in the back of my mind. I knew that if he refused to eat and drink I would be forced to bring him back to the hospital. Being home was an experiment. He was here on borrowed time. Dr. G. granted me a favor that she really did not want to concede to and from the sounds of what was going on in Joey's room, I knew that it would be hopeless to try to force the food issue at this moment. I decided to wait until later that evening before pursuing anything related to food or drink.

As evening rolled around I decided to bring Joey a little Jell-0. Knowing that his stomach was empty, I thought it unwise to overburden his digestive system. Entering his room, I found him just as I had left him several hours before. He was resting on his bed wearing the same jeans that I brought him home in.

"Joey, I made you some Jell-0, how about if you eat a spoonful or two?" He shook his head no. "Joey, please, you have to eat one mouthful or tomorrow morning I'm going to have to take you back to the hospital. You're home because we promised Dr. G. that you would eat and drink. So, try to help me help you."

"No, Dad, leave me alone!"

Now I was really scared. He was unable to sit up, barely able to move his head, and if he didn't start to eat he would be forced to re-enter the hospital. If that occurred, I knew, I was certain, he wouldn't make it. I could not allow him to succumb to his cancer, to quit. I had to break the cycle. He had to start fighting back. And then something came over me. My fear, now uncontrollable, took possession of me. I started to scream, "You are going to eat you little son of a bitch. You promised me that you wouldn't quit."

I was at a point where my emotions and worry were dominating my ability to think clearly. Without knowing what I was doing, I grabbed his head and banged it into the headboard. I began shouting, "We had a deal, I wouldn't quit on you and you promised not to quit on me." I was crying like I never cried in my life. I continued to scream, "You can't quit. Do you hear me? You can't quit. Not now, not ever. I never asked you for anything in your life but I'm asking you for this. If you don't care about yourself then care about me." I kept repeating these words until I became aware of what I was doing. Trembling, my sanity finally returned. I looked at his helpless sweet face and I began to cry, "Oh, Joey, I'm sorry." I rubbed his face and caressed his head. Sickened at what I had just done, I staggered into the hallway and sat on the top step outside his room. Doubled over with my face on my knees, I continued to cry, unable to stop. Then I heard a meek gentle voice say, "Daddy, please don't cry I'll eat for you, but please don't cry." With the help of the banister, I picked myself up and walked back into his room. I sat on Joey's bed and put my arms around him. I held him, not wanting to let go, not ever. I could have crushed him with love. I had to live with what I had just done and hated myself for having done it. I held him in my arms and wiped my tears aside. A few minutes later he ate a few spoonfuls of Jell-0. I knew that he wasn't going to survive on a minuscule amount of Jell-0 but it was a beginning, wasn't it? That night I had another conversation with God. I thanked him for holding my hand but now I needed a little more, I needed him to squeeze it. For the first time in days, I fell asleep.

The next morning Tammy awakened me by knocking on my door. "What do you want?" I mumbled still half asleep.

"It's not what I want. It's what Joey wants. He's complaining that he's hungry and wants to know if you will get up and make him something to eat?"

Sitting on the edge of Joey's bed, I didn't remember even leaving mine. "So tell me what are you in the mood for? Bacon and eggs, pancakes, baked Alaska, baked Kentucky? Anything at all." He laughed.

"I think that I want some French toast. Do you have any?"

"Joey, I have enough food down stairs to open a diner in Astoria."

"But, Dad, please don't let the bread stay in the eggs too long?" "They'll hardly get a chance to know each other."

Tammy remained with Joey while he ate his breakfast. He only consumed one slice of French toast but I felt like I had just won the lottery- no pain and eating.

"Okay God, thanks for the squeeze."

Later that afternoon, Joey asked if I could wash him and carry him downstairs. He wanted to watch television on the sofa. While he was watching television the phone rang. It was Claudine. After asking how her brother was feeling she began to inundate me with a series of personal problems. "Whoa, slow down, let's take one problem at a time."

"First, Dad, I am going to drop a class. If I withdraw from it now I won't be subjected to a penalty."

"What class is it that you want to drop? And why"? While thinking to myself, this should be good.

"I want to drop archeology."

"I didn't know that you were taking archeology."

"Well, it's an elective and you can't believe what they want me to do. They want me to participate in a dig."

"Where?"

"Right here! On campus! In the Bronx!"

"What are they looking for?"

"You got me, Pop. But I'm not jumping in some dirty hole looking for who knows what. The most I will do, I told them, is sit on the edge of this pit and dangle my feet."

"I must say, Claudine, you do have a point. I personally think that any cadavers that they find in the Bronx will be wearing Nikes and holding AK47's."

"Precisely."

"What class are you going to take in its place?" "German. It's the only class that has an opening."

"Good, take German. I'm sure the Reich could use you. You could be their best secret weapon since the V2 rocket. Fine, now that we have resolved that issue is there anything else that you want to talk about?"

"Actually, I have good news. I just got a part time job at the Met."

"Hey, that's great. It certainly fits in with your major," They thought Van Gogh was troubled; wait until they get a load of her, I thought.

"I'm also attending a party in Manhattan with some very important people from the Met, including a lot of benefactors. It's actually a charity function. The theme of the party is to save the Penguins and many of the people attending will be dressed as Penguins. What do you think?"

"I think that Penguins create their own problems by constantly pushing each other off of the same rock. Now if you don't mind I have enough problems around here without worrying about penguins."

When Claudine was finished bringing me up to date on what she thought was important in her life, I told her I would pick her up Friday evening so that she could spend some time with her brother and sister. I also thought it was imperative that I spend a little time with her alone. I discovered two things in raising children. First, it was essential that you spend time as a family, and second, it was also paramount to spend time alone with each child so that you could interact on a one to one basis. Plus, each one was always willing to give up all sorts of information about the other two. The secret to successful parenting is knowing. Knowing what? Knowing what they don't think you know.

Chapter 20

JOEY WAS STARTING to show some improvement. He was now eating; still his physique remained withered and limp. His strength had deteriorated. He was atrophic to a point where he was unable to walk. I had to figure out a way to restore his muscle tone. While Joey was resting on the couch one afternoon I approached him.

"Would you like to try to walk?"

"I don't think that I can do it on my own, Dad."

"I don't expect you to do it on your own. Here's what I have in mind. How about if we go outside on the deck? I'm going to place a chair ten feet away and with my arms around you why don't we try to make it to the chair? Don't worry I won't let you go." I could see that he was somewhat apprehensive, but was willing to give it a try.

Supporting his weight, we slowly made our way towards the chair. It felt more like a journey than a walk. Boy, what most of us take for granted, I thought.

"Would you like to remain out here a little while in the fresh air?"

"Okay, but only for a little while."

I let Joey remain outside for about fifteen minutes before picking him up and carrying him back into the house. "Joey, I was very proud of you. You really accomplished a lot today. Would you like to try it again tomorrow?" Apparently happy with his first venture outside, he said, "Alright."

We continued this exercises for the next two weeks, each day I moved the chair a little farther away measuring Joey's progress in inches. His eating also improved. Tammy complained that because of my constant cooking she was putting on too much weight. I told her that I was sorry but there was no stopping me.

One day I was in the kitchen when I heard the sliding glass door, leading to the deck, being opened. I didn't give it much thought until

I saw a figure outside. It was Joey. He was going to try to make it to the chair without any help. Holding onto the deck railing, he slowly trudged forward. Looking at him through the kitchen window I began to urge him on, "Yes! Yes! You can do it! Don't quit! Only a few more steps and you're almost there!" The closer he got to the chair, the louder I screamed. Finally, totally exhausted, he collapsed in the chair. I jumped up and down; my arms were flaring wildly in the air. While most fathers were cheering their sons on at their Saturday morning football games, I was home hoping that my son could make it to the end of the deck without falling. In my mind, his accomplishment was far greater than any touchdown ever scored. Today I celebrated the sweetness of my son's victory and I loved every second of it. I allowed Joey to remain outside looking up at the blue sky, watching the birds and enjoying the quietness and beauty of autumn. Yes, this was a good day.

Chapter 21

WITH CLAUDINE DUE for a visit, I knew that it would not be a very boring weekend because, along with her sophistication, beauty, and intelligence, came a commensurate amount of zaniness. I learned to shake my head in amazement at her antics and not get overly involved in her escapades. Actually, her unanticipated behavior was always welcomed. If nothing else it made for interesting conversation.

She too was startled at Joeys's appearance but that was to be expected. Most people looked at him with sorrow and apprehension. Cancer does not command respect. It demands it. Although people do not express their true feelings, unconsciously they have to be thinking, are there any cancer cells lurking in my body waiting to unleash their terror? People speak differently about cancer than other illnesses. So much so that their facial expressions and voice inflections change at the mere mention of its name. Its ferocity is viewed with disdained reverence. Sometimes only the first letter is used or they may bypass the whole word by whispering, "Do you know what she, or he, has?"

Cancer tends to be the ultimate equalizer. It's an equal opportunity killer showing no disparity because of size, race, gender, or affluence. If you are big and strong, cancer will say to you, "So how big are you?"

"I'm six-feet five inches tall." "And how much do you weigh?" "Almost 350 pounds."

"Wow! You're big. I'm only one little mutant cell. Are you strong?" "I can lift three hundred and fifty pounds over my head."

"I can't do that. Are you fast?"

"I can run the hundred in nine seconds flat."

"My goodness, that's fast. I'm really impressed. I can't do any of those things. Hey, would you like to fight anyway? Who knows, maybe I'll get lucky? And, oh, by the way, before we begin there is something I should tell you. Since we started our conversation something has changed.

"What's that?"

"There are now two of us."

All that "big" and "strong" means to cancer is that it can play its sadistic game a little longer. Within a short period of time, it will audaciously knock you down to size. It's not afraid of anything or anyone. It's a bully, but unlike most bullies, it has the teeth and the muscle to back it up.

Brothers and sisters are a wonderful lot. No matter what takes place in their lives they always manage to find time to bicker and tease each other. This was good for Joey. I couldn't treat him as though nothing was wrong, but they could. I was starting to learn that this was the best way to treat sick people regardless of their illness. Paradoxical as it may seem, laughing is a wonderful panacea when dealing with the sick.

Claudine wasn't home long before some bizarre incident took place. Having gone out with her sister, I noticed that Tammy came home alone.

"Where is Claudine?"

"She's in the dumpster behind the supermarket."

As I started to walk away something sounded funny about Tammy's sentence. Turning, I asked, "Did you say that she's at the dumpster behind the supermarket, or that she's in the dumpster?"

"In the dumpster."

"Before you walk away would you care to elaborate a little bit on this subject?" "Well, Dad, she went up there to donate her clothes to charity. She wanted to throw them into one of those big clothing dumpsters behind the supermarket. After she threw her clothes in the dumpster we started to drive away when she thought that she might have thrown a new pair of slacks in there by mistake. She was reaching into the dumpster trying to pull her clothes out but she couldn't reach in far enough. A few of Joey's friends happened to be walking by and saw what she was trying to do. They asked her if she wanted them to dangle her by her feet, and well, she fell into the dumpster. I didn't want to get into any trouble because if the police showed up who would believe such a crazy story. If they knew Claudine, they would understand how all this could have taken place. However, I wasn't going to risk that."

At that moment Joey interrupted, "I wonder if she was looking for the black slacks that are hanging on the doorknob in my room?"

How does this child get involved in all these bizarre incidents? I wondered. "Don't worry, Tammy, somehow it will all work out for her. It always does. I hear that there is a good movie on HBO tonight does anybody want to watch it with me?" Both Joey and Tammy joined me. The three of us enjoyed a great movie.

Chapter 22

I BLINKED AND three weeks passed by. With nervous anticipation, I tried to prepare myself for what was about to take place during Joey's next chemotherapy session. I hoped that he would not react as violently as he had after the first course. Before bringing him to the hospital, I tried to learn as much as I could about cancer and the bizarre world that accompanied it. If I wanted to take care of Joey, if I wanted to stand by his side helping him fight this serial killer of children, I had to know more than the little I knew. I couldn't learn the intricate scientific make up of cancer. I was too old for that. If I had known years ago that one of my children was going to be afflicted with cancer, I would have made science my vocation. But there was a lot that I could do to help even from the sidelines. Maybe, just maybe, one little minuet act on my part might be able to tilt the odds in Joey's favor. I wanted to do this the right way. There was a lot of information that I had to address, but I also had other household related issues on my mind.

It was a long time since I committed anything to memory, certainly nothing of this importance. In the past I had always been able to pass any test that came my way but now I was older and at times I thought I could hear the neurons shriveling up inside my brain. All I could think was don't screw this up it's too important. I began to do exactly what I said I wasn't going to do; I started to read, to learn about cancer. I learned that cancer could affect one's appetite, that mealtimes should be relaxed. (That will be a first around this house. Who would believe that even cancer had one virtue?) Joey should be allowed to choose his meal times. Smaller meals were better and soft food was preferable.

I discovered that his sense of taste might change and that he might suffer from dry mouth. I should also be prepared to substitute any foods that became unpleasant tasting and to be careful not to aggravate any sores in his mouth. I should avoid giving him anything tart. (A house without lemon meringue pie was beyond my comprehension.) And then I remembered I forgot to pay the automobile insurance. I believe I'm still in some form of grace period. I could do that later, I reasoned. Okay, next subject.

Nausea: For nausea, give him toast, sherbet, crackers and clear liquids. No fatty foods allowed. Serve food at room temperature, but not beverages, they should be served chilled. He should rest after meals. No food before chemotherapy treatments. (As though he would even think of eating something before chemotherapy.)

And then a thought jumped into my head. Did I mail in Claudine's college tuition for this semester? I'll check on that later too. Get back to vomiting. Stay focused. Don't stray. Nothing to eat or drink until his vomiting is under control then give him clear liquids, cereal, milk shakes and puddings. All right, that's enough with the intake part of his anatomy let's switch to the other end.

This was baffling, they had constipation and diarrhea listed in the same paragraph. Talk about yin and yang. Okay, let's take them one at a time.

Diarrhea: Give him food high in protein and calories, but low in fiber. Yogurt, and rice with broth seem to head the list.

Constipation: I should serve high-fiber foods, cereal, whole grain breads, and raisins. I wondered, wasn't it amazing that I had not seen one cannoli listed anywhere in either of these listings. Whoever made up the food list for cancer-related symptoms certainly wasn't Italian.

Wait! Did I call the oil company to have the heating system cleaned before the winter season comes into full swing? I'll add that to my have to do list. Concentrate, you can do it. Lactose intolerance, skip it, I'll get back to that one later.

Adjuvant Therapy: Simple, it's chemotherapy used in conjunction with radiation therapy. With my attention too scattered for me to continue, I decided that a temporary reprieve was in order. I was making a little headway. I already knew about white blood cells, red blood cells, platelets and several chemotherapy medications. I knew about unusual bleeding, rashes, changes in skin color, pain with urination, coughing that doesn't stop, headaches that occur in the morning, headaches that won't go away, changes in vision, hearing, lack of energy and unusual bleeding, that if he collapsed it might indicate bleeding inside his head. I had already purchased soft toothbrushes, and I knew not to give him aspirin or over-the-counter products containing salicylates. Not so bad, I was getting there, and tomorrow was another day. I knew that I would have to learn a lot more in order to be of any help to Joey. But I also knew that I would have to be able set my own pace.

I was about to put my literature away when I noticed one more word. This word jumped off the sheet hitting me squarely between the eyes, a plebeian of a word, a friend hidden in the midst of a hostile empire. *Remission*. Where did you come from? I marveled. "Want to be my friend? My island sanctuary?"

I made up my mind that no matter how much I read, and whatever else took place in my life, from this day forward remission would be my life preserver, the beacon of light that would guide me home to safety. Mr. Remission was proof that people survived cancer. Because without survivors, the word would not exist. I felt better. Have I had the oil changed in the car? Who cares!

Before entering the hospital for Joey's next chemotherapy session, I had to have his blood count taken. If his white cell count were too low, he would be sent home and told to return another day. If the immune system of cancer patients is too weak, they cannot receive a drug as strong as chemotherapy because having a limited amount of bacterial resistance would place the body in great peril. Dr. G. informed me that during this visit Joey would not have to undergo any tests. He was strictly there to receive chemotherapy.

Joey was again assigned a room; only this time he had a roommate, an older boy who I happened to notice during our last visit. His name was Thomas, and he was in the final stages of cystic fibrosis, a disease that attacks the respiratory system. Cystic fibrosis prevents those afflicted with the disease from a simple function that we all take for granted, breathing. His lungs would fill with fluid until the congestion filled his respiratory tract and he suffocated. It would claim his life. He received his sentence the day they diagnosed his disease. His fate was sealed, there would be no pardon and he knew it. So did his mother and father who sat diligently at his bedside. At nineteen years of age, Thomas had already lived beyond his golden years.

After assisting Joey onto his bed, I found a chair and sat near the faded curtains in the darkest corner of his room. I watched as a nurse began giving Thomas his physical therapy. She slapped him on his chest, back, and sides attempting to loosen his congestion. It sounded like a butcher trying to tenderize a slab of meat. Each slap caused him to wail out loud. His air passages were so inflamed that any movement irritated his raw tissue. It had to be torturous. I listened and watched, intruding without authority, on a moment in time that I had no right to be a part of. Seconds later, Thomas cried out, "I don't want to die. Please, I don't want to die. Give me my medicine." The nurse explained to him that the resident physician would not give him his medicine. She said that he was so weak that his medicine could cause congestive heart failure. "I don't care," he screamed, while begging for something to ease his pain.

I sat there motionless as his father walked over and picked up his son. Without saying a word he cradled him in his arms and returned to his chair. With no place to go, I again trespassed on their emotional closeness, spying on the love of a father as he held his boy, as he rocked him backed and forth, showering him with tenderness and love. I had an idea what he was feeling.

Later that night I discovered that Thomas's father and mother had cancer. Hearing this sadness, I was lost for words. I had always heard that God would burden you with no more weight than you could carry. After today I no longer believed that.

Waiting for Joey to receive his chemotherapy, I had the opportunity to meet Thomas's parents. His mother approached me. Looking up at me with kindness and love in her eyes she said, "Your son is going to live but mine is going to die." I didn't know what to make of her remark. I hadn't anticipated her comment or the moment. I wasn't able to tell if she was making a layman's attempt at prophesying the future or was she really possessed of some divine insight. All I knew was that I didn't have an answer. Could anyone have answered her? I asked myself what was going through the minds of these poor people? How did the two of them manage to get out of bed in the morning? How were they able to place one foot in front of the other? Unconcerned with their own inevitable fate, their love for their son was all consuming but after all was said and done, there was nothing for them to look forward to. When we lose a loved one, we live in our memories. Here there would be no one left to do the remembering. They were all going to die. To quote Mary, "I have never met two people with more grace." Overcome by the moment, I decided to take a walk across the street around the outskirts of Central Park.

Keeping the hospital to my back, I was careful not to turn for fear of catching a glimpse of it. Hoping to forget the sadness that was taking place inside, I watched the children at play. They were young, healthy and filled with the blessings of youth. I looked at the parents sharing in their children's fun. I wondered if they had any idea what was taking place in the building behind them? Did they know about Thomas and Joey? Did they know that playing was an untouchable reality to many of the children in that building? Instead of running and playing, they were fighting for a breath of air. I prayed that the happy children in the park would never see the inside of Falk 2.

I returned to Joey's room and found him resting on his bed still dressed in his street clothes. I looked at him, giving him a smile I hoped he would return but he didn't. Instead, he rested quietly awaiting his Benadryl and Ativan. Sitting on the foot of his bed was his nurse. She was tall, attractive, and seemed personable. During our drive to the hospital, Joey began to shut down all systems. It was impossible to get him to converse about anything. The only comments he made were to say, "Pull over, I have to throw up." Joey vomited every few minutes for the entire length of the Long Island Expressway and beyond. The thought of what was awaiting him began to take its toll. And so I was glad to see that he was conversing with his new nurse. To me, he looked terribly uncomfortable lying there in his jeans. "Joey," I said, "why don't you put on a pair of pajamas or something that you might be a little more comfortable in?" Joey acted as though I was invisible and he was deaf. Once again I repeated myself. Still no reply. I was about to stress the issue when his nurse, who was thin, had dark long hair and stood about five feet eight inches tall, and was about to leave the room, turned to me and said, "Why don't you mind your own business and leave him alone!" She then proceeded to blitz me with a few unrepeatable choice words and left. My jaw dropped as I watched her walk out into the hall. Annoyed that anyone would dare speak to me like this I pursued her into the corridor. "Excuse me, what's your name? And what's wrong with you?" I said.

"My name is Michele and I'll tell you what's wrong, and it's not what's wrong with me but what's wrong with you that I am going to talk to you about." At this point I knew that I had a tiger by the tail.

"Look, your son is in there fighting for his life. Every patient in this place handles his or her illness a little differently, can't you see what he is saying by leaving his street clothes on? He is telling everyone, including his cancer, 'I'm not staying here. I'm going home and nobody can make me stay here.' Why can't you let him fight his battle his way?

Why can't you get it?"

Thinking for a moment, I said, "You know, you are right. I just never thought of it that way."

"Well maybe it's time you started thinking."

"I guess I'm a little anal-retentive. I mean, my mother made me dry every drop of water out of the sink after I washed my hands." She turned her back to me and walked away. What a feisty mean nurse, I thought. I can see that I'm going to have to be on my best behavior whenever she's around. But I liked her.

Mary walked into Joey's room. I told her about my run in with Michele, who I now labeled, "The Mean Nurse." Mary laughed wondering how I managed to get into so much trouble in a children's cancer ward.

An IV was connected to Joey's arm. He moved, and dislodged it. It was reconnected, and again he shook it lose. The third time around it was reinserted into his hand. Michele and Carol secured it with several pieces of heavy adhesive tape. Next, he received his Benadryl.

"Remember," he ordered, "a slow drip." With the Benadryl flowing into his system, it was time for his Ativan. I watched as he became groggy; closing his eyes he eased into a relaxed sleep.

Laurie walked in, dangling from her hands were several colored vials of chemotherapy. Their bright red, yellow, and white colors almost made them look drinkable. At that moment Joey snapped out of his sleep, "What's that you have in your hands?" he asked Laurie.

"It's your chemotherapy."

"Is there anything new that I should know?" "No, the same as last time."

As he closed his eyes and started to fall back to sleep he murmured, "slow drip." Mary and I were astonished at the degree of his awareness. I thought about what Michele had said earlier. She was right. Whatever the outcome might be, he was going to do it his way. With his chemotherapy filtering its way towards his cancer he slept silently in his street clothes. I arrived home late that night and experienced the same empty feeling that I felt the last time Joey was in the hospital. Living in the hospital was wearing me down. I was tired and feeling every day my age and more.

It was early the next morning when I returned to the hospital. As I was walking towards Joey's room, I could hear him vomiting. I also heard a pounding, rapping sound, similar to an irate judge striking his gavel in a court of law. The noise thundered down the corridor. Opening Joey's door I saw Mary, "I can't stop him," she said. Joey was brutally banging his head on the metal partition that separated the two beds in his room. Still vomiting he managed to yell, "Leave me alone, leave me alone. I'm so sick." Once again blood started to flow from his mouth.

"Joey," I pleaded, "you are going to hurt yourself. Please son, stop it, please!" I held him while Mary ran out to find some help. Michele came running in and ordered a sedative. It wasn't long before he fell back to sleep. I looked at the metal room divider; it was dented from the impact of his head smashing into it. Mary said, "I have never witnessed anything like that before."

"I don't know. I really don't know. How is he ever going to make eighteen courses of chemotherapy? And we haven't started radiation yet."

With Thomas crying in his bed, and Joey attempting to rearrange the architectural design of the building, I thought, whatever this planet is that I'm on, I wish that it would stop spinning for a few minutes so that I could get off.

While Joey was sleeping, I called Tammy at home to see how she was doing. "I'm doing fine daddy. How is Joey?"

"Not bad, he's sound asleep."

"Oh, I'm glad that he is doing okay. Hey Dad." "Yeah."

"I love you."

"I guess that's why I wouldn't get off if I could." "Dad, what are you talking about?"

"Hey, Tammy." "What?"

"Me, too, you."

I called Claudine at Fordham. She expressed the same concern about her brother. But before hanging up she said, "By the way, the lime green Volkswagen bug has been towed away. It's in a nearby gas station and I can't get it out."

"How did that happen? Where did it get towed from?"

"From here. From Fordham. From the parking lot, she rattled back."

"I thought that you were allowed to park in the Fordham parking lot?" "You're right. We are."

"So?"

"Well, it wasn't exactly parked in that lot." "Then what lot was it exactly parked in?" "The Jesuit parking lot."

"Oh! I see. I somehow missed the day of your ordainment. How does it feel to be a Jesuit? Claudine, can we make this conversation brief? Tell me what you need?"

"Sure, I need you to come up here to pay the gas station owner so that I can get the Bug back. I would pay for it myself but I maxed out my credit card." "Okay, I'll be up there tomorrow."

"And, Dad, I aced my French test." "Wonderful, see you tomorrow."

I hung up the phone and shook my head. As I started to walk away, I realized that Claudine didn't have a credit card, at least not one of her own. The only credit card she had was the one I had given her to use in case of an emergency. I'll have to deal with this tomorrow, I thought.

Early the next morning I arrived at Fordham University. As I entered Claudine's dorm, I noticed that the main stairwell was cordoned off with bright yellow police crime scene ribbon. Looking up I could see bullet holes through the glass behind the stairs. It didn't take me long to realize that some sick individual was sniping away at the students from the abandoned railroad yard behind the dorm. This had not been the first time that an incident of this sort had taken place at Fordham. Although Fordham offered a wonderful education, and the campus was Gothic and beautiful in appearance, it happened to be in the middle of one of the highest crime areas in New York City. Just something else for me to worry about.

With my heart pounding, I ran up the stairs to make sure that Claudine was safe. As I walked into her room she said, with the emotional immunity of a real city dweller, "See all the excitement downstairs?"

"Yeah, anyone hurt?" "Nope."

"Am I the only one worried around here? Well, at least be careful until the police catch this sick puppy."

"I will, Dad," she sighed unconcerned.

We took a ride over to where the bug was impounded. The car had a look about it that said, "Can you please keep her away from me?"

"Claudine, I'm real busy with your brother so could you please make life a little easier on me for a while, and as long as you are taking it easy on me can you manage to take it easy on my credit card too. You know, think of us as a team, me, you, and my credit card."

"Sure, Dad."

"I promise you that I will be up here to take you out to dinner next week and then you can tell me all about what's going on in school and your life."

"What's your rush? Where are you going?"

"Home to sight in my riflescope. Looking at the bullet holes, I noticed that it's pulling to the left." "Real funny, Dad."

Driving back to the hospital, I thought about all the wonderful parents who traveled down this road before me, those who had raised children on their own and those who had given their unfailing love to all the Joey's in the world. They were my encouragement to go on, to move forward. Joey's radiation treatments would require that I drive a couple of hundred miles a day. Could I do it? I concluded that I could walk it carrying Joey on my back. Cancer wasn't taking my son. It didn't have that right or that privilege.

Chapter 23

I KNEW THAT when Joey tore out his IV he had sealed his own fate concerning the need for a Broviac. There was no way that Dr. G. was going to allow him to go on without one now. His hand was swollen from the IV needle. Plus, the uncountable injections were painful. Dr. G. was right; he needed the Broviac. To continue without one would be impossible. My problem would be convincing him that he needed it and informing him that he would have to undergo another round of anesthesia. Joey could be awfully thick headed when he wanted. (I wondered whom he inherited that trait from.) I was certain that this was going to be a hard sell. Once again I would have to resort to plan B, the bribe. I also knew that this wasn't the proper time to bring up the Broviac issue. He was too sick and too out of it for me to hit him with a little more bad news. I decided to wait a few days. Meanwhile, I told Dr. G. to make the necessary arrangements for his surgery.

After completing his second course of chemotherapy, Joey was too sick to come home the next day. On the third day, I went to the nurses' station to sign the release forms. Once again Michele was assigned as his nurse. I asked her to disconnect his IV so that we could be on our way. She refused.

"He's not fully hydrated so you're going to have to stay here a little while longer." "If I don't get him out of here now, we are going to hit rush hour traffic. I don't think you understand how far we live from here. Every minute is important. If we leave here a few minutes too late, a one hour and fifteen minute trip becomes a two and a half hour trip."

"He's not going anywhere until he is fully hydrated. I want him to still have his kidneys when he arrives wherever it is that you live. End of issue."

I knew better than to argue with her. She protected all these young adolescent children from impatient parents, young inexperienced doctors, and all others that might dare interfere with their welfare. After observing her taking care of her patients, I realized that she possessed a wonderful knack of being able to bring a smile to the children's faces by not allowing them to dwell in their suspicion. It wasn't unusual for her to break the tension in the room by murmuring a word just to the left of acceptable vernacular for all to hear. Her timing was usually perfect. Parents and children would look up at her and laugh. She in turn would say, "You know, I promised myself I was going to stop doing that; I really am going to have to work on it much harder." What she actually accomplished was to take the pressure off everyone, to change their moods. She was as stupid as a fox. But as far as I was concerned, I couldn't win with her. So, I thought, no use in trying. As she turned her back and started to walk away, I stuck my tongue at her. Then I wandered about, looking at my watch knowing that I would once again be stuck in rush hour traffic.

The trip home was a repeat of the last time except on this occasion I brought a gallon of water. Each time we pulled over I washed out Joey's basin. At least that little effort on my part made the trip a little more palatable. Finally arriving home, I said to Joey, "Boy I really showed that mean nurse who was boss, didn't I?"

Supporting Joey, we made our way up the stairs to his bedroom. He asked me to draw the shades and to leave him alone. As I left his room, I could hear him retching. Other then coming up to clean out his basin, I left him to dwell in the privacy of his silence. Much to my amazement, I was learning to give him the space he deserved.

Two days later I heard the shower running indicating that Joey was up and on the road to recovering from his second bout with chemotherapy.

"Dad, what's to eat? I'm starved." "You should be."

He proceeded to tear into the refrigerator making up for lost time. "Joey, would you mind if I run out for a few minutes?"

"No, go ahead."

I drove to a local travel agent and requested any brochures depicting pictures of various vacation locations designated for family use. After collecting my literature, I returned home.

Joey, I have been wanting to talk to you about something and I thought this might be a good time to discuss it."

"What is it Dad?" "You need a Broviac."

"I don't care what Dr. G. says I'm not getting one."

"Hold on a minute, there isn't any choice. Don't you want to make things a little easier on yourself?"

"I'm doing fine just the way I am."

"For the moment, but it's going to get to a point where you won't be able to do without one."

"Does that mean that I have to get anesthesia like I did the last time?"

"Yep. To have it implanted you do. But when they take it out they can do it without anesthesia. Plus, they told me that they would let you watch when they remove it. Doesn't that excite you? From your perspective, and the way you like to look at all the machines and doctoral procedures, this sounds like its right up your alley. Better than a trip to the zoo, right?" Returning to a more serious note I said, "Please, Joey, do this for yourself.

I'll tell you what I'll do, let's make a deal. If you don't want to do this for yourself than do it for us, and this is what I'll do for us in return." With that remark, I reached into my pocket and pulled out my travel brochures spreading them across the table like a deck of cards. "Take a look at these and let me know which one you would like to go to. I promise you that if you get your Broviac I will take you to a Caribbean resort of your choice." With that being said I left the room to allow him to sift through the travel pamphlets. With much reluctance, he gave his okay.

While Joey was having his Broviac inserted, I managed to get my hands on a booklet that technically explained what a Broviac was and how to care for it.

A Broviac catheter is a long hollow tube. It has an opening that is called a lumen and is made of soft silicone rubber. It is inserted into the large vein leading into the heart. It has a connector and an injection cap. A syringe can be inserted to the end of the connector. It also has a cuff that anchors the catheter under the skin to prevent it from slipping out. Tissue grows into the cuff to anchor it, forming a barrier to keep bacteria out. There are several uses for the Broviac. Its primary use is to allow patients, over a prolonged period of time, to receive special fluids, medicines, or to take blood samples for testing.

The Broviac operation lasted almost two hours. Again, I waited for Joey in the recovery room. The anesthesia once again made its presence known causing him to have an identical reaction to his previous anesthetic escapade. If it wasn't one thing causing him to vomit, it was another. The poor boy just couldn't win.

I found it difficult to look at him with this long thin tube snaking its way blow his skin protruding out from his chest. It took me some time to adjust to the visual appearance of this odd apparatus. I could see the clamp at the end, and although the concept of this device was functional it made me feel a bit queasy. My initial concern was that someone might accidentally pull it tearing a hole in the vein, or that the clamp would open up, and all of Joey's blood would spill out during the night. And then what? I thought. While all these worries were upsetting my karma, Dr. G. walked in the room. "While Joey is here I would like him to undergo his usual battery of tests."

"All of them?" "Yes."

"This isn't going to go over too well."

"I have to monitor his cancer. We need to keep a close eye on it. What's the sense of having you go home only to return in a few days?"

"Alright."

We began the whole series of tests all over again. Still sick from the anesthesia, Joey was really out of it. How he was managing to endure the personal onslaught of MRIs, bone scans, CAT scans, X-rays and several other tests was beyond me. The test that he seemed to dislike the most was the CAT scan with contrast. Sick to begin with, he was required to drink glass after glass of a chalky tasting liquid. He squinted with each sip that he took saying, "I hate this stuff, I really do hate it." With all this going on, I could see that there was something else disturbing him. "All right let's talk. What's on your mind?"

"Is the Broviac going to leave a scar on my chest?"

"I don't know, but I think that it probably will. Listen, if this is upsetting you, when this is over you can have some plastic surgery done. You also have to remember that as you get older the hair on your chest will cover any scar that you might wind up with." He didn't answer me. I thought, here was this poor boy fighting bone cancer that could at any second rear its ugly head and race through his body like a fire being fed by the Santa Anna winds and he was worried about a little scar. I guess it was better that he thought this way rather than display a defeatist attitude.

With his tests completed, and his Broviac implanted, we went home but not for long because he was due back in a week to receive his chemotherapy. Three days later I called the hospital to get the results of Joey's latest tests. I held my breath waiting for Dr. G. to speak. She said that Joey's tests showed no change but that he was still into the early stages of chemotherapy. She also said that she had not seen any signs indicating that his cancer had spread elsewhere, that it was still confined to his pelvis.

I guess it wasn't what I was hoping to hear. I was dreaming that she would say, "Guess what? To our surprise Joey's cancer is gone. There isn't any indication of it anywhere in his body. We can't explain it because we have never, in all our years of practicing medicine, seen anyone recover from Ewing's sarcoma this quickly." At which time I would rave, "I knew he could do it! I just knew it!" But that wasn't the case. Well, I reasoned, that was okay. I could go on like this for the rest of my life and so could Joey. I wouldn't give him any choice; he would have to go on. I would take him back and forth to Manhattan every day. I would clean up his vomit, and I would reassure him when his spirits were low that he could go on. As long as he was alive, I would be happy with whatever little of him I could have. No one was taking my son from me.

Chapter 24

BEFORE LEAVING THE hospital we were given a quick lesson on the care and use of the Broviac. One afternoon a traveling nurse stopped by our house to reinforce what we had already learned at the hospital. I was frightened that I might make some terrible mistake. I guess it showed. Joey, noticing that I was all thumbs said, "Why don't you let me do it? It's taking you forever just to draw a little blood."

"Fine, you're the mechanical one in the family. This should be right up your alley." With that, I stepped aside and watched him as he breezed through the steps of removing the tape around the injection cap. After cleaning it with alcohol and iodine, he carefully inserted a needle into the center of the catheter cap. With those steps completed, he drew his blood, flushed the catheter clean with heparin, and applied a new dressing to his chest.

The only step that he sometimes left out was to discard the syringe in the medical waste container. It wasn't uncommon for me to discover the needle lodged in my bed in the middle of the night- usually a painful discovery on my part. After repeatedly being stuck, I pleaded with Joey to discard his syringes in the proper manner. "You know, Joey, do what everyone else in the world does with their medical waste. Throw it in the reservoir." The Broviac was a big plus because I could now take Joey's blood to my nearby medical group to have it tested.

One afternoon I was in the kitchen when I heard Joey shouting my name. I sensed a bit of panic in his voice. I ran up the stairs, in Joeys's outstretched hand was a clump of hair. It had begun. He was moving up the ranks, assuming a new position in the hierarchy. Joey was being painted by the artist known as cancer and he was intent upon leaving his brush stroke for the world to see. "I guess I'm going to lose my hair just like the rest of the children in the hospital."

I smiled for a second while I searched for the right words to comfort a boy who next week, on Christmas Eve, would be fourteen years old. I knew there were no words to soothe a child who would soon wear a badge identifying him as someone afflicted with a terrible disease. He would now look different than most children his age. He had become a member of a club, a club that there was no resigning from. There were only two ways out. You either terminate your membership by living or it terminates you, forever.

I decided that honesty had worked for me up until now so why change. He wanted to understand the growth of cells and what chemotherapy did to them. I told him that all this meant was that his chemotherapy was working. "Joey, try to think of it this way. If the chemotherapy is doing this to your hair cells, then it must be beating up on your cancer cells too, and it's not going to stop until it kicks the cancer right out of your body." I went on to explain that his chemotherapy didn't mean to be cruel, but was unable to distinguish the difference between his cancer and hair cells. "Nobody ever said that chemotherapy was smart. You see," I whispered, "your hair cells really didn't leave but are hiding and when they feel safe they'll come out of their hiding place and all your hair will come back thicker than before." With all that said, I hoped that I was able to ease his mind.

Joey looked up at me. Apparently seeing that I was somewhat satisfied with my long dissertation on cancer vs. hair follicles he pulled out another clump of hair. Leering at it, with a perplexed look on his face, he finally said, "Hey, Dad, that was a great story that you told me. It really was one heck of a war that you had going on, meanwhile, my hair is falling out of my head in clumps. What are we going to do about it?"

So much for long stories, I thought, and I was so proud of my epic tale of carnage and concealment. Some kids just didn't appreciate a good cloak and dagger narration.

"Okay, you want an answer to your problem, I will give you an answer to your problem. I have a solution. Tomorrow I will have my barber come to the house and shave your head. This way you won't look like some sort of crazed rabid porcupine."

"Oh, no you're not!" "Why not?

Laughing, he said, "Dad, did you ever look in the mirror to see what you look like after he cuts your hair? If you're going to let your barber cut my hair, then I would rather look like this."

It was good to see him laugh. The children usually had the most fun when I was on the receiving end of their humor. "Yeah, I know you're right, but he's from my old neighborhood and I have to be loyal. If he doesn't see me every few weeks, he calls the house to make sure that I'm feeling okay. I couldn't betray him by bringing my head to another barber. He's been cutting my hair for a long time."

"We'll, he needs a little more practice. Maybe one day he'll get it right."

"You know, we don't need Vidal Sassoon to shave your head and if you don't get it shaved it's only a matter of time until someone calls the dog pound mistaking you for a mange dog. Here's another idea for you to ponder. Why don't I cut your hair myself? I still have an old pair of horse shears in the garage." Suddenly, my barber started to look a lot better. With that remark, I heard Claudine call my name.

"Come on, Dad, it's on." Which could only mean one thing, it was 7:00p.m. Time for Jeopardy. When Claudine was home, at 7:00p.m. everything came to a halt so that she could lure any potential victim into a game of Jeopardy at which they had no chance of winning.

"Sorry, buddy, I would love to talk to you about your hair, or lack of hair problems, but I have to run downstairs and for the first time in my life I am going to beat your sister at Jeopardy." I then explained I had discovered that Jeopardy aired an hour before on a cable network and that I had memorized all the answers or questions, whichever terminology was correct when referring to the rules of Jeopardy. A smile came across his face and then he said, "I bet you lose anyway."

"Impossible!"

Although my insides were being torn apart with worry, I wanted the children, especially Joey, to believe that all would turn out fine. The only way for me to accomplish that was by engaging in all our normal customary household activities. Each family, and person within that family, handles the travesty of cancer in a way that works best for him or her. I used humor as my crutch. To be able to make the children laugh even though we were surrounded by gloom seemed to put everyone at ease. An hour later I reported to Joey that his prediction was right. I lost.

Joey's hair continued to fall out. Soon the eyelashes and eyebrows that most women would have traded their soul for were no longer there. With no hair, and a tube protruding from his chest, he was continuing moving up the ranks. Witnessing Joey struggling through the transition of acclimating to his new appearance, I discovered a solution that seemed to work best. Actually, I didn't discover it. His sisters did. All I had to do was to leave the three of them alone and allow them to follow the same path that they had always gone down. They had made a career out of teasing each other. They were experts at it. I rationalized why not let them handle this. Tammy told him he looked like a newborn chicken that just hatched out of his shell. Claudine started to call him Q ball, and soon just plain old Q. The more they teased him the more he laughed. It wasn't long before he was having fun mocking his own appearance.

Each night after he fell asleep I sat in a chair next to his bed and watched over him as he slept. I reveled in the joy that he brought into my life and all the silly things he had done to bring a smile to my face. He made me feel good about being his father. I wanted to be with him. I could have sat there all night. But in the back of my mind I always wondered how much time we had remaining. I wished that I could have traded places with him, to take his cancer and put it into my body. I would have done that for him. Wouldn't any father? With my batteries charged, I left him hoping that he would dream the dreams that all healthy fourteen-year-olds dreamed tonight.

Joining the girls in the family room, I found them upset and worried. They had just gotten off the phone with their mother. She had told them that a friend of hers, a doctor in Missouri, said that unless Joey had an operation to remove his cancer he wasn't going to live. All I could think was why would anyone say this? Why would anyone do this? The second she stopped talking about cumulous clouds and news events she knocked this family somewhere into oblivion.

I spent the rest of the night trying to reestablish the girl's belief that Joey was being seen by the best doctors and that he was going to survive. I reiterated that they should allow me to do the worrying, "All I want from the two of you is that you continue to get good grades in school." Nothing is going to prevent you from having your brother to tease for the rest of your lives." With that said, I put on my coat and took a long walk mumbling every vulgarity I knew and some that I made up.

The next day I called Dr. G. to have a talk with her to go over the fact that Joey's cancer was inoperable and to eradicate all shreds of doubt. She re-confirmed what she had already told us and suggested that if Joey's mother wanted to discuss his cancer with her that she would welcome her phone call. I decided to write the children's mother a letter. I wanted to call her but I couldn't. The old ways were too ingrained in my fabric. "Please, do not fling any lightning bolts this way. They hurt." I wrote.

With that issue put aside, I was hoping for a quiet weekend. However, Claudine managed to get involved in another automobile accident. My car was again towed away. This time the damage was over seven thousand dollars. Two weeks later my auto insurance was cancelled along with my homeowners insurance, both written by the same company. I guess they figured it was only a matter of time until she drove the car through the house, or they may have remembered she had already done that with the MG: The way things were going I would soon be the only one living on Long Island insured by Lloyds of London. I needed a rest. I thought that I should try something a little less stressful than being a single parent like removing land mines in Bosnia.

Chapter 25

JOEY WAS MISSING the entire school year. He was a good student and always managed to pass all his tests and classes without much difficulty. All my children's I.Q. scores were well above average I expected A's in school and they delivered. I made a decision to call his Junior High School Principal and asked for an appointment to see if arrangements could be made to have him tutored at home. I knew that his tutoring schedule would be irregular at best. I reasoned that a little tutoring would be better than none at all. Any type of agenda that we previously tried to conform to in our household was a thing of the past.

Several of his teachers were sent over to the house to try to assist him with his schoolwork. As each teacher walked in, the expression on their faces typically exhibited their total dismay. None could believe that this was the same student that they grew to know and like over the last several school years. They said little in his presence; in private they expressed their concern and offered words of consolation.

Joey's study habits depended on whether he was feeling well enough to apply himself. If he did, he would hit the books and complete his daily assignments. Of course just when he was starting to roll along he began to run a fever and I was forced to call Dr. G. at the hospital.

"What's his temperature?" "Almost one hundred and one."

"Bring him right in and admit him through the emergency room. I'll leave instructions for them. In the meantime, we will get a bed ready for him somewhere in Falk 2." Dr. G. had made it perfectly clear that if Joey ran a fever of 100.5 or higher, he had to be admitted to Mt. Sinai.

During one of my own study sessions, I had learned that cancer patients had very little immunity to fight off infection. Their white cell count was in constant fluctuation. The white blood cells (WBC) helped to fight infections. Chemotherapy, while destroying the cancer cells also destroyed the white cells, or the healthy infection fighting cells. This decreased the body's ability to fight off infection. The white cell count was determined by blood tests. That is why it was important to monitor the white cell count before chemotherapy could be administered. When the count began to drop below normal it was called **neutropenia.** This was when the risk of infection was at its greatest. During this period, it was extremely important to try to prevent infection. It was imperative to practice good hand washing and to avoid the possibility of small cuts and abrasions. The body's temperature also had to be monitored. If the white cell count was too low, the patient's immune system needed to be aided with antibiotics. If it was too high, it could indicate leukemia and the possibility that the cancer was spreading into the bones and throughout the body.

If the red cell count was too low, it might indicate the need for a transfusion. Chemotherapy destroyed red blood cells too, causing anemia. It also killed the platelets that facilitated in the clotting of blood. Blood had to clot in order to prevent bleeding and to protect the body from injury. Signs of a low platelet count could be red freckles, increased bruising, nose bleeds that were difficult to stop, gums that bleed easily, and excessive bleeding from small cuts or scrapes.

The bone marrow acted as an important production site in the body. It was here where white and red cells were produced as well as platelets. Bone marrow was found at the center of the bones, especially the areas of the skull, sternum, ribs, backbone and pelvis. These were the holding sites for blood cells until they matured and were ready to perform their vital functions. Chemotherapy acts on these cells by interrupting their production.

During the course of treatment the term **nadir** might be used. This was the point when the cells in the body were at their lowest number. Once this period was over, the blood counts would begin to rise back to their normal level.

The last thing Dr. G. wanted was to take a chance that Joey's Broviac might be the cause of his fever. The only way to make that determination was to have a culture taken. If the Broviac was the source of the infection, then a regimen of antibiotics might be able to remedy the situation. If not, the Broviac would have to be removed. At a later date another operation would have to be performed to re-implant the Broviac. I couldn't take a chance on letting Joey go through all this again. After all, how many Caribbean vacations could I afford? My only problem was convincing him that he had to enter the hospital. He was aware that the results of the culture would take at least three days. Which meant three days of Falk 2 and all the negatives that came along with being there.

After an hour of doing battle with Joey we were finally on our way to Mt. Sinai. Joey stopped talking to me before we left the house. He was even angrier with Dr. G. who, in his eyes, was now assuming the role of villain. I understood that he needed to direct his anger at someone. He couldn't see his cancer but he could see Dr. G and the person that was once again driving him to Mount Sinai. Joey again went through his usual routine of vomiting along the Expressway. It was psychologically evident that he could not cope with the thought of the hospital.

The trouble with being admitted through the emergency room was the wait. A hospital emergency room, on the fringes of Harlem, on a Saturday night, could produce long delays. In this case, it was three hours before we saw the inside of Falk 2. Joey, now too sick to talk, turned his back to me and rested in his bed. As usual he was still dressed in his street clothes. I was unable to keep my eyes opened and much too tired to drive home, and so, I made a fatal mistake. I did what I said I would never again do; I decided to spend the night in Joey's room.

Falk 2 had not yet discovered the innovation of air conditioning or climate control. I attempted to open the window hoping that a whisper of Harlem air might find its way into the room. Unfortunately, I discovered that the window had been welded shut years ago by a careless painter who failed to distinguish the difference between the window track and the wall it was attached to.

As I opened the fold out bed, I could see that it duplicated, in every respect, the one that I slept in the last time I remained here overnight. That in itself frightened me. I covered myself with a blanket and tried to find a comfortable spot to position my aging body. As I moved to the right, I was stuck by a piece of metal wire protruding about one half inch out from the mattress. I couldn't tell if it was part of a spring or part of the frame. All I knew was that it hurt. If I wasn't being stuck by Joey's syringes in my own bed, I was being pierced by something else in another bed. I had forgotten what it was like, not only to get a good night's sleep but also to get a simple uninterrupted night's sleep. This bed was starting to make the last one look good.

I quickly designated the right side of the mattress a no sleep area. Sliding my body to the left side I discovered a matching wire. I wondered if this feature cost extra. I slowly wiggled towards the center of the mattress where it appeared to be safest. Okay, if I remain perfectly still, in the demilitarized zone, and refrain from coughing or sneezing, I thought that I might have a chance at surviving the night. Move too quickly in either direction and I would become a 185lb. shish kabob. These beds should have the same label that cigarette packs have on them. If I were ever fortunate enough to win the lottery, my first order of generosity would be to purchase a new fold out bed for every room on this floor. I closed my eyes thinking that no one would be able to sleep under these conditions. As my mind began to drift to another place, another time. I began to laugh. It had been so long ago that I forgot about Bernie. There was no doubt in my mind that Bernie could sleep here.

Chapter 26

I WAS KNOCKING on the door of O'Brien's funeral parlor waiting for someone named Bernie to answer and wondering why I was sent there to fetch him in the first place. After all, what could Bernie do against a giant?

I was assigned to foot patrol. My post was MacDougal Street in the Greenwich Village section of Manhattan. Actually, I was a rookie assigned to the police academy and was there, along with the other members of my academy class, on a training assignment.

It was 2:00 a.m. on a hot summer Saturday in July. Tourist and visitors continued to flock to the crowded streets of the village contributing a little more joviality to the already existing party atmosphere. I was standing on the corner of Bleeker and MacDougal when I noticed a commotion starting to take place down the street. I observed a man, not just an ordinary man, but a giant of a man that stood around six feet, eight inches tall and weighed well in excess of three hundred pounds. He was the biggest person, the biggest anything, I had ever seen. Adding to his flavor, this tyrannosaurus-like figure was dressed as a Genie, turban and all. Evidently he had a bee in his turban because anyone that had the misfortune to come within arms length was picked up and hurled into orbit. My concern was trying to figure out a way not to become his next victim. If I decided to shoot him, it probably would do nothing more than agitate him, and the last thing that I wanted to do was to screw around with this guy's serotonin level. Plus, I was a poor shot and would most likely miss him.

Well at least I remembered to bring my gun to work, and for me, that was an improvement. The reminder notes I left all over the house seemed to be working. I also removed the popcorn from the barrel and the cylinder was now able to open and close. In fact the range officer was wrong, it wasn't popcorn but crackerjacks that were stuck in my barrel. Some crackerjacks had fallen into my holster and when I put my gun back in, they became lodged in the barrel. The cylinder was quickly repaired too. All this was nothing to get upset over, at least to my way of thinking, but the range officer looked at this situation a little differently. Especially when I told them that I had broken the barrel by using my gun to hammer tacks into my carpet at home. I had never met a more sensitive group of individuals.

The only way that I qualified to carry this burdensome weight was by punching a bunch of holes in my target with my pen. I punched so many holes that I qualified as expert. Out of 50 rounds that I fired, I hit the target fifty-eight times. Not bad shooting, I thought. Now they told me that they were going to send me to sniper school. Great, just what I needed, a bigger gun that makes more noise. So rather than using my gun on Conan down the street, I decided to guarantee the safety of the innocent bystanders and myself by keeping a low profile.

It wasn't long before a radio patrol car from the sixth precinct pulled up. The driver started to wave his arms signaling me to approach the car. Judging from the urgency of his wave and the melee taking place down the street, I had a pretty good idea of what he wanted. Not rushing, I slowly walked over to the patrol car "What are you doing here?" he asked.

"I didn't want to go to Viet Nam."

"That's not what I'm asking you. Do you see that guy down the street?" "What guy?"

"The one dressed like Aladdin."

"Aladdin?"

"Yeah! The big black guy dressed like a Genie that's kicking the shit out of everybody that walks by."

"Oh, that Genie;"

"The Sergeant here wants you to arrest him."

"Me?"

"Yeah, you!"

"Why me?"

"It's your post isn't it?"

"Just for tonight. It's not like I'm thinking of moving here. Let me ask you and the Sergeant a question. Where is the bus?"

"What bus? What the fuck are you talking about?"

"The bus filled with cops carrying the bazooka that I'm going to need to help me arrest him." I knew that I could get away with almost anything I said because I was wearing the gray uniform of a rookie and still in the police academy. I was expected to know very little about anything and everything and I was about to deliver what was expected of me. Plus, I just turned twenty-one last month and was still cutting myself learning how to shave. I didn't appreciate the fact that these two idiots had every intention of sending me to Valhalla. If I wanted to commit suicide, I was quite capable of picking my own poison. I came on this job to eat free donuts, not to be the first rookie to land on the moon. A hero, I wasn't. That old Shakespearean verse, "Cowards die many deaths but heroes die just one," Well, he left out the part about cowards living to be a ripe old age. Let Shakespeare fight this guy. It's for sure I wasn't going to. It was time for me to out think these two clowns and to have a good time in the process. If they wanted to engage in a game of verbal masturbation that was fine with me. Instead of allowing them to pull my chain, I decided to pull theirs. They were screwing around with the wrong rookie.

"I would like to arrest him but I can't." "What do you mean you can't?"

"Well, it's not so much that I can't but more like I'm not allowed to. I'm not allowed to arrest anyone that another police officer, who is not a rookie, can arrest in my place. You know, like you."

With that, the Sergeant leaned over and said, "I've had enough of your arrogant bullshit. I'm ordering you to make the arrest."

"No disrespect Sergeant, but there's a directive from the Commanding Officer of the Police Academy stating that, 'Rookies cannot execute any arrests that might cause them to have to attend court thereby taking time away from their schooling.' They don't want our graduating from the academy delayed. It seems that the academy is very crowded and I guess they're in a rush to get us out onto the streets. Perhaps you should call the Commanding Officer at home. Do you have his home number?" I asked with as much innocence that I could muster up. I then decided to add a little weight to my spiel.

"The Academy has a Lieutenant on patrol somewhere out here tonight; maybe you should call him and ask him what I should do. I'm sure that he would be able to shed a little light on this subject." I knew that he wouldn't risk taking that chance. If there happened to be a Lieutenant on patrol, and there wasn't, the Sergeant would now place himself in jeopardy of having the Lieutenant order him to make the arrest. And judging from Kong's behavior down street, the Sergeant, and his driver, wanted to keep as far away from this one man wrecking crew as I did. What we really needed, I thought, were more people for him to throw around, to kind of tire him out. After all, nobody could keep up his present destructive pace.

With the ball in the Sergeant's court, I waited for his decision. Finally, the Sergeant's chauffeur turned to him and asked, "Shall we get Bernie?"

"Bernie?" he paused for a few seconds before saying, "I guess we have no choice, but who's going to be the one to get him?" "Let the kid go," the driver said.

"Good idea."

With that momentous decision now a part of the past, the driver turned to me and said, "Hey wise ass, go around the corner to O'Brien's funeral parlor and get Bernie. Just knock on the door until you wake him up. Now understand one thing," with a word of caution added to his voice he continued, "Bernie can be a little grouchy when he first wakes up."

"Yeah," the Sergeant interjected, "last night he was sleeping in the movie theater down the street when the porter came in to sweep the floors. Well, this guy was playing his boom box, and kind of woke Bernie up. Bernie pulled out his gun and put six rounds through the guy's radio. He works all day as a moving man and being a cop is kind of his part time job. He tries to get at least six hours of sleep each night. Just be careful kid he gets pissed off rather easily when his sleep is interrupted." They both started to laugh.

Then they backed out of the street eliminating the possibility that Godzilla might overturn their car as they drove by. And a few minutes later I found myself standing in front of O'Brien's funeral parlor trying to find a cop named Bernie.

I tapped on the metal doorframe with my nightstick and waited for someone to respond. With no one answering, I tapped a little harder. Still no answer. I now gave the metal frame a hard whack causing the glass to quiver. "Lets see if that gets some sort of a response," I said. Right about now I was beginning to wonder if I had been given the right information by the Sergeant and his chauffeur or if were they sending me on some sort of humorous wild goose chase. At that moment I saw a shadow moving about the dimly lit funeral parlor. I watched as the figure neared the inside of the glass door. Next, I heard the door latch being unlocked. I pushed opened the door and entered.

A small night-light produced just enough light to enable me to see the ludicrous figure standing before me. This had to be Bernie and he was stranger than previously described. He was wearing his pajamas. His gun belt and colt service revolver were around his waist. Instead of shoes he was wearing a pair of house slippers. This seriocomic sight had short-cropped matted hair in the back of his head. In the front it pointed straight up. His demeanor gave him the appearance of someone who was just jolted from a sound sleep, or a person that has been wandering aimlessly about the halls of a mental institution. Physically, Bernie was a throw back in time, something out of the Paleolithic Era. A real anthropological find. This was the missing link, hair and all.

Standing around five feet, eight inches tall he weighed approximately two hundred and fifty five pounds. He was barrel-chested and had no neck. His shoulders, unopposed, connected directly to his head that looked to be twice the thickness of a normal head, or, at least the average everyday head that I was accustomed to seeing on top of people's necks. Another feature became immediately apparent. Bernie was an ex pug. His nose and ears indicated that he had spent many a round in the ring. He was most likely hit at one time or another with everything including the kitchen sink. Add all this to the fact that Bernie carried refrigerators on his back all day long. Bernie was a formidable opponent for any man. I made a quick decision to try to remain on his better side, if I could find it. "What the fuck do you want?" he grunted.

My God, this guy doesn't even talk, he growls, I thought. "The Sergeant sent me here to get you."

"The Sergeant did what?"

"Sent me over here to get you. I told him to leave you alone and let you sleep. If it were up to me I'd let you sleep right through the winter but you know how Sergeants are." If Bernie was going to be pissed off at the Sergeant, so was I.

"That son of a bitch. He knows that this is my sleeping time."

"Prick," I added.

"Well, now that you're here what the fuck do you want?"

"Not me, I don't want anything. It's the Sergeant and it really wasn't just his idea to wake you. That piece of shit chauffeur of his was the one who suggested it." Chalk up one chauffeur, I thought.

"He did?"

"Yep, he said, 'Wake up that missing link: bastard.'" I felt like I was starting to see a little bit of daylight. With any luck I just might survive this whole encounter. "So, what the fuck does he want?"

"Well, there's this giant." Not allowing me to finish my story Bernie snapped, "what giant?"

Could there be more than one? Wasn't one enough? Was this area of Manhattan infested with giants and I was the only one who didn't know about it? "There's this guy dressed like a Genie, wearing a turban, and he's...." "You mean Sinbad? Is he at it again?"

"If you call turning people into ICBM's as being at it again, then he's at it again."

"That son of a bitch. It was just last week that I parted his afro. That's why he's wearing that turban. As soon as he starts drinking gin, he gets out of control and starts pulling the same old shit. Get me my flashlight while I get dressed."

As I started walking around the room looking for Bernie's flashlight, I grew curious as to where he bedded down for the night. Gazing about the room, all I saw were empty folding chairs. The only remaining object my eyes spied was, "Oh, no!" I gulped, "a casket!" Could this be Bernie's bed? At that moment, I felt Bernie's eyes burning a hole through my shirt. I slowly turned to face him. Seeing my expression he asked, "Do you think that there's something wrong with that?"

Now be very careful in answering this question I thought to myself. After all if a person is crazy enough to ask me if I think that there is anything wrong with sleeping in a casket, that should say a lot about his mental condition. Bernie's synaptic gap wasn't sparking.

"No, definitely not, as a matter of fact," I whispered under my breath, "that casket reminds me of the one I have at home. Of course yours is a later model with the crucifixes on the side, and all." Knowing that Bernie tuned me out a long time ago, I went on, "and if I should ever have kids, I'm thinking about getting them bunk caskets. You know just pile them right up to the ceiling. What catalogue company do you recommend? I hear that the Arlington mausoleum catalogue is a good one."

My mumbling now concluded, Bernie shouted, "Hey kid, have you found my flashlight yet?"

Yeah, it's right next to your bed."

"All right, bring it to me."

I picked up Bernie's flashlight. The weight of it caused it to fall from my hand. I picked it up again. I examined it and discovered that it didn't have a bulb, or any protective glass, and instead of the cylinder containing the five batteries it required to operate the flashlight it was filled with poured lead. No wonder why it fell from my hands. This was Bernie's equalizer. As though he really needed one.

I thought this should prove very interesting. On one side of the coin, I had a giant that looked like he just climbed down from the beanstalk, whose nightly entertainment comprised of hurling people into flight like clay birds at a skeet range. On the other side, I had a Cro Magnon vampire who was pissed off because he had to climb out of his casket. In addition, he carried a flashlight that was heavy enough to serve as the anchor on The USS Nimitz. I concluded that it was time for me to take a stroll through Washington Square Park.

Later, I heard, in the middle of MacDougal Street Bernie walked up behind Sinbad and knocked him out cold with one blow from his flashlight. However, because he knew Sinbad and wanted to get back into his casket he didn't arrest him, instead, he had him treated at the local hospital as an aided case and released. Yes, Bernie could sleep in this bed and think nothing of it.

Chapter 27

ALTHOUGH JOEY'S FEVER was gone by the next morning, he still had to remain in the hospital waiting for the results of his culture. I noticed that he was climbing more and more into a shell. He no longer spoke but began to use hand signals as a form of communication. I wasn't sure if it was too painful for him to speak or if he was emotionally withdrawing from everyone, and everything, around him. He even reduced his eye contact. As he stared aimlessly into space, it was becoming difficult to get his attention. Several of the nurses and therapists attempted to get him involved in some sort of creative therapy. Most of the other children would either paint or participate in some form of group activity. Once a week they would meet to talk about how they were feeling both physically and emotionally. They spoke about their highs and their lows. Their fluctuating emotions ran the gamut. Joey wouldn't leave his room; instead he remained on top of his sheets, tuning out all suggestions that he join the group for any and all activities. I was concerned but I also knew my son; when he made up his mind to do something it was best to let him be. He already proved this to me and to the rest of the hospital staff by refusing to change his clothes.

Joey was so unresponsive and set in his ways, that he wasn't a fan of the nursing staff. I could hear several of the nurses saying, "Who has him today?" I was surprised to hear Michele say, "I want him." I thought that was very nice of her. She seemed to have developed a rapport with Joey. She treated him just as she treated the other children, as though he wasn't sick.

"So, Joey, you don't want your lunch today? Good, I'll eat it. Don't fill out tomorrows order form until I tell you what you don't want to eat tomorrow," she would joke.

In her spare time, they would sit and watch television together.

He liked her company and, in spite of her feelings towards me, I had come to think of her as a special person and glad that she had taken a personal interest in Joey.

One evening while Joey was sleeping, I was standing near the elevator about to run out for a bite to eat. Michele was on her way home. Making an attempt to be nice I asked her if she would like to join me. I wanted to thank her for taking care of Joey. I was also kind of hoping that we could alter our relationship by getting things back on the right foot. Maybe if she got to know me, she wouldn't think I was such a bad person after all. Her response was a cold no. "What did I do this time?" I asked myself. All that I ever did wrong was ask Joey to change his clothes, and try to beat rush hour traffic. A few days later, several of the other nurses started to treat me coolly. I was baffled at the frigid treatment I was receiving. It would take me a while before I would figure out this behavior.

I was glad that this visit was coming to an end. It was an exceptionally difficult one for me because across the hall from Joey's room was a young boy named Robert. Robert was suffering from cystic fibrosis and he was here to die. In this capacious medical facility, there wasn't a room that contained a piece of equipment that could save his life. Among the hordes of medical intellects that swelled the laboratories and hallways of this learning institution, not one individual possessed the knowledge to prevent death from adding him to its register. Robert wanted it all to end. He lost the will to go on. There simply wasn't any more fight left in him. At nineteen years of age, life had worn him down. Instead of his lungs burning, bursting from the crisp December air, he was barely able to inhale a whisper of the fetid foulness of his hospital room. Robert was supposed to be stepping up to the batter's box. He was entitled to take a full swing at life. This wasn't the case. Fate had determined otherwise. It was the final inning for Robert. Soon the game would be over.

I was lost for words, but that was nothing new in this place. Here I was always lost for words. How does one explain something like this?

There wasn't a word or book that could explicate what was taking place here. Worse, there wasn't any way to tune out what was transpiring around me. Not a closet big enough, or a hole deep enough. By simply being here, you had to hear, you had to see the despair. But more, you had to live the sin of being helpless. Yes, there was nothing I could say, so I said nothing.

Once home, Joey retired to his room to be left alone in his world. Although he didn't receive chemotherapy he was still physically sick from the emotional and psychological impact of Mt Sinai.

I had just finished making him comfortable when I heard a knock at the front door. I opened it and saw a few of his friends standing on the front steps. They asked if Joey would like to take a walk with them, "a short walk," they said. I told them that he was too sick to leave his room. I suggested they stop by tomorrow, that he might like to join them for a walk at that time. Even though Joey was up and around, he had not ventured away from the house on his own. He wasn't strong enough and lacked the desire. I didn't think he wanted anyone in the community to see him without hair. I spoke to him about the possibility of wearing a wig but he rejected my suggestion. Several of the cancer children at the hospital opted to wear wigs. Joey chose not to, instead he wore a bandanna similar to the swashbuckling pirates of old. Even while wearing his bandanna the fact that he had no eyelashes, or eyebrows, was still noticeable to the naked eye. In addition, his complexion was pale and ghostly looking.

To my delight, his friends returned the next day. They sat with him as they had a few times in the past and joked about his baldhead. He played the part of the clown laughing along with them and at himself. They asked him to join them for a walk around the neighborhood. I could see that he wanted to accompany them, but remained a bit reluctant. After a few minutes of prodding on their part, he looked at me and asked, "Dad, do you think I can go?"

"Of course you can go. A little fresh air will do you a world of good."

I was outside talking to his friends when they did something that would live inside me until the day I leave this earth. Each one took out a bandanna and put it on their head.

Now, they all looked alike. They weren't going to allow their friend to be different. I wanted to grab those boys and hug them. "Thanks boys. Thank you so much," I said. Joey took his short walk with his friends. He returned home feeling tired, but it was good to see him participating in something that he hadn't been able to do for so long.

Someday, maybe he would be able to run just like he used to. It was possible, wasn't it?

Christmas was soon upon us but it would be a very different Christmas for all of us.

We had gone through difficult holidays before when the children's mother left but this wasn't comparable to any other depressing or worrisome time of our lives. This was very different. Joey's survival was the issue this Christmas. How could the significance of anything in the past be comparable? It couldn't.

The family gathered together on Christmas Eve to give thanks just as we had done in the past. This year we celebrated the holidays at the home of my brother Sal and his wife. He remarried years ago, owned a beautiful waterfront home on Long Island Sound and was blessed with two wonderful children from his second marriage. His two daughters from his first marriage had decided to live with him too. He was a lucky man and his children were fortunate to have two selfless parents.

I admired his achievements and success. Many times I reflected back to what my lawyer had said a few years ago. "If you want to be happy then concentrate on your future. Time and the flaw in people's personalities who perpetrate evilness will take care of the rest." He was right. It did in my brother's case. His ex-wife never attained the happiness she sought. To the contrary, her life ventured down many a bad street. In simple terms, "she backed the wrong horse." This year I would not be able to rejoice in the spirit of Christmas. All I could do was move my lips and pretend. To make matters worse it was Joey's birthday, his fourteenth.

That night I couldn't take my eyes off Joey. Regardless of where I looked, my eyes always came back to him. When your child has cancer, you spend your life anticipating that at any moment something is going to happen. Exactly what you anticipate you're not sure of, but you worry and you check anyway. You have an uncontrollable need to know that your child is feeling fine. Satisfied that he is, two minutes later you ask yourself is he still O.K? All you do is check, check, and check again. Cancer does that to parents. Why? Because cancer is so strong that it reaches outside of the child, touching people in ways they never dreamed possible. You won't read about it in any books but you will live it.

I watched as Joey opened each of his gifts and I thought who would ever have believed a year ago that this would have taken place in his life, in our lives. Frail, ashen, and wearing his bandanna, he kissed everyone and thanked them for being so generous. I read the sentiment of those who kissed him in return. I knew what they were thinking. As Joey was cutting his birthday cake, blowing out the candles, and making the customary birthday wish, we all wanted next Christmas to be different.

I came up with my own theory that my luck would change as the New Year rolled in. Yes, I was having bad luck because it was an odd year. An even year would rectify all my problems. Sounded pretty good to me, I convinced myself.

From my bed I watched the ball at Times Square as it gradually brought in the New Year. Everyone was partying and all I wanted was one good night's sleep. What an exciting single life I'm living, I thought. It was five minutes past mid-night when I was jolted by the phone. It was Tammy.

"Dad?"

"Tammy, what's going on?"

"Dad, I don't know how to tell you this but while the car was parked someone hit it, and crushed in the front door.

"Tammy, before you continue let me take a wild guess. You took my car to wherever it is that you are and not the Bug.

"Dad how did you know?" "It's a reoccurring dream. I'll be there in a few minutes."

Chapter 28

JOEY WAS GROWING bored being at home. I thought I would never hear the day that he would come to me and ask, "Dad, do you think that I could try going back to school?" I thought about it for a few minutes then asked him "would you really like to try going back to school?"

Do you mean it?"

"Yes, I mean it. I miss my friends."

"Fine, then tomorrow you start school."

My emotions varied. I wanted him to attend school, but I would be a bundle of nerves anticipating problems that would probably never occur. I was especially concerned about his Broviac, worried that someone might accidentally rip it from his chest. But how could I say no to him? I couldn't place my worries ahead of his decision to move on, to try to resume his life.

I watched from behind the window of the house as he walked to the bus stop. It reminded me of his first day of school when he was just a little boy. I knew, at that moment, that my day would be a long one. I would have bitten my nails down to the quick but I had already done that. Later that day, I saw him walking down the street towards our house carrying a big box. "What's in the box," I asked "It's a cake. Dad, when I arrived at school they all cheered and clapped as though I was some sort of hero or something. Then they brought out this big, kind of like, birthday cake. Everywhere I went in the school there were posters that said, 'Welcome back Joey.' Why do you think they did all that?"

"That's an easy question to answer. When someone hits a home run people cheer. Joey, you're a home run."

Two weeks later Joey's class took a trip to Washington D.C. Dr. G. would not allow him to accompany them. We were sitting in the house when the doorbell rang. It was the UPS deliveryman. He was holding a long cardboard cylinder addressed to Joey. Enclosed was a picture of the entire Junior High School class on the front steps of the capitol building. They were holding a long banner that read, "We miss you Joey."

I was beginning to understand how eighteen courses of chemotherapy could conceivably be prolonged into three years of treatment or more. Joey was constantly running fevers requiring more hospitalization than I had anticipated. Often now, his white cell count was low delaying his chemotherapy. In-between courses of chemotherapy he was undergoing MRI's, bone scans, X-rays and a multitude of other tests; including an echo cardiogram to determine if his heart was damaged and his least favorite test of all, the CAT scan with contrast. On one occasion, they mistakenly performed his CAT scan, to his delight, without contrast. When Dr. G. found out that the contrast was omitted she raised the roof with the CA department and instructed Joey to retake the test. On that day I gave him plenty of room. I don't think that I had ever seen him so angry.

A short time after his last chemotherapy session, Joey began to urinate blood. I feared, as did members of his medical staff, that his cancer had spread. It was decided that he should remain in the hospital for several additional tests hoping that the results would give us some insight as to why he was encountering this problem. A determination was made that the chemotherapy was eating away at his bladder, kidneys and urinary tract. I could see that he was tiring of the whole hospital scene. I didn't know how much more he would be willing to tolerate before he decided that he simply had had enough. I don't think that I could have endured it this long. It was two years since he was first diagnosed with cancer. His spirit was dwindling and yet the cancer remained in his body.

Many of the children we had met were no longer there. All around us cancer was unleashing its fury, taking its toll of victims, feeding like an out of control Pac-Man. All that remained were their graffitied names on the walls and their memories; stories about who they were and what they were like.

Some children died at home while others died on the pediatric floor. When a child died on the ward, a noticeable change took place. I saw and heard parents crying. Doctor's and nurses congregated together. The prevailing storm, much like a hurricane, was followed by a calm. In the end, there was one common denominator, sadness. Yes, it was always followed by sadness.

In some cases, the children were personally familiar with the child who died. They may have known him from their numerous stays at the hospital or from off day visits to the hospital clinic. Regardless of how hard parents tried to keep the news from their children, they usually found out about it through one means or another. Very little around us remained a secret. I made up my mind that if Joey knew the child I would mention it to him before he received word from other sources. Then I followed it up by explaining that he was doing extremely well and mentioning names of children who were now in remission. I didn't know of any other way to handle it. This was all trial and error to me. One hell of a way to learn anything.

I wasn't able to escape the news that a child had died. I could sense it a mile away. I hated the fact that I was so street smart. What managed to get by other people never eluded me. I knew what people were talking about down the hall, in every room, and in every corner of this place. If I happened to be engaged in a conversation with someone, I was still aware of what was transpiring around me. I couldn't tune it out. I tried, but I was never successful. I didn't miss a thing. I had been a cop too long. My survival skills were too finely tuned to miss anything. Whether it was of importance or not, I knew about it.

Many times I saw parents crying. Usually different parents who happened to be standing on the same floor, in the same place, and crying the same tears the parents who preceded them cried. They were just different faces.

Cancer patients and their families battle cancer one day at a time. A satellite view is not part of the package. It's prohibited by the nature of the disease. If a patient has a good day, you live that day for all its worth. You bleed it, because tomorrow is without promise. It's not a selection on a menu.

The parents that I met were nice people. None of them were given a choice saying, "If you refrain from, or engage in, a specific type of behavior you are running the risk that your child could be afflicted with cancer." These parents were walking around wondering what they did to bring this diabolical disease into the lives of their children, and for not discovering it earlier. But how could they? They were looking for sprained ankles, torn ligaments and pulled muscles. Some faulted themselves for their child's cancer. They knew that the odds were in cancer's favor and they also knew that every action they took to thwart its aggression hurt their child. In simple terms, when you treat cancer you harm your child. Your child is cancer's shield, its refuge. Cancer is cruel, it's smug, and it's coy.

I wanted to aid the parents that I met but I didn't know how. If I did I would have helped. One night I was standing outside of Joey's room. Time had moved on, Joey had just concluded his twelfth course of chemotherapy. He was scheduled to begin radiation treatments next week. This course of chemotherapy was an exceptionally difficult one for him. He was vomiting and urinating blood and had just finished battering his head into the wall. With the vomit and bile dripping from his nose, he tried to relieve his pain by causing more pain, only to a different area of his body. I called for help and a nurse ran in to give him a sedative. I didn't know how long he would sleep. All I knew was that I couldn't remain in his room for another second. I needed to be someplace else.

Standing in the hall, leaning against his door, I scanned the corridor of Falk 2. I could see the children in their beds. Some were receiving chemotherapy; others were being treated for different serious afflictions, most with strange names that I was unable to pronounce. All were life threatening.

The air, depending on which way you tilted your head, smelled of a combination of vomit, antiseptic medication, and human excrement.

All I could think was, this place never let's up, the volume is always turned up high.

I was standing there for about fifteen minutes when I heard a commotion, yelling and crying coming from the opposite side of the nurses' station. I watched as a woman in her late thirties exited a room. She was crying, walking about the hall appearing dazed, and in a great deal of emotional pain. As she found her way to where I was standing, I could see that she was completely distraught. She began to say something but her hysteria muffled her ability to speak, or at least communicate her problem to me. I automatically reached out and put my arms around her. I had always found it upsetting witnessing someone crying. It didn't matter if you were a woman, or a man, if you were crying somehow you would find your way into my arms. Such was the Cancerian in me. I told her that I would be glad to listen to her, but she would first have to calm herself if she wanted me to help her, or at least hear her. "Why don't you tell me what's going on?" I asked.

"It's my son."

"What about your son?"

"He is cursing at me and he won't stop. He's never spoken to me like this before. Never!"

"How old is your son and what is he being treated for?"

"He's sixteen and he is being treated for cancer."

"Where is his cancer? I mean, what type of cancer does he have?"

"His cancer is in his face and his bones around his face. They've already removed half his jaw bone, and now it's..." she was unable to finish her sentence.

From what she told me, I had a pretty good idea of what was taking place. The boy's cancer was spreading. He had reached a stage where life was becoming too much to handle. He couldn't bear to get up in the morning. I wondered how, and where, a sixteen year-old child would find the courage to look in a mirror that reflected half a face, half of what he used to be. And why should he ever want tomorrow to come? There was only one place for him to go to unleash his anger. Only one person's love was strong enough to tolerate his bitterness, his mother. She wasn't going anywhere. He knew that she would never stop loving him no matter what he looked like or how he behaved. She would hold him, love him, and kiss what little of his face remained to be kissed. To her, he would always be her wonderful handsome son. He had to strike out at someone. When you're sixteen and dying you have a right to be angry. I didn't know what to tell her. I wasn't a mother. As my deep as my love was for my son, it ended where hers began. She carried her son in her womb, sharing in the pain of his birth, and now she remained on the sidelines, helpless, as cancer desecrated her creation. I wanted to help her but I could only say what my heart told me to say. I could only tell her what I believed I would have done had I been in her place and I wasn't even sure of that.

"Let me ask you a question. Before your son became stricken with cancer, did he ever speak to you as he did tonight?"

"No, never. He wouldn't think of it. He's a wonderful boy."

"From listening to you, I didn't think you would have anything but a wonderful child." I thought to myself, aren't all these children wonderful? Every boy and girl that I met in this place was extraordinary and likable. "Let me make a suggestion, whether you decide to follow my advice is entirely up to you but hear me out anyway." I told her that her son loved her very much, that she was the only mother he had. But that didn't mean she had to stand there and let him hurt her. He wouldn't expect that of her. She had to be the mother she always had. That was the mother he wanted, the mother he needed, and the mother he knew and deserved.

I didn't know how but somewhere inside her she was going to have to find the strength to go back into his room and show him that she was still his mother and that he was not to speak to her like that, not now, not ever. If she had to raise her voice louder than his, then so be it. She had to finish this thing now because it was not tonight that we were talking about but tomorrow and the next day. Her son needed her to keep her dignity because he needed to keep his. He needed his old Mom back, that wonderful woman who always had a way of making things better, and he needed her now more than at any other time during his life. I knew that if she quit on herself she would also quit on him. But who could really blame or fault her for wanting to quit? It's just that the rules didn't allow it. Quitting was never an option given to parents.

I held her for a while and finally said, "When you're done take a walk back over here, put your head on my shoulder, and cry. It's okay, I'm not going anywhere." She did as I suggested. That night I cried too. I cried for her and for her child. It wasn't long before her son passed away.

Chapter 29

JOEY LOOKED AS though he was going to sleep through the night. I was extremely tired and needed a night's rest so I decided to go home. My mind was fixed on his pending radiation treatments. I was aware that both of us would have our strength taxed to the limit.

It was 2:00 a.m. when I pulled into the driveway. As I entered the house, I tripped over two male bodies sleeping on the den floor. Not knowing who they were I immediately came to the conclusion that Claudine was home and whomever these people were, and whatever their reason for being here, had to do with her. I elected to worry about it in the morning.

Early the next morning, I heard Claudine knocking on my bedroom door. She wanted to know how Joey was feeling. "Fine," I said. "Now before you leave my bedroom, would you mind telling me who those strangers are camping out in my den?"

"Oh, I met the two of them at a party last night in Manhattan and they needed a place to spend the night. They're heading out to the Hamptons today. One is named Mario and the other is Carlos. Both of them are from Spain and they're studying dance at the Joefrey Ballet."

"Good, I'm glad that they are dancers that should make it easier for them to pirouette out the door. And make sure that they leave my DVD and television before they leave. Let me make one thing clear to you. I'm not running a halfway house for homeless dancers. Now, pay very close attention to what I am about to tell you. I do not want any strangers in my house when I'm not home. That includes circus clowns, jugglers, gypsies, members of assorted cults, midgets, Cyclopes, fish and anything that needs air to survive.

Understand? And, Oh, I forgot unicorns, unless they're house broken. I don't want any of them in the house either."

"Yes, Dad."

It's always, "Yes, Dad," and then everybody does as they want around here anyway.

I wondered what the color of the sky was in her world.

Regardless of what is transpiring around them, teenagers feel their needs are paramount to what may be taking place in the rest of the world. They develop a selfinduced protective shield. In our present situation, I believed this to be healthy. It made it possible for the girls to remove themselves from the reality of Joey's illness. It also assisted me in keeping occupied with other events that I considered comical situations.

After Claudine's friends departed I sat down with the two girls hoping to bring myself up to date on what was transpiring in their never mundane lives. Claudine informed me that she was being inducted into the honor society at Fordham. I was delighted to hear the news and said that I would make the ceremony. Tammy was getting ready to attend her high school prom. She was venturing out that afternoon to pick out a dress with her girlfriend and her friend's mother. I vowed to be home to see her off to her prom. She also wanted to fly to Arizona to tour Arizona State University where she was thinking of attending college. "Party school," I said.

"Dad, how did you know that?"

"What I find amazing is that you children think that I know so little about everything." I informed her that I wouldn't be able to accompany her because I didn't want to leave Joey alone. She understood. Fortunately, her Aunt Donna volunteered to chaperon her. However, I promised to fly to Arizona when it was time for her to start her school year. That seemed to make her happy. My life was filled with promises. I kept them all.

I would miss Tammy while she was away at school. I respected her and liked her.

She possessed the typical middle child personality, the mediator, the friend, the smooth running wheel that never required grease. She was looking forward to going away to college and I would not laden her with the thought that her brother might not be here when she returned. Those thoughts were for me alone. I would think them in the privacy of my bedroom, alone in my car, and in the quietness of a crowd. I would not share them with anyone, especially my children.

We had all journeyed far as individuals because we were first, and foremost, a family. I would not allow anything to jeopardize that. In running the household, I never created any doubt as to who was in charge. I also learned that the children reflected my moods as much as I reflected theirs. At times I may have disappointed them. But who in this world hasn't been disappointed by others? Whatever their decisions, I wanted them to feel as though I was standing there beside them. Not limited by objection, or prejudice.

They had the right to do, or become, anything they wanted in life.

It was only a few days prior that I noticed Tammy was visibly upset. With so much transpiring around us, I was unable to pinpoint the cause of her sadness. After a few minutes of probing, she told me that she had been pressured by a friend to accompany her to an abortion clinic. To Tammy, life was precious but her age and loyalty to her friend demanded that she remain silent. It was a bad choice on her part, and although I understood the terrible predicament she was placed in, I told her that I was disappointed that she had not come to me for guidance.

I knew her friend, and was aware that her parents were intolerably strict. At every opportunity, their daughter rebelled at their rigidness. I remembered her telling me how much she wished that I were her father. She said that I listened and at least we had fun in our household. I'm not sure of the advice I would have given her. But she was right, I would have listened. If I learned anything being a single parent, it was that one parent willing to listen superseded two parents who were not.

Throughout my life, I had seen the best and the worst of mankind.

I also learned that bad things happen to good children and caring parents. It's just that they tend to happen less. I also believed that the most difficult phase in raising children was transcending those years where their youthful exuberance was running at full throttle. For a single parent, it stands to reason that this period was twice as difficult. The secret to success is selflessness, love, the ability to listen, humor, a blackjack, and a pocket containing one huge rabbit. A mere foot would never suffice. It also didn't hurt if God, in his infinite wisdom, sent you an airborne division of archangels.

It was early morning and the girls were just finishing their breakfast when I heard Tammy ask, "Claudine, are you ready?" "Ill be ready in five minutes." "Ready for what?" I asked.

"Oh, Claudine is taking me for a driving lesson in your car."

"Tammy, do you know how you children are always complaining that I never pay attention to you when you speak. Well, this time I heard you but just to make sure I heard you correctly why don't you repeat what you said a few seconds ago?"

"Claudine is taking me for a driving lesson."

"Okay, that's what I thought you said. Do you realize that taking a driving lesson from Claudine is like asking Jeffrey Dohmner to come over the house to show you how to carve the Thanksgiving Turkey? Are you crazy?"

"Well, Dad, somebody has to take me, and you're too busy." "But, you already have your driver's license."

"I do, but I want t try driving your car. C'mon let her take me?"

"Good luck, and I suggest that you might consider having a Saint Christopher armored suit made before you climb into that car with your sister."

It wasn't long before I discovered that my fears were all unwarranted. They never made it out of the driveway. Passing an opening in the fence, I could see a white object pointing skyward. It was my car. Somehow they managed to run over several railroad ties wedging them under the car. They also flattened my mailbox. I guess they didn't want to inform me of the prospective launching of my car because the two of them were working feverishly trying to remedy their present situation. Shaking my head, I walked to the front of the house. I jacked up the car, removed the railroad ties, went to the post office, paid for a postal box, and returned to the quietness of the hospital.

Chapter 30

PROMISES ARE IMPORTANT. They should be kept. After all, when we promise someone to do, or not to do something, we are giving our word that we will fulfill our obligation. I didn't break my word, not to anyone. My word was good. So I felt bad that I had not delivered on my promise to take Joey on vacation. I tried my best to deliver on my pledge, but Joey had been too sick to make the trip. The few times I thought that he was feeling well enough to go, Dr. G. wouldn't allow him to travel. "It's too risky a trip. If he should become sick in some desolate Caribbean hospital what are you going to do? What about the risk of bacteria? Those places are loaded with any one of a million forms of bacteria," she said.

Dr. G. was right. I had learned that bacteria could cause serious infections to cancer patients, especially in children with low blood counts. Most bacteria that we come in contact with don't usually cause infections to a normal healthy person but they could infect a child whose blood counts were impaired. Children with implanted catheters run a much higher risk of bacterial infection than those without this device. But, infection could occur in any child undergoing cancer treatment.

Then there was opportunist infection to consider which may not cause infection in healthy children, but could cause serious infection in children whose immune system was affected by cancer or its treatment. They included fungal infections, thrush or yeast infections, and pneumocystis pneumonia. Ordinarily, it was difficult to prevent exposure to these organisms because they were all around us. The hot humid climate of the Caribbean was home to this type of bacteria. If that wasn't enough to consider, I knew that Joey would also run the risk of viral infection. Viral infections were no more than minor infections, that is, unless you had cancer. In that case, they took on a different perspective of a more serious note. When a child showed signs of an infection, they were usually placed on a medicine called Bactrim to help ward off pneumocystis pneumonia.

The problem with viral infection was that viruses were extremely hard to identify and could not be treated with antibiotics. Minor viral illnesses in a child with normal blood counts were allowed to run their course. The cause of infection could be difficult to find in children receiving cancer treatment. Children with low blood counts and other signs of infection (such as fever) were treated with antibiotics regardless if a virus or bacteria happened to be suspect.

There were also rashes to consider and a host of other issues. If we wanted to go on vacation, we would have to take a truckload of medication with us for his Broviac. Each time Joey ventured in and out of the water he would have to clean his Broviac and apply a clean bandage. I was also worried about the strong rays of the sun. Joey's skin would burn and fever would most likely follow. As much as I wanted to keep my promise to Joey, I had to break it. Joey, to his credit, never mentioned the fact that I had not kept my word. He would never bring it up. It was not his way of doing things. He was too nice a boy to ever try to make anyone feel guilty. But I felt guilty nonetheless. I watched him work on an old gas operated scooter. My driveway looked like Sanford and Son lived here. I don't know how he did it but somehow he managed to breathe new life into this old scooter. I told him that he could ride it through the fields behind the house, but not to ride it around the local streets.

An hour later there was a knock on the front door. It was Joey and he was accompanied by a police officer.

"Yes, officer, can I help you?" "Is this your son?"

"Sure is."

"Well, he is riding this scooter illegally."

"Joey where were you riding the scooter? You weren't riding it through the streets were you?"

"No, you told me not to."

"Excuse me," the officer said. "He can't ride this scooter at all. I'm going to have to insist that you tell him not to ride it again. In a year or two he'll be legal, he could ride it then."

"I'm sorry I can't tell him that, nor will I. I will tell him to be very careful riding it and to enjoy himself. That's all I will do," I said.

The officer looked at me, not used to having someone publicly defy him. He didn't know what to make of my statement. At that moment, Joey walked by with his bandana removed. The officer gave a double take. He looked at him and at me and asked, "Does he have?"

"Yes."

"Tell him to have a good time and to be careful out there." "Thank you officer, I will."

During our last stay at Falk 2, I knew that we would not be returning for a while because Joey was scheduled to begin radiation treatments. We said our good-byes to the hospital staff. I had grown very fond of many of them, especially Michele. I admired her resolve, her kindness and love for these unfortunate children whose lives met with a catastrophic turn of events.

I discovered that Michele's opinion of me had changed one day while she thumbed her way through Joey's medical file. To her amazement she had detected that Mary was not my wife, but my sister-in-law. I had assumed that this was a well known fact. Over the years I had grown accustomed to the neglect that the Joey's mother had shown him. But it was inconceivable to the people who worked here, who witnessed firsthand the constant pain and anguish of these poor children, that a mother had not visited a son afflicted with cancer. If men found this concept difficult to understand, women had even a harder time comprehending it.

The more I knew about Michele the more I began to like her. I learned that Michele was recently divorced. She lived in an apartment in upper Manhattan. Until her father's recent death from diabetes, she had commuted on a daily basis to her parent's Long Island home where she aided her father who was trying to adjust to life after having his leg amputated. I wondered how one leaves a personal tragedy of that magnitude and comes here where the sorrow in every room outdoes the sorrow taking place in the next. Still, with all the despondency occurring in her life, she gave to these children whole heartily without reservation. No, there weren't any deals with Michele, what you saw is what you got, and what I saw was wonderful.

One evening, wanting to ask Michele a medically related question I said, "Would you like to join me for lunch?" That's not what I wanted to say, I thought. I continued, "We could meet at Jones Beach Saturday afternoon." I couldn't believe how nervous I was. I had disarmed gun-totting robbers with less trepidation. "You know you don't have to go if you don't want to," I added.

"Did I say that I didn't want to go?" "No."

"Then why don't you relax and let me answer your question?"

"Right, that's what I'll do, I'll relax." What's relax?" I asked.

"I would like that," she replied.

"You would?"

"Yes, I'm not as bad as my bark."

"Thank God." I smiled as she walked away.

A week after our first meeting, we enjoyed a Broadway play and not long after that she stopped by the house to pay me a visit. Yet, as much as I enjoyed her visits, it was Joey who won her heart. To my surprise and delight, she invited me to her apartment saying that she wanted to make me a special dinner. She also warned me that she was the world's worse cook.

Well, I was warned, but how bad of a cook could she be? I thought. I should have heeded her warning. She was indeed the world's worse cook. An Irish lass trying to conquer the secrets of meatballs and spaghetti. I walked over to the stove to stir the sauce, the large wooden spoon stood in the middle of the sauce, erect, not quivering. Attempting to move it, I realized that it would have been easier to row a boat. I was certain that my digestive system was in deep trouble. I took a bite. My eyes crossed as I attempted to force down the food. I gulped a glass of water swallowing the contents in my mouth whole. This stuff is a population killer, I hope it never gets in our reservoir system, I thought.

"So how is it she asked?" "Fine, I mean good."

"You don't like it. Do you?"

"No, I like it," I said. While thinking what we needed here was a United Nations inspection team. Why should war-like nations develop anthrax when they had this stuff available?

"Would you like to take some home for Joey?" she asked.

I forced myself to say, "Sure." Just what he needed, I thought, chemotherapy in a jar.

It wasn't long before we became good friends. Sometimes I would meet her on her day off. We would take long walks on the beach as we talked about a whole host of issues. At other times, we would talk on the phone for hours and when all that I was able to feel was despair, she was there for me at any hour of the day or night. She was teaching me how to do something that I had forgotten how to do, to trust again. It felt good. Michele was special and I knew that the first time I met her. I was growing very much in love with her.

Michele called me at home one afternoon and asked if I would like to accompany her to a birthday party the following Saturday. "My pleasure," I responded. The party, as it turned out, was for one of the young cancer patients, a sixteen year old boy named Antohny who had been afflicted with Osteosarcoma. In his case, cancer of the bone of his lower leg. Fortunately, surgery, in conjunction with chemotherapy, saved his life.

As we entered the catering hall, we were greeted warmly. Michele was treated as though she was royalty and I received a special hug from Anthony's parents; one reserved strictly for the parents of club members.

Upon seeing Anthony, I remembered him from Falk 2. I had always wondered what became of him, but I never found the courage to ask. Michele explained that he had been in remission and everything was going well for Anthony and his parents. I guess the look on my face gave my thoughts away because she squeezed my hand and said, "they do make it."

"You don't know how much I want to be the one giving the party," I said. "You'll have your party. You'll have your special day."

"Promise me that you'll be there."

"I promise that I'll be there to share it with you."

I needed to hear those words from her. It felt good not to be alone.

Joey's five weeks of radiation treatments turned into nine weeks. I knew a lot about chemotherapy, but radiation was all new to me. I was ambivalent and apprehensive, not so much because he was going to start radiation but because he would have to cease chemotherapy treatments for a while. I didn't realize that I would feel this way, that I wouldn't want him to stop chemotherapy. I felt that as long as he was receiving chemotherapy he was safe from the bandit within his body. Chemotherapy was his police officer. Now the police officer was going on vacation. With its absence, could radiation be able to hold its own? It was cutting in on the dance, but did it know the steps?

The radiologist in charge of Joey's treatment was Dr. White. I had never met her, nor would I. Very few patients ever met radiologists. They, because of the nature and location of their work, roamed the inner hallways and the deepest depths of medical facilities. Technicians followed radiologists' orders. They were the ones that patients saw on a regular basis. I had no idea what radiologists looked like. Did they resemble the rest of the members of the homo sapien race or were they Vulcan in appearance? The problem created by their absence was that there was no one that I could talk to about his treatment. Which meant no answers to many questions. That wasn't good, at least not in my way of looking at things.

During Joey's first visit, an area was mapped out on his body scheduled to be radiated. This was done by placing dye marks under his skin resembling a tattoo or a connect the dot game. The radiation itself would entail no more than taking a simple X ray of a targeted area. The plan was to gradually decrease the area being X-rayed. This was referred to as coneing. The reason a wide area, usually outside of the suspected cancer area, was radiated was because of the possibility that a few cancer cells might be lurking about. One cell missed today could be the one that leads the charge tomorrow.

Day after day we would arrive at the radiology department only to be told to return home without Joey receiving treatment. The excuses were always the same. We are overbooked. The X-ray machine is broken, and so it went on and on.

I spent endless hours sitting in the reception area waiting for Joey while he was being inundated with radiation particles. The patients sitting next to me, waiting their turns, were not a pleasant sight. Some were missing limbs, many had their voice boxes removed and others looked as though they would not survive the day. I tried not to talk or look in their direction. I wanted them to remain nameless and faceless. I didn't want to know anything about them. I didn't want to know if they were married, if they had children or the name of their cat. I knew what cancer could do. I had my fill of it, I didn't need to see or know any more. The coldness of the labs chilled me to the bone and the smell of the chemicals used to develop film glued itself to my nostrils making me want to vomit.

At first, Joey's radiation treatment had little negative effect on him. It appeared that it would be less iniquitous than his chemotherapy. After a few treatments, his skin started to redden. Dr. G. had mentioned to me that radiation treatments, especially the dose that he was scheduled to receive, could cause serious problems to his internal organs. I had to wonder what more could be done to this child. He was already bleeding from each end of his body. Dr. G. was very concerned that his reproductive organs might be permanently damaged. I told her that issue did not concern me. All that I wanted her to do was to kill his cancer. "Keep my son alive."

After the first few weeks of radiation I could see a big difference in the way he felt; not for the better. The little strength he had before he began radiation treatments was now gone. He suffered from diarrhea and a few weeks later his hip and pelvis were beet red. I asked him how he compared radiation to chemotherapy. "No comparison, Dad, radiation is easy compared to chemotherapy." He made me laugh. He was my hero.

One particular afternoon, just before leaving the hospital, I felt a migraine of the highest order coming on. As I drove home, my headache was drilling its way down to my little toe, forcing me to pull the Cougar off to the side of the road where Joey and I vomited competitively at calibrated intervals. Talk about father and son activities; I was certain that a game of horseshoes sure had this beat. I don't know how I managed to complete the trip home, but I did. Arriving in our driveway, Joey said, "hey, Dad, let me help you out of the car for a change." He grabbed my arm, helped me up the stairs, and into the bathroom where I proceeded to vomit until I could not vomit anymore. "I'm so sick," I said. He looked at me and answered, "Boy are you a wimp." He was right. I felt like this for one day. He felt like this, and worse, on an average of ten days a month. I couldn't do what he did. Very few people could.

With Joey's radiation therapy completed, it was time for him to resume his chemotherapy treatments. With a free week remaining before we re-entered Mt. Sinai, I asked Tony and Mary to keep an eye on him while I fulfilled my promise to accompany Tammy to Arizona. I would only be gone for a weekend but that would give me enough time to get her situated in her dorm.

Upon arriving in Arizona, I Immediately discovered one thing. The tolerable climate rumor we had all heard so much about was just that, a rumor. Humidity or not, one hundred and fifteen degrees was too hot. To cool off, people who lived in Arizona traveled to Kenya. I couldn't touch the steering wheel of my car. I wasn't able to sit in a pool chair without scalding my arm on the metal frame. The bottom of my feet burned walking in the shade. More importantly, there were no people to be found anywhere during the day. I discovered that they were all inside or underground in their air-conditioned houses, too afraid to venture out. I told Tammy that the only reason the pioneers decided to build a town here was because their horses died from the heat heading west leaving them no choice but to remain here. Two days later with my promise kept I returned to New York and Joey.

While touring ASU with Tammy, I had made a decision that when I returned to New York I would take a few classes at Stony Brook University. My mind was stagnating. Plus, with endless hours spent idly sitting at Mt. Sinai I thought that I should at least read something worthwhile. I didn't care what classes I signed up for, that wasn't the issue. Years ago I had received my college degree in dental technology but my college days were a bare glimmer in my memory bank and I had promised myself that one day I would finish my education.

I applied to Stony Brook University. While registering I was asked if there were any particular subjects that I might be interested in. "It didn't matter," I said, "as long as one of them was abnormal psychology." I told the registrar that I wanted to try to gain a better understanding of my children. An hour later I registered for three classes totaling nine credits. I guess my real reason for doing this was because I wanted a reprieve from children and cancer. I needed a few moments to be me in a world where I wasn't a provider, or a Dad, but a whole person that had a personality of his own complete with likes and dislikes. A person, who didn't have all the answers to every problem, but had his own problems that required answers. I needed time alone. Not a lot of time. I wasn't going anywhere. I never would.

During my first day of classes, I wandered over to the cafeteria to purchase a cup of coffee. I noticed a few demonstrators marching outside protesting what they believed to be the high cost of State tuition. I believed that compared to what I was paying for Claudine at Fordham, and Tammy at ASU, this was a bargain. I sat down to enjoy my cup of coffee when one of the demonstrators approached me.

"You know we are protesting the cost of tuition. Would you like to join us?" She asked. I laughed. She said "If you're scared, don't be, nothing will happen to you, everything is relatively quiet. Have you ever been to a demonstration or a protest before?" she inquired. I didn't answer but remembered. "Your name, Sir?"

"Spock, Dr. Benjamin Spock."

"What do you do for a living?"

"I'm a Pediatrician and author."

I proceeded to the next person and asked, "What is your name sir?" "Robert Bly."

"Are you employed and if so what do you do?" "I'm a poet, author and professor."

I moved on. "Your name?"

"I'm Reverend Sloan Coffin."

"I think I know what you do for a living."

"Next, you are?"

"Galway Kinnell, and I'm a professor and poet."

Another six inquires and I was finished.

The crowd had swelled to over one hundred thousand and was getting larger by the second. All were protesting the war in Viet Nam. I was standing, or leaning, in a nice secluded doorway hoping to keep the low profile that I valued so much. I don't know what went wrong but suddenly the crowd of blue around me opened up and I was standing face to face with a Police Department Chief. He approached me and one other officer. He ordered us to direct a group of men who were sitting on steps of the White Hall Street Induction Center to move. If they refused, they were to be placed under arrest. Of course I was told to give them their legal rights under the law, something that I had trouble doing because I could never remember all of the rights that they were entitled to. I was still working on the Ten Commandments. Usually I would mumble my way through them until I came to one that I thought I knew. I would then speak a little louder so everyone around me might falsely perceive that I knew what I was doing. I tried my best to convince each of these individuals to move, but they weren't going anywhere. All I wanted was to go back to the comfort of my doorway and remain out of view because I was having another bad gun day. Once again I forgot my gun at home. It wasn't as though it was lost or anything. I knew it was in the house, someplace. To hide the fact that I didn't have my gun, on the way to this demonstration, I stopped at a local delicatessen and purchased a bottle of coke. I asked the storeowner to pour the contents down the sink. I then shoved the empty bottle into my holster. The delicatessen owner looked at me with a strange worrisome look on his face. Poor fellow, I thought, if he knew me better he wouldn't be so concerned. I didn't have a gun but at least I had a bulge under my winter blouse.

Trying one last time to persuade the protesters to move, I then called for a Paddy Wagon, loaded my new friends into the rear, and jumped in with them. The officer that was assisting me sat up front with the driver. I told my prisoners that if they cooperated we could all conceivably be home before dark. Looking at them, I could tell that something was obviously wrong. I noticed that with every move I made they flinched, each raising their hand to protect their face and head. Finally, I asked, "What in the world is wrong with you people?"

One of them replied, "When are you going to beat us with your stick?" "Beat you with my stick? What do you mean beat you with my stick?" Another demonstrator voiced, "Why don't you just shoot us?"

Somewhat bewildered at their behavior and comments I said, "Look fellows, I have no idea what you're talking about. First of all, I'm not going to hit anyone with this stick." Actually, I was having enough problems trying to learn how to twirl this ridiculous thing. Every time I thought that I was getting the knack of it, I hit myself in the shin. It usually happened when someone was asking me for directions and I was trying to show off. In great pain, I would wait for them to leave then fall to my knees rubbing my shins. My legs were all black and blue. I had made up my mind that I would never swing or twirl it again. Secondly, I didn't have enough rounds in my coke bottle to shoot anyone. I asked if one of them would care to tell me why they had this great concern that I was about to hurt them. I told them not to hold anything back, that I would be glad to listen to whatever they had to say. Personally, I thought that they had been punished enough by having to sit on the filthy concrete steps at the Induction Center.

They spoke and I listened. All of them had just returned from the Democratic National Convention in Chicago. The violence between police and demonstrators elevated to a level where many police officers and protesters had been severely injured. After listening to them, I had a clearer view of their fears. I told them that it was my turn to speak and I wanted all of them to listen to me. More importantly, I wanted them to believe me. I gave them my word that no one would shoot them, hit them with a stick, or place a finger on them. This I promised. In return, I asked that they each help me process the necessary paper work as quickly as possible. I was hoping that with any luck we could be able to beat the rush and be out of Central Booking before it became too crowded, if not, it was going to be a long night for all of us.

At the time, they may have not realized it but each of them were doing to me exactly what they were accusing me of doing to them, they were unfairly stereotyping me. None of these men knew my views on the war. I was in a blue uniform; therefore I possessed their idea of a blue uniform mentality. How unfair of them. They were intellectuals afflicted with a proclivity to be just as prejudice as everyone else. They had not known that two years prior, on September 28th, with my college draft exemption expired, I had received my draft notice to report to Fort Hamilton. It just so happened that on September 25th, while I was sitting home contemplating which toe I could best function without, the police department called informing me to report to the Police Academy the next day to be sworn in as one of New York Citi's Finest. I was informed that my draft orders would be canceled thereby saving one little toe from a horrible fate. The next week I received a letter from the draft board canceling my orders along with a request to mail them back their fifteen-cent token.

I looked at Dr. Spock and said, "Would you mind if I call you Ben or Benjamin? I keep getting you mixed up with the fellow on the space ship, you know, the one with the pointed ears."

"Fine, call me whatever you like."

"That sounds great. Now here's the plan." I told them that I would gather the necessary forms. I would then pass the paperwork through the bars of their cell so that they could fill out their own arrest sheets.

I instructed that if anyone had a question to please shout it out. I believed that with their cooperation we would be able to fly through all this nonsense rather quickly. I told Benjamin that in a few hours he would be back in his office seeing patients or writing another book. Next, I told the Reverend that he would be back on his pulpit preaching fire and brimstone. Last, but certainly not least, I informed my Poets that they would be back on their porches, sitting in their rocking chairs in the Adirondacks, writing poems that nobody understood. I also asked if they could explain to me why all poets live to be at least 103 years old. At least my remarks made them laugh. I put them at ease. I liked them. I was only twenty-two years old but they looked to me for guidance and help. They trusted me. I wouldn't betray that trust.

As the night moved along, we became bogged down with the flaws of an inadequate, antiquated system. Prisoners started to flow in by the hundreds and our hopes of an early departure diminished into a, "could have been." It was late evening, I was hungry, and of course I realized that my wards must have been hungry too. I decided to throw the rules of the department out the window as I had done so many times in the past.

I wandered out of Central Booking in pursuit of a McDonald's. I asked another police officer, whom I trusted, to keep a watchful eye on my prisoners and to make certain that nothing happened to them in my absence. Before leaving, I took their food orders. I was forced to clip their wings when they asked me to bring back three different flavored shakes. "One flavor only," I shouted. I told them that if they didn't have any money that I would pay for their food. "You can mail it to my house at a later date," I said. My prisoners were the only ones who ate that night. I made friends and hoped that I was able to touch their lives in a small way. Just as they had touched mine.

Two weeks later two books arrived at the precinct station house. One was from Robert Bly. The title, "The Light around the Body." He wrote, "For Joseph, who arrested me and cared for us all during the Induction Center demonstration November, with great humanity and thoughtfulness-To a good man. Robert Bly." The other book was from Galway Kinnell titled, "<u>What a Kingdom It Was.</u>" He wrote, "To Joseph who led a poet through hell. With gratitude, Galway Kinnell." Those books are in my bookshelf and treasured.

I saw Benjamin Spock once again at his trial in Boston. The Government charged him, along with many other demonstrators, with Conspiring To Overthrow The Government Of The United States. Boston was chosen as the venue for the trial. According to Federal law, wherever a person first engages in a conversation or act that could be viewed as a conspiracy, that is the location where the trial must be convened. As I was walking to take the stand, I stopped to say hello to Spock. I asked him that if he should ever again decide to overthrow the United States that perhaps he could save his first remarks for his next visit to Hawaii. He smiled giving me a wink.

Much to the dislike of the U.S. Assistant Attorneys and the FBI, the trial ended in a dismissal for all defendants. I didn't like many of the members of the prosecuting team. They were alligators that ate their young. They climbed the ladder of success on the backs of many decent people and each other. Some of them had lost their perspective, failing to see the big picture. Their aggressiveness blinded them and Spock meant no more to them then another notch on their gun.

One night I was invited to join these individuals for dinner. They spent the evening briefing me on what my testimony should be when I took the witness stand. They also wanted to know any information that I had learned about my prisoners during the arrest process. "All I can say is that I know they all drink chocolate shakes." I did not share their views that these were evil men and I would not compromise the truth, and so I did not make a big a hit with the FBI or the U.S. Attorney's office. During the course of the night, I listened as they expounded their theory that the most dangerous man in the country was Martin Luther King. They were certain of this because it was a God-given opinion handed down from no other than the divine one, J. Edgar Hoover himself, a man who spent sixty percent of his time at the racetrack and the remaining forty percent dressing as a Victoria Secret Model.

These men and I were different. They grew up having their own bedroom with a window that overlooked a green yard. They hunted pheasant in the cornfields of Kansas using a twenty gauge side-by-side Charles Daly shotgun. They fly-fished the streams and rivers of New England. Their fathers smoked pipes and they all had English Setters that warmed themselves in front of a fire. They had no idea what it was like to be pushed out of a single bed in the middle of the night by their brother. If someone in my neighborhood was handed a Charles Daly shotgun, he would walk to the closest bank and say, "Stick 'em up." A fly rod would have had a piece of gum stuck to its tip. It would then be used to remove coins through a subway grating. And all the dogs I knew had mange and teeth that were used for biting people. None of them knew that the bookie, Charlie, could be found every night between the hours of 7:00p.m. and 8:00p.m. in the front of Maxie's candy store.

They didn't know that you could break the devil's dishes by stepping on the cracks of a sidewalk. They weren't aware that if your pretzel fell on the floor you could kiss it up to God, that he would make it clean. And they didn't know that if your ball happened to take a bad bounce finding its way over Mr. Randazzo's gate, he would pick it up, smile, and cut it in half with his switchblade knife. Of course, later that night, Mr. Randazzo's garbage pails would disappear never to be found. No! none of these men had any idea about the reality of life.

Time proved Spock had been right and they were wrong. We were fighting a war that we never had any intention of winning; a limited war with unlimited dying. And where I came from, you never engaged in a fight that you had no intention of winning.

Spock, Bly, Kinnell, and the rest of them were aware that America's youth were being led down a disastrous path. They saw the flag draped caskets, the tears of parents as they greeted their children for a final good-bye. In retrospect, I realized their protest was never about what they wanted, but more about what they didn't want. They were pleading for a young generation to be able to live to an old age, as old as the politicians and generals that were whisking them to their deaths. They objected to having mantels arrayed with photographs of what was the innocence of America. Instead, they wanted mantels beautified with America's grandchildren. They had the courage to tell young men what their parents should have been telling them but did not. They thanked me. I should have thanked them.

I looked up at the young girl standing in front of me and said, "It's not that I'm afraid to join your protest, but that I'm older. Good luck, I wish you well."

Chapter 31

IT WAS ONE of the coldest winters I was able to bring to mind. I always hated the cold, barely managing to tolerate it. The girls had recently sent the Bug to the happy Volkswagen junkyard in the sky. I was afraid that my no longer new car might decide that it had suffered enough at the their hands and refuse to start. I knew that I had to have a spare on hand, especially if Joey needed to be rushed to the hospital in the middle of the night.

After taking a family consensus, the children decided on a Jeep Wrangler. I worked out an insurance payment plan with them and gave them my okay. The next day I went out and leased a bright yellow Wrangler, thinking that I was doing motorists a favor by giving them plenty of advance warning that Claudine was on her way.

Tammy was home on winter vacation and I overheard a conversation that she and Claudine intended to spend the day shopping at the local mall. My intention was to leave for the hospital before noon. Walking out the front door, I was hit with a wind chill factor hovering below zero. Looking for my car, I discovered that it was nowhere to be found. I saw the yellow Jeep parked by the curb and thought it was nice of the girls to let me try driving our new car.

I took my keys out of my pocket. I went to unlock the front door but was met by nothing but air. "Where are the doors?" I shouted. I kept walking around the car looking for the doors. I knew that they couldn't be in the glove compartment. But where were they? With no other options remaining, I headed off to the hospital in below zero weather in a car without doors. Before leaving the house, I wrapped several scarves around my face and blankets around my body. Other drivers starred, shaking their heads as I drove by. I wondered, could they possibly think that I always drive around like this, that this was intentional on my part? Didn't they know that I had daughters? If driving to the hospital was torturous, coming home was far worse.

When I finally arrived home that night, my eyes were white; my eyebrows frosted, and I was barely able to walk. As I entered the house, I found both Claudine and Tammy sitting at the kitchen table.

"Hi, Dad, wow you look awful! Tammy said.

"Hey, Dad, did you notice that somebody had stolen the jeep doors during the night? Claudine asked.

Making a valiant effort to unlock my lips I said, "You have to be kidding! Why did you girls take my car! Can't you see that I'm frozen?"

"Dad, what did you expect us to do? Drive around in a car without doors? Haven't you noticed how cold it is outside" they answered.

Joey couldn't go on much longer. Cancer is not that kind. I had a feeling that we were nearing the finish line. One way or another the race would soon be over. Joey began to falter. He told me that he didn't want to return to Mt. Sinai for chemotherapy. Forcing him into the car, I continued to drive to the city but it was becoming close to impossible to get him into the hospital. He lagged behind vomiting up and down Fifth Avenue, Madison Avenue, and each side street that we crossed. I pleaded with him to keep moving, to catch up, but he ignored me.

The hospital that at first appeared so vast and huge had diminished in size and scope. The corridors, with their striped walls, were as familiar as the face that I shaved each morning. Walking through the hallways, I knew how many steps there were between each color code in our path. Secret stairwells that allowed us to journey from one medical department to another were a breeze to negotiate. The sad part was that Joey knew them as well as well. Yet, when I told him that we had an appointment for a CAT scan he said, "I don't know where the CAT department is."

My tolerance was at an all time low. My calculations told me that

I had driven fifteen thousand miles in ten weeks. In the middle of Fifth Avenue, I began screaming, "How can you not know where the CAT Department is? You've been there sixteen times. Cut the crap." Still, he delayed. I was angry. I was angry at him, at his cancer, and at the world. Joey had had enough and so did I. We had been playing cancer's sadistic game for too long. It was beating us into the ground, into submission, not all at once, but a little at a time. There was no doubt in my mind that it was winning. Everywhere we went it reminded us that it was there.

The week before we were in a supermarket when some children called their mother to show her the boy without hair and eyebrows. "Girls, you're right," she whispered, He doesn't have any hair." Anger started to build up inside me. I was ready to explode, to blast the children and their ignorant mother. Years ago, I would have but now I was a different person quieter in many ways, mostly weary. Two days later, Joey stopped in a store to purchase a music tape. The owner told him, "Hey kid, the next time you come in bring your skin head friends with you." Joey was often mistaken for a skinhead subjecting him to verbal, and on one occasion, had it not been for Tammy coming to his aid, physical abuse. Fighting the ignorance of society was part of the battle that we had not foreseen and something we could do little about. I didn't have the time to educate people, nor the inclination. I was too drained.

A few days after this incident Joey became involved in a bitter battle with Claudine over some trivial matter. The subject of their argument wasn't the issue; it merely served as the catalyst for an impending showdown, and although Joey was not equipped with Claudine's verbal artillery, he was holding his own. I decided not to intervene knowing that there comes a time in every young boy's life, who has two older sisters, when he finally says, "Enough, I've had my fill!"

Joey had never resented doing for his sisters; he resented being asked in a tone that insinuated that he had no choice but to do. I knew that once their battle was over, life would somehow go on.

I was a single parent who had lived through felonious episodes of anger brought on by who's turn it was to put gas in the car, illegal borrowing of sweaters and shoes, and the gravest sin of all, phone glutting.

Joey's cancer had afforded him little immunity in household arguments. Over the last few years, the girls had learned to live with their brother's cancer. The novelty of his illness had worn off a long time ago. To them, he was no different than their girlfriends' little brothers. Except that he had less hair, a strange tube protruding out of his chest, and he disappeared several days a month to who knows where? But he always came back, and he always would.

I had learned a long time ago that the social issues in the girl's lives took precedent over all other matters. God had encased them in a protective armor called youth and neither blight, disease nor nuclear attack could dent or scratch their shield. Joey did not seek his sisters' pity, nor would he accept it. God, in his astute wisdom, had encased Joey with the same youthful protection. I had lived through these battles before, and I would somehow survive this one. Plus, I knew that there was a lot more meaning to Joey's outburst than a fight with his sister. He was growing tired of playing host to the merciless savage that prowled within him gradually stripping him of all that he was, all that made him special and wonderful. Before my very eyes, cancer was making him old, less tolerant of others, and it was doing the same to me.

As we entered the CAT department, Joey intentionally procrastinated in drinking his contrast. "Would you please cut it out?" I roared. "Stop being a brat and drink that before I pour it down your throat." He reluctantly drank it. Then he looked at me with a sad face. I felt sick. What are you doing? I asked myself. What kind of human being have you become? I reflected thinking what my life would be like without Joey. I knew that if I lost him, that no matter how hard I had tried in the past the only thing I would remember was what I had just done, the way I had just treated him. Joey was fighting harder than anyone I knew to stay alive and the last thing he needed was an impatient son of a bitch like me yelling at him. I was wrong and I wanted to fix it between us right there and then. I wanted to hold him, and tell him that I was sorry. But more, I wanted to reassure him I would never behave like that again. If it made him happy to crawl down Fifth Avenue, well then, he should crawl. And if he wanted some company, I would get down on me knees and crawl right alongside him. That was the way it should be between us. The only way it could be.

A few minutes later Joey walked out from taking his CAT scan. I looked at him with his little baldhead and I melted with love and sorrow. "Joey, are you okay?" I asked in a way that begged his forgiveness.

He shook his head, "Yes."

A tear ran down my face as I said from the deepest part of my soul, "Joey, daddy loves you, I was wrong and I'm sorry."

He smiled a smile that said, "I know, Dad, it's okay."

We returned to the hospital the next week for his scheduled chemotherapy session.

Joey was assigned a room on the long corridor, the one that extended out from the nurse's station of Falk 2. This wing of Falk 2 was occupied by five children. They were, in many ways, as diversified as children could be. Three girls. Two boys. The girl in the room next to Joey was from an Orthodox Jewish background. She was suffering from Leukemia. The other boy, a few rooms down, on the opposite side of the corridor, was black and resided locally. His name was Denver. He and Joey were about the same age. He too, was suffering from Leukemia. On Joey's side of the corridor, and only two rooms away, was a teenage girl named Lori. She was afflicted with Ewing's sarcoma. Same cancer, almost in the same location as Joey's. The last child was Tina. I could hear her parents and relatives conversing in Italian. She was afflicted with Rhabdomyosarcoma, a cancer that attacks the muscles. All had been battling cancer for too long. Michele was walking out of Tina's room, on her way to visit Lori, when I stopped her and asked, "How's Tina doing?" "Not well. She replied."

Tina's cancer was noticed one day while she was playing basketball in the school gym. A small lump, or bump, appeared on her forearm, something that the average person would think little of. Her cancer, Rhabdomyosarcoma, was a soft tissue sarcoma stemming out from the muscle cells. It usually occurred more in males. It affects children between the ages of two and six. Being a teenager made it more difficult to treat Tina's cancer. Michele had previously told me that they were fighting Tina's cancer like they were fighting Joey's, "Using the big guns." I had asked her what she thought about Tina's chances. Trying to protect me from the truth she told me that it was cancer and that they were playing a wait and see game. I knew that Michele loved Tina very much.

Michele didn't have children but she had mentioned to me that Tina was the daughter she would have wanted. She loved and spoiled her, and Tina loved it.

I had discovered that Tina wanted to work behind the candy counter of her local movie theater so that she could talk with her friends when they stopped in to see a movie.

She missed them very much. Not too much to ask for, I thought. Her wish came true when a few of the nurses rallied in her defense. They convinced Dr. G. to temporarily waive her concern about Tina being exposed to bacteria and viruses in a crowd. Several of the nurses stopped in to visit her at work. There she was with her wig on, smiling, happy as a lark, talking with her friends. A few of the nurses also attended her confirmation party.

Tina, like many of the cancer children I had met, was worried that her illness was a burden to her family. I remained in a perpetual state of admiration thinking these children could teach the world a wonderful lesson of humility, compassion and love. But first, the world would have to be willing to learn.

My attention now returned to my conversation with Michele. I said, "Thanks for caring, for caring about Tina, Joey, and me."

"Don't you ever forget that I cared about Joey long before I cared about you. He's special. There's not a mean bone in his body. "Remember, no matter what happens around here in the next few days, don't lose faith. Please, don't lose faith."

"Okay, I won't." I had a feeling that she was trying to tell me something. A bad feeling."

Lori, like Joey, at first was misdiagnosed. She was being treated by a chiropractor who failed to make the right call. Finding the right doctor when you have cancer and treating it early was the name of the game. But what parent was looking for or thought that their child might have cancer? Lori's parents each had children from a previous marriage. Lori consummated their marriage, adding richness to their lives by tying the families together making them one. She fulfilled her parents' dreams, giving more meaning to their existence than they ever thought possible. They adored her and she them. Lori's dream was to become a bride. She enjoyed looking through bridal magazines, trying to pick out the one wedding dress that she thought she would look best in. She would have complimented all of them.

It was easy to like these children. They made it easy. I didn't know how the nurses and doctors did their job. I had seen people die, lots of them, but this was different. Here, you were whirled into the lives of the families and they yours. When a doctor or nurse entered a room, the parents looked at them as though they were going to pull a rabbit out of a hat and save the life of their child. To them, these doctors and nurses were the bridge to a cure. But how did these mercenaries of hope sleep at night? Where did they stow all the faces? They were extraordinary people making life easier for each child and every parent. Parents came here searching for Lourdes. Sometimes they found Armageddon instead. The final chapter was about to be written on each of these children. Cancer was about to make a decision. It would either go into remission or it would climb the summit claiming victory.

During what felt like a lifetime at Mt. Sinai, I had seen most of these children either in the corridors, their rooms, or in one of the many testing areas of the hospital. I knew they had cancer. At first I wasn't aware of the type of cancer they were battling, nor the severity of their illness. Cancer took on many faces, similar only in the respect that it was constantly attempting to extend its territory.

Unchecked, all cancers were fatal. But, with today's advent of chemotherapy many children had a fighting chance. The ability to survive depended on several factors. The type of cancer. The length of time it was left unchecked. The acceptance of chemotherapy by the body. The individual's will to fight, and about one million other conditions that most likely had nothing to do with anything at all. I heard some people suggest that God's will was part of the pie. While others, of a less religious belief, felt that it was no more than a roll of the dice. I personally believed that all these components played a vital part. I also knew the only thing that mattered was the bottom line. You either lived or you died. If eighty-five percent of patients afflicted with Acute lymphocytic leukemia (ALL) lived and my son died, screw the statistics. They meant nothing to me. I would pay homage to anyone or reason that allowed my son to live. And I would curse and urinate on the grave of anyone who took him from me. I was led to believe that Joey had less than a fifty percent chance of surviving Ewing's sarcoma.

For arguments sake, if he had fifty percent and two children were diagnosed free of Ewing's sarcoma what did that mean? Did it mean that Joey and the child after him would die in order to adjust the statistic? I couldn't fall into the statistics trap. No parent could. It would drive them crazy. No one used up another person's turn to live or die.

This was Joey's fifteenth chemotherapy session. Still, he remained in his street clothes sleeping on top of his sheets. From the second we pulled out of our driveway, all communications stopped. Not a word was said. By this time, I understood his handsignals. If he pounded on the mattress, somewhere on the ward food was being served or the elevator door opened containing food. It then became my job to make certain that no food found its way into his room. Other movements meant that he could hear his chemotherapy being collected at the nurses' station. When it was time to take him home, he would sometimes slap the armrest of his wheelchair. This was to let me know that I had him facing the wrong way, that he wasn't facing the elevator door. I did as he asked.

Social workers and psychologists asked if they could speak with him. He shook his head no. To them, he was an enigma, someone that they wanted to study. They wanted to know why he withdrew into himself. Each composed a theory that would explain Joey's innermost thoughts concerning this behavior. I finally said, "Why is everyone guessing? Why don't I go to the source?" So, prior to his visit, I did. While we were alone in the car I asked, "Joey, everyone wants to know why you stop talking when you enter the hospital. I promised them that I would ask you." Then came the complicated answer that all the psychologists and social workers had been waiting to hear. "Dad, I'm too sick to talk. If I talk, then I throw up. So, I try to keep quiet."

"Thanks, son. I'll pass on your message to all the scholars, perhaps they can do a thesis on this complex problem and have it published in The New England Journal Of Medicine."

I left Joey alone in his room while the nurses connected the IV line to his Broviac. Returning a few minutes later, he was nowhere to be found. I wondered where he had disappeared. Searching for him, I found him in the recreation area of the hospital. He was seated next to a six-year-old boy. Joey was helping him color. I entered the room and said, "So here you are. What's going on? I've been looking for you and I see that you've made a new friend."

"He's having trouble coloring so I thought that I would help him out." "You know he looks like a little you."

"Well, we all look alike around here."

"Have fun, I'll see you later, and you too," I said to the little boy, who was lost in his creative work. I sat in the lounge waiting for Joey to undergo his chemotherapy. Denver stopped in to say hello. He was well like by the nurses and physicians. I liked him too, a polite boy, he was warm and friendly.

Denver was suffering from Leukemia. I learned that there were three basic types of Leukemia along with several odd, not so common strains. Acute Lymphocytic or (ALL was the most common type accounting for over 75% of all leukemia. The next was Acute Myeloid

Leukemia (AML), one fifth as common as (ALL). The last, Chronic Myelogenous Leukemia (CML) affected less than 5% of leukemia victims. The highest success rates in treating leukemia dealt with Acute Lymphocytic Leukemia (ALL). A person did not want to hear that they had AML and they wanted to hear even less that they had CML, a death sentence by most standards. Denver had AML. He had been fighting a gallant battle. I admired his courage and his up-beat personality.

A week later, I was taking Joey for an echocardiogram when I ran into one of the nurses from Falk 2. I told her that Joey was due for his chemo treatment within the next few weeks. I asked her if Denver was scheduled for his chemotherapy as well. Denver had purposely stopped in Joey's room to say good-bye during his last visit. The nurse didn't answer. Sadness filled her eyes. I understood.

It wasn't long after that the little girl in the room next to Joey died. Leukemia had taken her. I never had the opportunity to meet her, only to see her pushing her IV through the hallways of Falk 2. In a way, I was grateful that I didn't know her. I was tired of the pain and fear that accompanied knowing. It had come to a point that I would remain standing, staring at Joey's bed, wondering if the last child who slept in Joey's bed had lived or died. If the bed had the ability to speak, what would it say?

I would then tell myself, stop it. Don't do this. Don't give in to it. Life goes on. Yes, for some people.

Joey ran, then he no longer could.

I raked the leaves, then they were gone.

I raked them again, and again they were gone.

And, I raked them one more time.

I watched the snow, then it was gone.

I watched it again, and again it was gone.

And, I watched it one more time.

I watched the trees bud flower and bloom, then they were gone.

I watched them again, and again they were gone.

And, I watched them one more time.

I burned from the sun, and then it was gone.

It burned me again, and again it was gone.

And, it burned me one more time.

And, Joey still could not run.

Chapter 32

ALL OF JOEY'S tests still indicated that something was still abnormal. The nuclear particles and dyes still affixed themselves, lighting up this area. I was wishing that it was bone erosion caused by radiation to the area, but I knew differently. So did Joey. He was becoming increasingly depressed. His youth was no longer a positive factor. With enough pain even the young become old.

My thoughts blurred, I had lost count of his chemotherapy sessions. One seemed to blend into another. All I knew was that we were back on Falk 2. But tonight was different; there was meanness in the air. Something horrible was about to happen. The hair on my neck stood up. The cop in me was on guard. But there was nothing I could do. Cancer was about to reestablish its dominance. It was awakened, angry, and on the move making its way down the corridor, hungry, searching for a victim, a child. It sneered at each parent knowing that it could not be stopped. The only question that remained was whose door would it come knocking on?

I sat with Joey, alone in his room. Mary and my brother had not yet arrived. I was hoping that they wouldn't be delayed. Tonight I wanted company. Soon the silence of Joey's darkened room was broken. I heard weeping that turned into crying, then wailing that turned into shrieking. I walked out into the hallway. Tina's mother and aunt were barely able to hold themselves up. Had it not been that each was entwined in the arms of the other, both would have fallen to the ground. Cancer had found its mark. The little girl who not so long ago had noticed a small lump on her forearm, the child whose sole dream in life was to sell popcorn to her friends in a movie theater was gone. Did she ask for too much? Was it really too much to ask for? I knew that sometimes God said yes, and sometimes He said no, but couldn't He have said yes one more time?

I wanted to know why this had to happen? I needed someone to answer my question. But no one had an answer because no one understood it anymore than I did.

My heart filled with compassion for this child and her loved ones, but my mind was filled with fear. Cancer, tonight, shook every parent here, showing them what it was capable of doing. It brought them to their knees humbling them like common beggars. I could only think would Joey be next? Would I be the one in the hall crying, and who would be there to hold me up? I felt like I was in a game of Russian Roulette, only all the cylinders in this game were loaded. I didn't want to play games like this anymore. I wanted out of this game, to grab Joey and flee, to go a place where they didn't play games like this. I sat in the darkest corner of Joey's room glaring at the door. A good cop always faced the door to see the unexpected danger before it could see him. I had done this before, I was good a it. I was ready anticipating that at any moment the door might open allowing the evilness down the hall to enter. Then it dawned on me, it was already in the room.

Joey, sedated, slept through the night. It was early morning. He was still sleeping.

I poked him trying to wake him. He didn't budge. So, I poked him again, only harder.

This time his eyes opened. "Let's get the hell out of here. I want to go home." "Dad, I'm so sick, I can't move."

"Joey, you're the one who always wants to flee this place and now you're too sick to move. Is this what you're telling me?"

"Dad, please, I have to vomit. I can't pick my head up."

"You can vomit in the car. I don't care if you vomit all over the back seat, the front seat, and anywhere else you care to vomit. I want to get out of here and I want to go now.

I'll carry you if you can't walk. I'm leaving to find a nurse to disconnect your IV. Get ready to leave this place."

I walked out into the hall to find a nurse. Along the way I bumped into Dr. G.

"Doctor, I'm leaving with Joey. We will see you when we come back from our Caribbean vacation.

"You know how I feel about that."

"Yes, I do, but we're going, so work with me. I have a promise to keep." "I can see that you have your mind made up."

"Yes, it's made up."

"Okay, let's talk about what you have to be careful of."

"Thank you for understanding."

When I finished my conversation with Dr. G., I walked back into Joey's room. I sat in the same chair in the same corner of the room that I sat in last night. Usually the light of day gave me the ability to take another step forward. Today it didn't help.

While I waited for Joey, I looked out his window. I saw the hordes of people crossing the street, the impenetrable wall of traffic slowly making its way down Madison Avenue. I wanted to scream, "You people have no idea what's going on up here. If you experienced only one second of the pain that these children and their parents have lived with, you wouldn't allow this horror to continue. You would assemble your forces and put an end to it." But no one looked up. No one heard me because no one was listening. Sunday, I attended church. I needed help, lots of it. I was never a steady churchgoer. Like many others, I used the old excuse that I had led a good life not harming anyone or anything. God understood that I would prefer to sleep late on Sunday mornings rather than sit in a church pew listening to someone expound theological nonsense. Occasionally, I would attend Sunday mass, but I was never really there. Instead, I went through a series of automated motions hoping to fool anyone that glanced my way while I dozed and dreamed of far away places and material conquests. Now, I was in God's house asking him for a favor that I didn't deserve. The other children's parents, I was sure, were far more religious than I, and were more likely suitable to receive a blessing. I sat there wondering if God saw through my ploy. Did he know that I was a counterfeit? That I was a convenience worshiper? Was he about to say, "Sorry you had your chance don't come around now because you need a favor. Where were you last Sunday? and the Sunday before that? I've seen people like you before that only come around when you need something and once your prayers are answered you return to your old ways."

Of course I would rebuke by saying, "God this time it's different. I promise I will never sleep late on Sunday. I will be the first one in the door and the last one to leave your church. Can't you grant me this one favor?"

The thought that I had not fulfilled my promise to take Joey on vacation was upsetting to me. Tina's death added to my guilt. After all, she had the opportunity to live her dream of working in a movie theater. Wasn't Joey entitled to his brief moment of happiness too? Wasn't he in need of a sabbatical from constant hospital stays, chemotherapy and worry?

After packing our luggage, I filled a carry-on satchel with adhesive tape, gauze, heparin, bandages, syringes, a small waste container, alcohol and beta dine swabs. I hoped that we wouldn't be detained at customs for suspicion of being international drug smugglers and headed off for the Turks Cacaos Islands.

Allowing my imagination to run free, to take control of reality, I envisioned a huge sign posted in the customs area of the airport that read, "This is a cancer-free Island. All forms of cancer must be checked at customs along with firearms and time bombs. They will be returned to you upon your departure." At which time I would say to Joey's sarcoma, "See you in a week. Just don't hold your breath waiting."

Joey wearing a T-shirt to cover his Broviac, and a bandanna to hide his baldness, spent the afternoons wading in and out of the tepid turquoise water of the Caribbean. On several occasions his bandanna became wet causing it to slip off his head. I teased him telling him that he reassembled a white marker buoy bobbing about. Each time that he came out of the water he disappeared to our room to clean his Broviac and to change his bandage. A few people approached me voicing their curiosity and concern about the boy that looked so different than the other children running around. Most of them were very sympathetic and compassionate. Their well wishes and comments were comforting.

My time was spent positioned under a palm tree preparing for my final exams, reading my textbooks on "The Theory of Personalities and Abnormal Psychology." I kept looking for the chapter that explained why daughters are hell bent on sending single fathers to the great hereafter but I couldn't find it. If nothing else, I came to the conclusion that I was a histrionic manic/depressive schizophrenic sociopath with suicidal tendencies. Well, at least I wasn't bulimic so I put down my book and decided to have lunch.

As our week at in the Caribbean drew to a close, I wished that we could have placed our lives in limbo; to somehow slow up time, to delay the inevitable, a life again dominated by cancer. Soon, our reprieve would be over. We would return to the mayhem we left behind. Returning to the airport, Joey's cancer was waiting for him, ready to climb on board to finish what it had started three years ago.

As we boarded the plane Joey's slipped into silence. I could tell that something was wrong. He didn't have to utter a word I knew what he was thinking, how he was feeling.

He was quitting. I sensed that he had had enough. No one I ever met in my life would have been able to tolerate three years of bone cancer and its horrifying by products. When we first started all this, I didn't know about cancer, that it could be this devastating. I didn't know that it could dehumanize and humiliate the human spirit. I had learned a lot.

We arrived home late that night. The next day I called the hospital. I was sorry that I did.

The news that I heard devastated me.

Lori
The Girl Who Dreamed of Becoming a Bride

Tomorrow, the sun will rise. It will slowly warm the earth gently touching it with its morning rays. Twelve hours later it will be chased by the night shadows into the western sky. It happens every day.

Tomorrow, the tide will rush in. It will clap the highest dune, then quickly make its retreat to the safety of the sea. It happens every day.

Tomorrow, people will be jolted from their sleep by the surprising sounds of their alarm clocks. They will stagger from their beds, shower, have their morning cup of coffee, and arrive at work with only a few minutes to spare. It happens every day.

Tomorrow, young boys and girls will attend school. Boys will dream of becoming major league baseball players, and girls will browse through bridal magazines. All these things will take place tomorrow, except for Lori. Last night, Ewing's sarcoma changed its mind. It took what it had no right to take. It took Lori from us. It wasn't fair but cancer never is.

Today, will be like no other day in the life of Lori's parents. In their world, the sun will not come up, the tide will not clap the highest dune, and there will no longer be a little girl who dreams of becoming a bride.

Today, the world is not as beautiful as it was yesterday.

Chapter 33

JOEY'S NEXT BATTERY of tests, including his chemotherapy, was due in two days. He appeared extremely melancholy. Refusing to speak, I left him to dwell in his quietness. It would only depress him to talk about it.

The night before his hospital admission I found him sitting on his bed dressed only in his underwear. His Broviac was uncovered dangling to within inches of the floor. I could tell he was fading. I sat down next to him. I asked him, "Are you okay?" He didn't answer; instead he starred aimlessly into space.

I began to rub his shoulders. His bones were protruding, jetting out, and obstructing the smooth flow of my hand. After a few minutes I turned, dropped to my knees, and faced him. His jawbones were vivid, accentuated by his recessed cheeks. His dimples were now more noticeable because of his thinness. I looked into his sunken eyes; beneath his illness there was still the boy with the extraordinary good looks that could have broken a million female hearts. All one had to do to see it was to look deep enough, to look beyond his cancer.

"Joey, talk to daddy. Tell me what's bothering you?" I waited but he didn't answer.

"Joey, please let me in. Tell me what you're feeling? Maybe I can help you?" He slowly altered his stare until our eyes met.

"Daddy, I'm not going back to the hospital. I can't go back there again. I just can't. I'm tired of all the tests and the chemotherapy. I don't want to throw up anymore. I hate that place and the way it smells. I don't care what anyone says and I don't care what happens to me. I'm not going back there."

"Joey, I hear what you're saying. Believe me I understand, but you can't turn your back on this. You can't pretend that you don't have cancer, that it never came into your life, because it did."

I told him it hadn't beaten him, that it was getting tired of trying. I explained that his cancer never dreamed that he would be this tough an opponent and how it had used every weapon in its arsenal expecting him to quit. "Joey," I said, "It discovered that you weren't an easy mark."

Holding him, cherishing his fragile life, I went on, "Son, I have prayed everyday that God give me your cancer but he hasn't. You are the only one who can finish this thing. I can't do it for you."

I had never felt more helpless than I did at that moment. Over the last few years, I had witnessed and lived every second of his pain with him. Yet, as much as I loved him, I realized that I was no more than a spectator with a box seat. I could only cheer him on.

His cancer wouldn't come out to fight me. I didn't even know what it looked like. But, I could tell. I could smell it. I could taste it. This cowardly bastard had its bags packed. It was ready to go elsewhere. Sadly, Joey was the only one who could show it the door. He was the only one who had the key. It was time for him to open that door and kick it out. It was time for him to give it "the evil eye." All he had to do was move forward. Soon, he would never have to come back here. With time he would be able to close his eyes and never see this place again. The rest of his life would be his to live as he chose. One day he would get married and have children of his own. I was going to make it a point to tell them about their father and the time he fought the battle of his life, the time he beat cancer. I had the speech. All I was asking was for Joey to give me the opportunity to deliver it. He couldn't deprive me of my dream. He couldn't allow cancer to take that away from me. That moment belonged to me. I earned it.

"Dad, I know it's still there."

"It probably is, but this scoundrel is ready to crawl away. You have to finish him off. Joey, I never told you this but God, in his own way, told me that you were going to be afflicted with cancer and now He's telling me that it's all over. It's one of those things that I know a lot about. There is a reason why God took the others and has allowed

JOSEPH TRIOLO

you to live. I don't know why, only He does, but God has a plan for you. It wasn't your turn. He doesn't want you. Now he's showing you the path that will take you home. Walk down it."

Two days later we entered the hospital. Joey's mental and physical state were quickly waning. He remained in his bed motionless awaiting his chemotherapy. To me, it was life saving medication. To him, it was sickness beyond belief that few people could tolerate. Still, he was willing to go for one more ride on this incessant roller coaster. I was sitting in a chair next when his door opened. It was Michele carrying his chemotherapy just as she had so many times in the past. I could see Joey's eyes following her. Michele suspended his chemotherapy from his IV pole and removed the cap from his Broviac. Seconds later, with my eyes fixed on the IV line, I kept beat with each drop of chemotherapy as it began its slow descent.

Closing his eyes, Joey slowly drifted into a semiconscious state. He would remain that way unless he sensed some impropriety about to take place. Looking at him one would never anticipate his degree of awareness. Only those who had previously witnessed this episode of his life realized, that at this moment, his senses far exceeded that of most people.

I knew that it wouldn't be long before he began to vomit. I searched for and found a clean basin to have on standby. I was hoping that his reaction to this course of chemotherapy would not be as severe as his last. I was wrong. It wasn't long before his retching began. Soon, the blood began to run from his mouth and his nose. A few drops at first, followed by a heavier flow. Within seconds he began to slap the safety railing of his bed. I understood his signal and quickly replaced his basin with a clean one. Seconds later he again slapped the bed railing, this time he struck it harder. We repeated this scenario a dozen times.

With the vomiting now at an intolerable level Joey began to punch the wall. He was dry heaving so violently that he commenced to choke. His body muscles and reflexes were rigorously contracting. I was frightened.

"Take it easy."

"I hate it. I'm so sick. God, I'm so sick." "I know, Joey, hang in there son."

I watched him as he slowly picked his head up and with one quick motion he slammed it into the glass room divider. I jumped on top of him to hold him down. "Joey, stop it. Don't do that."

"You don't know how sick I am."

"You're been here before. You can handle it."

"No, Dad, I don't want anymore. I don't want any more."

"I hear you. I understand what you're saying. Try to close your eyes and let the medication put you to sleep. It will put you to sleep in a few minutes. Don't fight it try to relax." I lowered his bed railing and sat on the edge of his bed. Reaching down I rubbed his head and face with the palm of my hand. Finally, sleep claimed him.

With my heart broken, I walked out into the hall and leaned against his door. I could feel the tears running down my face. The thought that he was too tired, unwilling to go on, was too much for me to accept. My days of screaming, pleading and bribing him were over. I would continue to try, but it would be useless. I had played my last hand and I knew it. Without his total resolve to fight, cancer would make its move. I would lose my son.

Without direction I walked about the hall. I had to walk. I needed to move but I didn't feel like I was moving. I was in different place on the ward but I hadn't any idea how I arrived there. Circling the nurses' station, I recognized their familiar faces. The children and parents I saw were new. They were the new arrivals. Part of the never ending flow of replacements.

The young old timers were gone. No longer would I see them wandering the halls of Falk 2. All that remained were their names covering an already too crowded window shade. I would never be able to accept their deaths. But what was I to do with the memories? Where was I to store the faces that burned within my mind never to be forgotten? Where did they all go, these beautiful children that were dreaming of tomorrow but living for today? I guess they went home to a place without pain. For them it was over. They now would be able to live a life free of X-rays, MIR's, bone scans, chemotherapy, and cancer.

For their parents it was over too. No longer would they exit the Falk 2 elevator and rush to their children's rooms blinded by fear and anticipation of what was awaiting them. No longer would they have to witness the vomiting, the crying, and the sadness that cancer had brought into their children's lives. No longer would they have to watch their children walk the fine line between life and death. Cancer, uninvited, invaded their lives and trampled their dreams. All this was part of their past. Yet, I would rather live with the bile, the blood, and the misery of cancer than spend the rest of my life without my son.

These parents, these poor lost souls, would now be forced to do what I prayed I would never have to do, spend a life time waiting to be reunited with their children. Until that time they would have to learn how to survive in their darkness. If God were merciful, He would hasten away their years.

I walked back to Joey's room but could not enter. I leaned on the door allowing it to hold me up. Tears were still racing down my face. Seeing me, Carol approached.

"Are you alright?"

"No, not really."

"What's wrong?"

"It's Joey, he's quitting. I guess he's beyond fighting."

"I know, he's been through more than most."

"Yes, he's seen them come and go. Three years on this roller coaster, non stop, without a break. I can't tell you the pain that I'm feeling right now. I can't leave him here to spend forever by himself. You don't know how I've prayed it would be all over, that God would have heard my prayers and returned him to me. I guess I didn't pray hard enough."

My eyes blurred from crying. I had difficulty distinguishing the figure now standing behind Carol. Wiping the tears from my face, I noticed Mary, next to my brother, trying to catch my attention. I ignored her. I was too dazed to concentrate on anything or anyone other than my own emotional devastation.

As I leaned forward I could hear Mary murmuring something. It was indistinguishable. I assumed that she was trying to cheer me up. She had always been my pillar of strength. However, the smile on her face offered me little comfort.

I could see her coming closer, "Joe, listen to me. Pay attention to what I'm trying to tell you. Joe it's, gone. Joe, it's gone. Can you hear me? Joey's cancer is gone. I just met Dr. G. in the hall. The tests came back. There isn't a speck of cancer anywhere in his body."

My eyes opened wide. "His cancer is gone?" "Yes, yes."

"Oh, God! Oh, my God!" I pulled Mary into my arms. Then I reached out for my brother. I needed them to hold on to. I began to tremble, to shake. At first slowly, then uncontrollably. The three of us began to cry. Now, finally all of Joey's tomorrow's belonged to him. Three long years of a living hell was over. My son, my wonderful beautiful son, found his way home. He took the right path. "God, said yes."

"Do you want to tell Joey?" Mary asked. "Yes, sure. Sure I'll tell him."

I rushed into Joey's room. He slowly picked up his head to look at me. "Joey, I have something that I want to tell you."

"Dad, I'm too sick, please don't talk to me. Not now."

"Okay, it can wait until tomorrow. We now have tomorrow. Try to go back to sleep." He closed his eyes falling into a deep sleep.

I walked into the lounge. My body emotionally depleted; I had trouble standing. I found a chair and collapsed into it. Tony was close behind. He sat down next to me.

Looking at him I said, "You know, we're sitting in the same chairs that we were sitting in the day we found out Joey had cancer."

"You remembered where we were sitting?"

"Do you want to know where Mary, Dr. G., and Carol were sitting?" "It's unbelievable that you would recall something so irrelevant." "Nothing about that was irrelevant."

Tony asked, "do you want to call Mom and Dad to tell them the good news or shall I call them?"

"You call them. Remember, I couldn't tell them that he had cancer so I asked you to do it. Now I want you to tell them that it's gone. I owe you that."

When Tony was finished with his phone call I called each of the girls. We cried together sharing the good news. I told them that they had their "little guy" back.

Sometime later Tony and Mary went across the street to toast Joey. I would never be able to thank them for all that they had done. They wouldn't expect me to.

Late that evening I went back into Joey's room. Sitting in a chair, in the darkness, I relived the last three years. Mostly I thought about the other families I met along the way.

I wondered why God had decided to save Joey while so many other parents went home alone. Surely they were better people than me. I guess I would have to wait for that answer.

The next morning, for the first time in over three years, I didn't mind the drive to Mount Sinai. Not the traffic, the weather, or even a parking ticket, would upset me today. On my way into the hospital, I saw several construction workers walking about. Parked in front of the Falk building was a crane with a demolition ball attached. I asked one of the workers what was going on. He told me that they were going to demolish the Falk Pavilion. I stood there for a few seconds glancing up at the building. It's good, I thought, it's good that they demolish this place. Although I knew no wrecking ball would ever be able to obliterate my recollections of the bravest children I had ever met, the club members who now shared in death what they were unable to share in life, *happiness*.

I walked into Joey's room. "Good morning son. How are you feeling today?"

"Sick. Really sick."

"You look sick but maybe I can give you some good news to cheer you up. All your tests came back. Joey, you no longer have cancer. It's gone. You did it son. You won. You beat the devil at his game."

As he picked his head up off his pillow his eyes flicked in my direction. He wanted to speak but couldn't. He was too sick. Slowly a grin came across his face.

"Do you know what this means to me? I'll always have someone around to fix the VCR. I leaned over, placed a hand on each side of his face, and kissed him. "I love you," I said. "I love you with all my heart. Now rest and go back to sleep. Let me know when you are ready to go home."

I walked out into the hall. I could see Dr. G. walking into a room across the hall. Before the door closed, I heard her say, "So tell me, where is your pain?" I wondered, how does one thank a person for saving their child's life. It was too big a thank you for words. To me, and many of the other parents, she was our angel of mercy.

Two hours later, I followed into Michele into Joey's room. "Take your time disconnecting his Broviac. Today I'm not in any rush."

"You're not in any rush?" She said laughing.

"No, why should I be? Everything that I want, and need, is right here in this room." Although, at this moment, I knew it wasn't meant to be between us. Her divorce was too raw. She was still asking how long it took to heal from a divorce. She needed time for her wounds to mend, to finish the old before she would be able to start the new, and yet, I loved her.

I embraced her, smiled, and said, "Thanks for being my mean nurse." I watched as she disconnected Joey's IV and helped him dress. Dr. G. had already informed me that an appointment would be made to have Joey's Broviac removed.

Michele left and returned a few minutes later with a wheelchair. I pushed Joey's wheelchair in the direction of the elevator and for the first time in years I faced him towards the nurses' station. He raised his arm to slap his wheelchair, to let me know that I erred, but stopped. Behind the nurses' station stood the entire staff of Falk 2. On top of the desk was a large cake with candles. The doctors and nurses blew out the candles for Joey and said their good-byes.

Leaving the hospital, I paused to look up at the sun I had forgotten what its warm rays felt like on my face. It felt good. I was alive, able to breathe deeply without worry.

As we started to cross Madison Avenue, I put my arm around Joey to support him just as I had always done. He stopped walking. Pulling my arm away he said, "I can do this by myself."

"Yes, you can. Joey, you can do anything you want."

It was a year later while I was thumbing my way through an over-stuffed post office box that a post card fell to the floor. Its foreign print was distinguishably Italian. I read the message. It said, "I'm vacationing in this little town in Sicily and I can't stop thinking about you. I feel your presence everywhere I go. I love you Michele." It felt good to have my friend back.

I collected my mail, walked out to my car, and leaned on the hood. "You're still at it," I said. But then that old Sicilian was always at my side watching over me, over us, sharing his warmth, his love. I prayed that maybe one day we would be able to again share a glass of his homemade red wine.

Chapter 34

SEEING THE CROWD of people filtering out from the commencement area, I wanted to share with them all that I had learned, to take my past and to place it in their present, to allow them to see the world through my eyes, from within my memory, my soul. What more beautiful gift could I give then to share with each of them the preciousness of a child? Someday perhaps I could find a way.

Looking around, Joey's good looks made him easy to find. As he approached me, for a second I thought I saw that little boy inside his fur lined blue parka. To me, he will always be that little boy. I opened my arms and gave him a hug. Only now I could feel the power of his youth as he hugged me in return.

"Hey, Joey, I said, "Did I ever tell you that you're a home run?" "A million times Pop."

"Well, have I ever thanked you?" "For what, Dad?"

"For being my son."

"Thanks, Dad. Thank you both."

I turned to my wife and said, "Michele, do you know that this is the second happiest day of my life?" She smiled. She understood.

Yes, today was a beautiful day. The sky was bright blue. Spring was in the air. But nothing will ever compare to the day I learned that God gave me back my son. That wonderful day when he came home to stay.

When Cancer Takes

Without our children

our dreams are no longer of tomorrow

Instead, we must live in what was,

in what might have been

And yet, we take solace in knowing the pain

of yesterday is gone

Our flower stripped of its petals

Our life now void of light,

Filled with the shadows of darkness

We impatiently wait for one moment

when we can see them smile, hear them laugh,

hold their hand, and say,

"Come into my arms. I love you. "

Author's Comments

WRITING THIS BOOK was an extremely painful undertaking. It brought to life many unpleasant memories. I wrote it with the hope that it might make a difference in the lives of others.

For years, during Joey's illness, the only way I was able to fall asleep at night was by writing the day's events. I wrote notes on lined paper, plain paper, and tissue paper. I then stuffed my writings in a drawer intending to never take them out. Years later, I changed my mind.

This book forced me to relive my past by bringing me back to a time and place that I had no intention of ever revisiting. Calling to memory, each child's face, I wept. I was touched by God. He caressed me. While I was holding Joey's hand, He was holding mine, never letting go. I was never alone. I guess God had as much faith in me, his child, as I had in mine. And I have always wondered why? Why, to all of it. I think that God answered that question when I received a letter from Dr. G. It read, "Thank you for sending me a copy of your writing. I want you to know that I think it is quite remarkable. The intensity with which you expressed the emotions that you experienced was incredible, very vivid, very moving, and very real. I like to believe that I am pretty empathetic and understand the terror a parent must feel when they face their child's illness, but your text raised my awareness once again. It also brought back many memories for me, how young Joey was, for example. Also Denver, Tina. You clearly understood how all of these kids touched all of us...and the special place Tina held in our hearts... as I see she affected you as well. Just yesterday I was talking with the father of a young five-year-old with a newly diagnosed Ewings sarcoma of the sacrum (another bone that cannot be removed). I couldn't help but tell him about Joey (and your manuscript)...and I believe it was a real comfort to him." Signed... "Yours, Dr. G."

I now knew the purpose behind God's plan, why he allowed Joey to live. When a child reaches that point, that unacceptable moment, when cancer erases all hope, Joey would be the beacon of light that would encourage other children to find their way home. His survival would allow them to live with the thought that there was once another little boy who had the courage to try just one more time.

My gift would be to the wonderful parents who, in the middle of the night, when the shadows and the relentless intimidation of cancer kept them awake, when their flow of tears were more than anyone dreamed possible, maybe, through my story, I could reach out to them and ease their pain. Then I will have realized my purpose.

People ask me how has all this changed my life. I learned that in the scope of our totality, our existence, that we are all blind to what tomorrow may bring. Most of all, I learned that children are God's special gift, his tapestry.

I grew up in a generation where having children was a common event. They were produced in conveyor belt fashion where their arrival was met with little fanfare. I was a kid from Brooklyn trapped within the confines of my past and limited by my patriarchal stereotypical view of life. To make matters worse, I was a cop callused by all that I had seen. As a young parent, the need to provide for my family kept me busy with work and away from home. Later, because of my many responsibilities as a single father, I found my emotional self-pity at an all time high. I lacked compassion and tolerance for others, especially my children.

Then one evening, from out of the night, cancer targeted our home. In entered *the hunter,* stalked Joey, and plundered the sanctity of his body. From that moment on, I would never be the same. I spent each day for the next three years not living with fear, but with helpless terror. I had the occasion to intrude on the privacy, the life and death of others. What I witnessed was hard to describe. I could never pass on to others how I felt at that time of my life. My attempts would fall short. I am simply not that good a writer. But all I have to do to remember is close my eyes and allow myself to drift back to a time of tears, and sadly the faces all return.

I have learned that the trivialities of life are simply that, trivialities. Traffic jams that delay our way home, a canceled airline flight, or a failed business deal that needed one more signature are disappointments, but when we compare these setbacks to seeing a mother or father leaving a hospital for the last time *alone,* those other issues amount to no more than a small crimp in our lives. If only everyone would spend one day in a children's cancer ward. If only they would allow these children to touch their hearts, to enter their souls. If only!

I like who I am, the person that I have been transformed into. A metamorphosis took place allowing me to shed my hardened shell and I never want it back. The air is cleaner in my world. The sun is warmer, and a child's laugh is hardier.

Perhaps, I have become the person that I am today because of all that I have seen, or maybe I realize that cancer is still out there somewhere waiting, and that thought humbles me. I do know that I wake up each and every morning in a house where cancer no longer dwells, and that's one hell of a way to start a day, and so I bleed it for all its worth. Yes, I love life more. I hold my children tighter, and I thank God for having entered my heart.

Not a day goes by that I do not think of my son, and not a day goes by that the thought of him does not bring a smile to my face. Somewhere within all this incomprehension I found peace. Do I live in a Pollyannic world? To quote Michele, "You are the happiest person I know." She's right. I am. And that's the way I'm going to stay. I don't need a lot out of life. God gave me back my son. Could a man have received a better gift?

I am certain that there is a test awaiting all of us. For those that must face life's crisis alone, I can only say that when you least expect it, a special person will enter your life, hold you, and show you how to love again.

The children I wrote about needed help. It's too late to help them but it's not too late to help those that have and will continue to take their place. Children are God's irreplaceable gift. We all have an obligation to see to it that they have a childhood free of cancer.

Peace and happiness to all the children.

CPSIA information can be obtained at www.ICGtesting.com
Printed in the USA
LVOW08s0829071016

507774LV00003BA/48/P